# Rock and Sand

*An Orthodox Appraisal of*
*the Protestant Reformers and Their Teachings*

ARCHPRIEST JOSIAH TRENHAM

# *Rock and Sand*

*An Orthodox Appraisal of*
*the Protestant Reformers and Their Teachings*

*The rain came down, the floods came, and the winds blew,*
*beating hard on that house. Yet, it did not collapse, because*
*it was founded on the rock.* (Matt. 7:25)

NEWROME
PRESS

Archpriest Josiah Trenham

ROCK AND SAND
*An Orthodox Appraisal of the
Protestant Reformers and Their Teachings*

© 2015 Archpriest Josiah Trenham

Edited by the Rev. Fr. Michael Monos and Nitsa McClatchey
Cover drawing by Goce Illievski

ISBN 978-1939028365
Library of Congress Control Number: 2015900110

***Newrome Press LLC***
PO Box 30608
Columbia, Missouri, USA, 65205

Tel: 573.823.7272

Email: info@newromepress.com
Web: http://www.newromepress.com

# CONTENTS

# Dedication

*To Christopher and Sophia Hetrick
without whose encouragement and
sacrifice this text would not exist.*

# Acknowledgments

*Special thanks to His Grace,
Bishop Basil, Fr. Peter Heers,
and Monk Menas of
St. Anthony Monastery,
Florence, AZ*

*Forgive me.*

His Grace Bishop BASIL of Wichita and Mid-America

# *Foreword*

> Everyone therefore who hears my words
> and does them, I will compare to a wise person
> who built his house on a rock. The rain came
> down, the floods came, and the winds blew,
> beating hard on that house. Yet, it did not col-
> lapse, because it was founded on the rock. But
> everyone who hears my words and does not do
> them will be like a foolish man who built his
> house on the sand. The rain came down, the
> floods came, and the winds blew, beating hard
> on that house; then it collapsed, and great was
> its downfall. (Matt. 7:24-27)

While the imagery employed in the Parable of Rock and Sand is quite effective in affirming the wisdom of hearing and the importance of incarnating the Gospel of Christ – that is, after all, what our Saviour was address-ing – the same imagery can be used to describe the various bodies which profess to proclaim that Good News. Hence the title of this book, authored by my beloved spiritual son, The Very Reverend Josiah B.G. Trenham (Ph.D. *Dunelm*).

What *is not* discussed in this book is the Rock, Holy Or-thodoxy – the One, Holy, Catholic and Apostolic Church, the Body of Christ (1 Cor. 12:27) built by our Lord Himself upon the Rock of the True Faith (Matt. 16:18). Countless volumes have been written about the Orthodox Church, against which the "rain" and "floods" and "winds" of two millennia have beat, leaving Her unscathed, "a glorious church, not having spot, or wrinkle, or any such thing ... holy and without blemish" (Eph. 5:27). And after the greatest of storms – "The Perfect Storm," if you will – which is yet to come, the storm which shall culminate in the great and last Day, the Church shall be revealed by Her Bridegroom to be in truth the Bride of the Lamb (Rev. 19: 7), the New Jerusalem (Rev. 21:2).

What *is* discussed in this book are some of those bodies which, having been established only over the past several centuries, stand upon unstable and shifting Sand. May the Reader find it edifying for mind and salvific for soul!

† Bishop Basil
Diocese of Wichita and Mid-America
Antiochian Orthodox Christian Archdiocese
of North America

# *Introduction*

Over the last 50 years, there has been a significant increase in global population. Meanwhile, the world itself has become "smaller" due to new modes of communication which have altered the way humans interact. This phenomenon of globalization has lessened traditional cultural barriers and religious distinctions between East and West. In much of the developed world, homogeneity has given way to a heterogeneous cosmopolitan society. This is dramatically evident in America, the world's most religiously diverse society.

The rapid societal changes due to globalization are providing new opportunities for Westerners to become acquainted with Orthodox Christianity through social encounters with believers and the widespread availability of Orthodox literature in Western languages. However, globalization has also presented new challenges for Orthodox believers living in the West. Orthodox Christians often interact with Protestants[1] who invite them to Bible studies

---

[1]  On the origin of the word "Protestant" MacCulloch (2003) writes, "It originally related to a specific occasion, in 1529, when at the Holy Roman Empire's Diet (imperial assembly) held in the city of Speyer, the group of princes and cities who supported the programs of reformation promoted by Martin Luther and Ulrich Zwingli found themselves in a voting minority:

1

and home groups, preaching with zeal and devotion, often calling upon them "to be saved." Such encounters leave the Orthodox believer wanting to respond to the Protestant's lack of familiarity with traditional Christianity. However, since most Orthodox Christians know very little about the historical roots of Protestantism and the myriad of forms it has taken in the 21st century, they are unsure how best to reply.

This book has been written for three purposes. First, to provide the Orthodox reader with a competent overview of the history of Protestantism and its major traditions, from its beginnings in the 16th century to the present day. This overview relies heavily upon the Reformer's own words as well as the creeds of various Protestant faiths, in order to avoid misrepresentation and caricature. Second, to acquaint Orthodox and non-Orthodox readers with a narrative of the historical relations between the Orthodox East and the Protestant West. Finally, to provide a summary of Ortho- dox theological opinion on the tenets of Protestantism.

---

to keep their solidarity, they issued a 'Protestatio', affirming the reforming beliefs they shared. The label 'Protestant' thereafter was part of German or imperial politics for decades, and did not have a wider reference than that. When the coronation of little King Edward VI was being organized in London in 1547, the planners putting in order the procession of digni- taries through the city appointed a place for 'the Protestants', by whom they meant the diplomatic representatives of these reforming Germans who were staying in the capital. Only rather later did the word gain a broader refer- ence" (xx). The word "evangelical" was the word widely used and recognized at the time for what we now would call "Protestant."

## *The World at the Time of the Protestant Reformation*

The Protestant Reformation cannot be understood without a cursory grasp of the political, social, cultural, and ecclesiastical developments that created 15th century Europe. The Crusades were especially important during this period. The Crusades, begun in A.D. 1095 and continuing into the 13th century, were envisioned, organized and carried out by Western Christians with the express purpose of liberating the Holy Land from Muslim control as well as repelling their advance into Christian lands. Though they experienced limited successes, especially the First Crusade which was a joint endeavor with the Christian East, in the final analysis they were a failure. This was made evident when the Queen City, Constantinople, fell to the Turkish Muslims on May 29, 1453, and the Great Church of Christ (Patriarchate of Constantinople) found itself captive to Ottoman rule. Further Turkish incursions into the heart of Europe showed the European peoples that the Muslim threat was closer to home than Jerusalem.

Fifteenth century Christendom was also suffering from centuries of internal division. The Great Schism of 1054, the most sorrowful event in the history of the undivided Church, left the East and West eucharistically alienated and tragically divided. The Sack of Constantinople by the Crusaders in A.D. 1204 created an enduring animosity towards Western Christians. Previously Eastern Christians believed that their Western brothers had fallen into a regrettable heresy, but now saw them as little better than barbarians.[2] Two papal sponsored councils, Lyons in 1274 and Ferrara-Florence in 1438-9, failed miserably at reuniting East and West, and also demonstrated the degree to which the Latin church had become wed to its many theological innovations. Furthermore, the centuries-long separation between Christians of the East and West led to a profound ignorance of each other. This ignorance, borne of theological and political separation, impeded meaningful contact and dialogue between reform-minded Latin clergymen and Orthodox leaders. Though we will document official Orthodox interaction with Protestant leaders of the 16th and 17th centuries, such contact was rare.

## The Papacy and Roman Catholicism
### at the Time of the Reformation

Most examples of ecclesiastical histories authored in a Western context are distinctly biased. The traditional western historiographic categories of "Dark Ages," "Middle Ages," Renaissance," and "Reformation," have little meaning in the East, and in fact have now been widely discarded in Western academia. The fall of Rome in A.D. 410, a seminal

---

[2]    The Orthodox could also be brutal, as is witnessed by the massacre of the Latin community in Constantinople in 1182 during which the majority of the 60,000 strong Latin community was massacred or forced to flee, and 4,000 sold into slavery to the Turks. Fossier (1997), pp. 506–508.

event for West and Western Christians, was not as significant in the East nor did it create the beginning of any "Dark Ages". The Eastern Empire was spared the incursion of many Northern barbarian hordes who were repelled by the walls of Constantinople and instead went toward the West. Furthermore, as Western Christians in the 5th-9th centuries were struggling to survive and trying to sustain an educated and informed faith, the Orthodox East demonstrated remarkable theological and pastoral vigor and never lost its connection to classical or patristic learning.

Prior to the Reformation, the papal West entered into a scholastic period in which theology was conformed to philosophical paradigms and detached from its traditional ascetic milieu. Theologians became academics,[3] and bishops political lords. Detached from the Orthodox East and its insistence on patristic continuity, papal innovations – theological and practical – abounded. These innovations, advanced by a newly articulated and aggressive view of papal supremacy, were supported by a collection of forged historical documents known as the *False Decretals*.[4] These *Decretals* are a collection of canon law written under the

---

[3] A good example is Peter Abelard (1079-1142) who became the theological and philosophical scholar *par excellence* while carrying on a sexually immoral relationship with the nun Héloïse. This relationship was memorialized in a collection of letters which have been published regularly over the course of the last millennium. *The Letters of Abelard and Héloïse* Ed. Michael Clanchy (2004), Penguin Classics: London.

[4] *Collectio falsarum decretalium Isidori mercatoris.*

pseudonym "Isidore Mercator," a reference to the 6th century St. Isidore of Seville. In fact, the decretals were compiled in the 9th century, most probably in France. The first section of the *Decretals* consists of letters purported to be written by pre-Nicene popes from St. Clement of Rome (A.D. 96) to St. Miltiades (A.D. 314) during whose pontificate Emperor Constantine became a Christian and issued his Edict of Milan granting toleration to Christians. These forged papal letters were fabricated in order to place the ever-growing claims of papal arrogance and supremacy into the mouths of early saint-popes and thus establish the papal novelties as ancient Christian faith.[5]

Besides the aforementioned counterfeit papal letters, the *Decretals* also included a document called the *Donation of Constantine*. This falsified imperial decree is said to have been written by Emperor Constantine the Great to Pope Sylvester I (314-35), and includes an account of the Emperor's conversion to Christianity, as well as an enumeration of the privileges bestowed upon the pope and his successors. These privileges included supremacy over the churches of Antioch, Alexandria, Constantinople and Jerusalem, dominion over Rome and all Western provinces, supreme

---

[5]   Met. Panteleimon Rodopoulos (2007) writes that the publication of these Pseudo-Isidorean ordinances provoked a "radical change" in the canon law of the western church, in which papal decrees began to be listed in canonical collections immediately after Scripture and before the Canons of the Ecumenical Councils as sources of canon law, p. 80.

judge of the clergy, chief of whom were to have rank as senators, and the Imperial crown.

Pope Nicholas I knew of these *False Decretals* and used them in his disputation against St. Photios the Great, who so vigorously contended for Holy Orthodoxy. Throughout the Western Middle Ages, these spurious documents were generally considered to be authentic, and served to establish the innovative deceptions of successive popes. They were first explicitly used in a letter to support the papacy in A.D. 1053 by Leo IX to Orthodox Emperor Michael Cerularius. Cardinal Nicholas of Cusa,[6] an influential German Roman Catholic churchman of the 15th century exposed the false provenance of these documents. Martin Luther was aware of Cusa's work and obtained a copy as a young theologian,[7] which certainly influenced his thinking on the proclaimed rights of the papacy. Their authenticity has been universally rejected for hundreds of years, even by the papacy.

### *The Holy Roman Empire in Relation with the Papacy*

Politics played a definitive role in the enduring success of the Protestant Reformation. The Imperial princes of the

[6]   Nicholas of Cusa (1401-64) was a reforming German cardinal and humanist, with deep interests in reconciliation with the Greek East. He was a papal legate in Constantinople prior to its fall to the Turks. He was a firm opponent of indulgence preaching and his *De Concordantia Catholica* was probably the most influential piece of Conciliarist literature. Duffy (1997), p. 183.

[7]   In February 1520 Luther read Ulrich von Hutten's edition of Valla's treatise which showed the famous *Donation of Constantine* to be a forgery.

15th and 16th century[8] were upset by the taxation policy of the Roman Church, as well as its political encroachment into German sovereign estates. During this time, local diocesan bishops were competing for control with Eurpean political powers, and the early Protestant leaders found a receptive audience amongst rulers who were pleased to hear that Rome had no temporal rights over Germany. These rulers were assisted in this cause by a reform movement from within the Roman Catholic Church of the 14th-16th centuries called Conciliarism. Conciliarism, which asserted that ecclesiastical authority lay not with the Pope, but with the ecumenical/general councils of the Church. The appearance of the Conciliarist movement was contemporaneous with an effort by certain monarchies in Catholic Europe to assert their authority over the papacy. Resistance to papal authority was in the air of Western Europe and was supported by the kings of France and Spain. A strong argument can be made that the Protestant Reformation itself was more a land grab by the Protestant princes than about ecclesiastical renewal, and that without their cooperation Martin Luther would have been a flame that quickly ignited, but then rapidly dissipated. With this summary of the historical background to the period, we will now turn our attention to the Protestant Reformers.

---

[8]    Since 1485 in Saxony (long before Luther posted his 95 theses in 1517) the electors of the Holy Roman Empire had rejected the Pope's right to sell indulgences in their estates.

Philip Melanchthon, Martin Luther, Johann Bugenhagen and Gaspard Creuziger, four German Protestant theologians shown working on Luther's translation of the Bible.

Martin Luther

# 1

# *The Life of Martin Luther*
# *Founder of the German Reformation*

### *Childhood*

Luther was born in Eisleben in Saxony on November 10, 1483, and baptized on St. Martin of Tours day, November 11th – hence his name. His father, Heine, was a miner, and ran a prosperous peasant family. His mother Margaret was from a reputable family. Luther was one of nine children, but only five survived to adulthood. He was educated at Magdeburg and Eisenbach, and then Erfurt University (1501-5) where he became a nominalist.[9]

### *Vocation to Monasticism*

Luther was a student of law, but had a near death experience during a lightning storm that altered his life course. During the tempest, he prayed to St. Anne with an oath that he would become a monk if she saved him.[10] Such took place, and in 1505 he entered the monastery of Augus-

---

[9]   That is, he followed the 14th century Englishman, William of Occam, in denying the independent existence of Platonic forms, and became highly critical of a faith overly subjected to reason and scholastic categories.

[10]   Oberman, p. 92.

tinian Hermits/Friars in Erfurt. This Latin religious order lived according to the Rule of St. Augustine of Hippo. Established by Pope Alexander IV in 1256, the Augustinians were well represented in Western Europe, and many of the German Reformers were members of this order.[11] Luther's monastery had about fifty monks, and many of these were well-educated. The German monasteries were at the center of the conflict between Roman centralism and territorial autonomy.

### Priestly Ordination

Luther was ordained a Roman priest in 1507. His father rode into Erfurt with twenty riders for Martin's first mass, and bestowed a generous sum of money on the monastery. During this first mass Luther had one of his most fundamental religious experiences. He was struck by the majesty and holiness of God, and was unable to finish the canon of the mass.[12] Only the wise and calming guidance of the master of novices was able to convince him to finish. Many of Luther's Roman Catholic adversaries would later reference this incident in their attempt to portray Luther as a psychologically impaired person due to an unfortunate upbringing.

---

[11]   Brecht (1981), pp. 51-69. The Augustinians still exist today, though in a much less glorious and influential condition.

[12]   Brecht (1981), pp. 72-73.

## Professorship

Johannes von Staupitz, the Vicar General of the Augustinians, insisted that Luther finish his doctorate in theology and sent the young priest to Rome in 1511. Luther's visit
to Rome was a dream fulfilled, and yet at the same time
was personally very disturbing. He wanted to say mass
for his mother in St. John Lateran Church on a Saturday
since this would bring her great relief in purgatory, but the
line of priests was too long. He wanted to free his grandfather from purgatory so he scaled the Holy Staircase[13] on
his knees, with an "Our Father" on each step, but having
reached the top was left wondering if the act really had
helped his grandfather. He also heard in Rome, for the first
time in his life, outrageous, grotesque and public blasphemy out of the mouths of clerics, sometimes even during the
masses. He was scandalized by the mockery of the saints
and joking about the eucharist by the Roman clergy.[14]

Upon return to Germany, Luther became a doctor of
theology and professor at the University of Wittenberg.[15]

---

[13]  *The Scala Sancta*, or Holy Stairs, are reputed to be the steps that led up
to the praetorium of Pontius Pilate in Jerusalem, on which the Lord Jesus
Christ stood during his Passion on His journey to trial. St. Helen, the mother of St. Constantine the Great, is said to have brought the stairs to Rome in
the 4th century.

[14]  Erasmus of Rotterdam had visited Rome five years previous and wrote
unambiguously about the blasphemy he heard there. Ten years later Ignatius
of Loyola was advised against going to Rome. Oberman, p. 149.

[15]  Brecht (1981), p. 125.

During this time, according to his own testimony, Luther "devoured" the writings of St. Augustine.[16] His first lectures in the University were lectures on the Psalms (1513-1515). He made efforts to learn Hebrew and Greek.[17] He gave himself to Scripture study, and on his deathbed said that no one should believe he has tasted the Holy Scriptures sufficiently unless he has spent one hundred years doing so. During this period of his life, Luther was tormented by the question of whether he was or was not among the elect or predestined.[18]

### The 95 Theses of October 31, 1517 and Papal Indulgences

The Latin theory of indulgences was articulated and given official status by Pope Clement VI in his papal bull *Unigenitus* of 1343. In this bull Clement articulated that the treasure of salvation accomplished by Jesus Christ is "entrusted to be dispensed" through blessed Peter and his successors – the popes of Rome. Indulgences were to be

---

[16]   The first scholarly printed edition of all of Augustine's known works was made by the Basel printer, Johann Amerbach, begun in 1490 and taking sixteen years to complete. MacCulloch (2003), p. 111. This new work stimulated much new interest in Augustine's writings.

[17]   Luther used Erasmus's Greek Edition of the New Testament in 1516.

[18]   This question tormented many a Protestant Reformer. In Orthodoxy the faithful are called *the elect* by virtue of being united to Christ in Holy Baptism and being members of His Holy Body, and pray that they may persevere in such status in order finally to be numbered amongst the elect in God's eternal kingdom. See the prayers for churching/enrolling a catechumen, and the prayers in the baptismal service.

applied to those who had confessed their sins, and who, by the supposed demands of divine justice, must suffer penalties for their sins either in this life or in purgatory.[19] The granting of an indulgence was designed to relieve this punishment due to temporal sins. Pope Clement VI also argued that the treasure has been *increased* by the merits of the Mother of God and the saints. This *treasury of merits* was increased by works of *supererogation*.[20]

In 1476, just seven years before Luther's birth, Pope Sixtus IV in his bull *Salvator noster,* first applied indulgences to the souls in purgatory. Anyone moved to sympathy for departed loved ones or relatives thought to be suffering the fires of purgatory for expiation of punishment (which by divine justice is due them for their sins) could purchase indulgences by giving money for the repair of St. Peter's. This would win relief for the souls in purgatory.

By Luther's time the indulgence machine was running at high speed,[21] and its regulation for Luther was made by Archbishop Albert of Mainz whose *Instructio summaria*

---

[19]   Here we see the fundamental erroneous presupposition upon which the practice of indulgences is built, i.e. the notion that in order for God to maintain His holiness and justice, He must administer retribution even to sinners who have confessed and been reconciled to the Church by priestly absolution. We Orthodox Christians do not believe any such "necessity to punish" binds God whatsoever.

[20]   In papal theology, supererogation refers to those works that go beyond the law of God and are as such completely voluntary acts, such as consecrated celibacy.

[21]   Brecht (1981), pp. 175-183.

Albert of Mainz

of 1515 gave specific instructions for the sale of indulgences.[22] One could have so many absolutions for so much money, even of those sins that were traditionally reserved for judgment by the Apostolic See. Contributors need not be confessed or even contrite themselves, for their offering was considered to be an offering of the departed person himself.

The indulgence preacher Fr. Johann Tetzel (1464-1519), serving Pope Leo X, who needed indulgence monies in order to renovate St. Peter's, was preaching in the Brandenberg territories near Wittenberg. Fr. Tetzel particularly raised Luther's ire with his crass and hyper-dramatic preaching, which many considered to be an abuse of the simple listeners in order to plunder their funds. Here is an example of Tetzel's preaching,

> Do you hear the voices of your dead parents and other people, screaming and saying: 'Have pity on me, have pity on me...for the hand of God toucheth me' We are suffering severe punishments and pain, from which you could rescue us with a few alms, if only you would.'

---

[22]  Janz (2008), pp. 56-59.

Open your ears, because the father is calling to
the son, and the mother to the daughter.[23]

And so the indulgence preacher's message was summarized by the Reformers in these words: "Your coin into the
treasury jings, and a soul from purgatory springs."

Sale of Indulgences

On October 31, 1517, in response to the prevailing ecclesiastical environment, Luther posted ninety-five theses on
the door of the Castle Church in Wittenberg.[24] This ac-

---

[23] Oberman, p. 188.

[24] The door of Castle Church in Wittenberg is to this day a major shrine
memorializing Luther and Protestantism. It should be noted, however, that
the door is not original. The original was destroyed by fire in 1760. Mac-
Culloch (2003), p. 123.

tion has been considered by many Protestants throughout their history to be a significant day, dubbed "Reformation Day."[25] Here follow some thematic excerpts from the *95 Theses* themselves:[26]

### Tenets of Luther's
### 95 Theses or Disputation on the
### Power and Efficacy of Indulgences

*Thesis 1* affirmed that repentance is to be the characteristic of the Christian's entire life, not just a matter of base financial transaction and a formal act of contrition.

*Thesis 5* asserted that the Pope had no ability to remit any penalties at all except those imposed by his own authority or that of the papal canons.

*Thesis 8* noted that penitential canons are traditionally imposed on the living and never on the dying.

*Thesis 12* asserted that traditional canonical penalties were imposed before absolution to give the penitent a test of his repentance, not following absolution.

*Thesis 38* affirmed that papal remission and blessing should be properly valued as a proclamation of the divine remission of sins.

---

[25]  Services and festal celebrations are often held on this day by traditional Protestants. As a young Protestant myself I participated in celebrating this day, and even made a pilgrimage to Wittenberg to see the door itself.

[26]  The English translation of the *95 Theses* may be found in Schultz (1967), Vol. 31, pp. 25-33.

*Thesis 62* affirmed that the true treasure of the Church is the Gospel, not a so-called treasury of merits.

*Thesis 82* posited that if the Pope has power to empty purgatory then he should do it for the sake of love and not for money.

The *95 Theses* are not an articulation of fundamental Protestant dogmas, and could be assented to as much by an Orthodox (on principle) as by a Protestant. The posting of theses for debate on the door of the Castle Church was not unusual in Wittenberg, but was a typical academic exercise as a call for debate, and this was the usual place to post such things. Over time Luther's post came to be viewed as a manifesto of reform. The theses were reproduced and distributed widely throughout Germany within weeks. It was not the *95 Theses* themselves that had such a revolutionary effect on posterity, but rather the subsequent debate on the question of the fallibility of councils, the supreme power of the pope, and the right to admonish the church on scriptural grounds to change her ways.

At about this same time Luther wrote his work *A Sermon on Indulgence and Grace,* which became the first bestseller of the Reformation, being published all over the Holy Roman Empire and reprinted more than twenty times in two years.[27] In April 1518, Luther defended his positions in the

---

[27]  Brecht (1981), pp. 208ff. *cf.* Oberman, p. 192. Luther refused to take any royalties on his writings throughout his entire life. He lived off a salary provided him from the Elector.

Heidelberg Disputation during a meeting of the chapter of his order, and won over to his views the Dominican Martin Bucer. At this disputation Luther articulated forty theses and then offered proofs of his more elaborate theological positions, including: the Law of God cannot help man be sanctified but brings wrath and condemnation to everyone not in Christ; the Law commands but provides no grace to accomplish what is commanded; faith accomplishes everything by the act of believing; free will exists in name only after the Fall; in order to receive the grace of Christ one must despair of his own ability; human good works are not good unless done in faith and by grace; and a true theologian must reject reliance on Aristotle (and acknowledge Plato's superiority) and human philosophy. Luther also articulated what would become the three fundamental slogans of the Protestant Reformation: *sola fidei* (faith alone), *sola gratia* (grace alone), and *sola scriptura* (Scripture alone).

## *Excommunications*

Martin Luther himself said he was excommunicated three times: once by his Augustinian order; once by the pope; and once by the emperor. It was assumed by his interrogators initially that Luther was not smart enough to have produced the works ascribed to him, and that perhaps he was a front man figure for a more accomplished mind like Erasmus[28] or someone of nearly that stature. Luther was tried *in absentia* in Rome for heresy, and summoned to appear before the pope. His political benefactor, Elector Frederick III of Saxony,[29] succeeded in getting the venue changed from Rome to Augsburg. There Luther appeared before Cardinal Cajetan.

Frederick III of Saxony

Refusing to recant, he fled and took refuge under the protection of Elector Frederick. In 1519 Luther debated Fr. Johann Eck (1486-1543) at the Leipzig Disputation, where he denied the primacy of the Pope and the infallibility of general councils.[30]

The denial of the infallibility of general and ecumenical councils became a standard Protestant position, and provides a prism through which to understand the Protes-

---

[28] Desiderius Erasmus 1466/9-1536. He was the leading humanist and most renowned scholar of his age. A great student of Greek, who prepared both a fine edition of the Greek New Testament with a classical Latin translation, together with numerous editions of patristic works. He was highly critical of the corrupt papal church, but rejected the Protestant movement.

[29] Luther and Lutheranism were kept viable by the political support of three successive Electors of Saxony: Frederick "the Wise" (1486-1525), John "the Steadfast" (1525-1532), and John Frederick "the Magnanimous"(1532-47).

[30] Brecht (1981), pp. 299-348. This denial of the infallibility of general councils should not obscure the fact that at this time Luther himself sought

tant faith itself. It was clear to the Reformers (and to the Orthodox) that post-schism Latin councils and popes had contradicted one another. In fact, there were for substantial periods in the post-schism Roman Church two and sometimes three rival popes at the same time. The Western Church was deeply entrenched within a centuries-long debate on authority, which pitted the Latin monarchs of the West against the Papacy.[31]

Given this reality of fallible Roman councils, was there no alternative for Luther to the drastic affirmation that all general councils are fallible? We Eastern Orthodox posit a *tertium quid*, a third option. We posit that the post-schism Latin councils are fallible and full of contradictions because the papacy fell away from the one, holy, catholic, and apostolic Church, and, in so doing, lost its participation in the infallibility of the one, holy, catholic, and apostolic Church. Luther's theological affirmation that all general councils are necessarily fallible is an assertion that contradicts scripture itself (Acts 15). Such a teaching also leads to

the Emperor to convoke a general council to solve the theological divisions of his time.

[31] The Council of Constance (1414-1418) effectively brokered a compromise between the papacy and the western monarchs in which the monarchs agreed not to push the theories of ecclesiological conciliarism, if the pope would allow the monarchs effectively to oversee the church within their realms. Hence, when Luther appealed his condemnation to the Holy Roman Emperor and sought a general church council to decide on the theological matters at hand, his proposal was already irrelevant. MacCulloch (2003), pp. 38-42.

theological chaos, and the positing of some new and novel infallible authority other than the one, holy, catholic and apostolic Church in ecumenical council. This infallible authority would become the Scriptures privately interpreted, and this standard has proven over the last 500 years to be no standard at all.

### Erasmus and Luther

Desiderius Erasmus

The great humanist Erasmus remained a Roman Catholic and endeavored to reform the Church from within. Martin Luther established some of his theological clout by an association with humanism,[32] utilizing the linguistic and theological tools of the Renaissance. Martin Bucer (1491-1551)[33] tried to link Luther and

---

[32] The term "humanism" is a 19th century scholarly invention. It was not used at the time of the Reformation, nor did it have anything to do with the modern notion of a humanist as a person who rejects revealed religion. In the 16th century a scholar who had particular interest in the liberal arts was called a "humanista." The vast majority of humanists of the fourteenth through sixteenth centuries were sincere Christians who were enthusiastic about the rediscovery of ancient and classical texts. The humanists were not Protestants, nor were they interested in overthrowing the established ecclesiastical order. MacCulloch (2003), p. 76.

[33] Bucer, pronounced Butzer, became a follower of Lutheran teaching in 1521, obtained a papal dispensation to dissolve his monastic vows and marry, and became one of the most educated and articulate of all the Reformers.

Erasmus, but neither had much time for the other,[34] though
Luther read Erasmus's work faithfully and more frequently
than any other author.[35] Luther was unable to be protected
by humanist associations, and was condemned by the Pope
on June 12, 1520, in the papal bull *Exsurge Domine.* This
bull of excommunication censured forty-one theses drawn
from Luther's works to date.[36]

## *Pope Leo X's 'Exsurge Domine'*

In the preface to the bull, the pope criticizes the misinterpretation of Protestant historiography, and laments that
these heresies are arising in the heart of the Holy Roman
Empire, which has been so loved of the pontiffs and has
been so faithful to the papacy. In the preface the pope argues that some of the German heresies "expressly contain
the heresy of the Greeks and Bohemians."[37] The "heresy of

He served as rector in Strasbourg until falling out with the city council in
1548 and moving to Cambridge, England, to take up the post as Regius Professor of Divinity. He died in 1551, and was buried in St. Mary's Church,
Cambridge. In 1557, during the reign of Mary I (Tudor-called 'Bloody
Mary'), his body was exhumed and publicly burnt.

[34] Erasmus wrote against Luther's denial of free will, and Luther countered
with his *The Bondage of the Will.* In this text Luther denied the classical
doctrine of free will, and terribly embarrassed his protégé Melanchthon,
who saw to it that Luther's denial of human freedom stayed out of formal
confessions and in the background of theological dialogue with the papacy.

[35] Brecht (1987), pp. 78-84. Luther often referred to Erasmus in his *Table
Talks.*

[36] Brecht (1981), pp. 348-388.

[37] Janz (2008), pp. 381-383.

the Greeks" is a reference to the Orthodox, and revolves around our criticism of papal supremacy and of the Latins' innovative sacramental practice. It is *not* a reference to our dogmatic denial of the *filioque*, since unfortunately Luther accepted this worst of all Latin heresies.[38] The "heresy of the Bohemians" is a reference to Fr. Jan Hus and his Bohemian followers. Hus, together with the English cleric and scholar John Wycliffe, is considered by Protestants to be a morning star of the Reformation.

John Wycliffe (1330-1384) was an English philosopher and theologian at Oxford who found inspiration in the Bible and the Fathers rather than in scholasticism. He argued that the Bible was the sole criterion of doctrine and attacked the authority of the pope. He also attacked Latin monasticism and called on the English government to reform the English church. He went so far as to criticize eucharistic doctrine, which undermined much of his authoritative position in En-

John Wycliffe

glish society. His followers were dubbed Lollards, which means a 'chanter' or mumbler of prayers. Though Wycliffe

---

[38] Siecienski (2010) notes that Luther's acceptance of the creed with the *filioque* was explained in large part by his acceptance of the Augustinian Trinitarian model and the supposed Athanasian Creed, p. 174.

was never condemned by English synods due to his significant political protectors, his followers and teachings were soundly condemned. He contributed to the English Reformation by providing areas and minds receptive to Lutheranism, and was very influential in the Hussite uprising in Bohemia.[39]

Jan Hus [John Huss] (1372-1415) was born a peasant, entered Prague university in 1390, and took his Master's degree in 1396. In 1401, he was appointed Dean of the Philosophical Faculty. He had been ordained to the priesthood in 1400, and became a famous preacher at Bethlehem Chapel in Prague. Wycliffe's writings were familiar to the Czechs since Anne, sister of King Wenceslas IV, married Richard II of England. Hus was attracted to Wycliffe's teaching on predestination. Initially, Hus was supported by his Archbishop, but forty-five of Wycliffe's propositions were condemned by the Prague faculty in 1403. The papacy at this time was divided between two rival popes, and as a consequence the Czechs were divided with different papal and political loyalties. Hus was excommunicated in 1411, and summoned to a council in 1415. After seven months of imprisonment, at the Council of Constance on July 6, 1415, Hus was burned at the stake, his guarantee of safe conduct being disregarded. Hus became, and remains, a Czech national hero and martyr. The Hussite movement demand-

---

[39]  For more on Wycliffe see Evans (2006).

ed a vernacular liturgy and insisted on communion being served in both kinds.[40] Luther followed Hus on these principles. Various contemporary ecclesiastical groups trace their lineage from Hus including the "Bohemian Brethren" and the Czechoslovak National Church. Wycliffe was posthumously condemned at the same time as Hus at the Latin Council of Constance in 1415.[41]

For Martin Luther, Jan Hus was St. Jan Hus. Luther referred to words which Hus was reported to have uttered in prison as a prophecy of himself. Hus said "They might now be roasting a goose (for Hus means goose), but in a hundred years they will hear a swan sing, which they will not be able to silence."[42] Luther considered Wycliffe and Hus to have challenged primarily the immorality of the papacy while Luther himself was an attacker of false papal doctrine.

Having established a historical context in the preface, the papal bull moved next to document Luther's errors. The papal criticisms of Luther contained in *Exsurge Domine* in-

---

[40] These Hussites were utraquists, from the Latin *sub utraque specie*, "in both kinds."

[41] For more on Hus see Spinka (1968). Both Wycliffe and Hus are memorialized to this day. Today there is a famous Protestant mission organization focused on translation of the Bible into all the languages of the earth which bears the name: Wycliffe Bible Translators. Wycliffe supported the use of the vernacular; however, he played no direct part in translating the Bible into English. This was a project of his disciples. Many contemporary memorials to Jan Hus exist throughout the city of Prague, as well as a good number of small Hussite churches.

[42] Oberman, p. 55.

Jan Hus in Prison

clude the following: his severely limited tolerance for purgatory; his denial that the Scriptures teach purgatory altogether; his attack on the objective work of sacraments apart from the faith of the one believing; his encouragement of a false assurance; his teaching that priests have as much authority in the confessional as the pope and that a layperson could also function as a confessor; his tolerance of Bohemians as schismatics and his refusal to brand them as heretics; his approval of the distribution of the eucharist in both kinds; his charge that indulgences are pious frauds; his denial that the Roman Pontiff is the Vicar of Christ over all the churches of the entire world instituted by Christ Himself; his support of some theological articles of Jan Hus that were condemned at the Council of Constance; his teaching that even in doing good works a man sins; his opposition to the burning of heretics; and his opposition to the war against the Turks. For these errors he is "condemned" and "damned."

Luther could not bring himself to repent of his teachings and enunciate those six simple letters the pope wished him to speak: *revoco*. Luther burned the papal bull, together

Martin Luther burning Papal Bulls

with various books of scholastic theology and canon law. Excommunicated by the papal bull *Decet Romanum Pontificem* on January 3, 1521,[43] Luther was summoned before the Diet[44] of Worms, where he again refused to recant. His articulate refusal has been memorialized in these famous words:

> Unless I am convinced by the testimony of Holy Scriptures or by evident reason – for I can believe neither pope nor councils alone, as it is clear that they have erred repeatedly and contradicted themselves...my conscience is captive

---

[43] Janz (2008), pp. 383-386.
[44] A 'diet' in this context means an official assembly.

to the Word of God. Thus I cannot and will not recant, because acting against conscience is neither safe nor sound. Here I stand, I can do no other.[45] God help me. Amen.

Luther's response was circulated in print throughout Germany. From this time Luther began to teach that the

Papal Bull
Excommunicating Luther

Pope was the Antichrist, a notion that had been in circulation for some time amongst the radical Franciscans. This radical affirmation would become standard Protestant fare, and even became codified in some Protestant confessions.[46] On May 26, 1521, the Holy Roman Emperor banned Luther, and called for his arrest. Elector Frederick rescued Lu-

---

[45]   MacCulloch (2003) notes of these two phrases "Here I stand, I can do no other," 'the first editor of his collected works, Georg Rörer, felt compelled to construct two tiny summary sentences in German, which have become the most memorable thing Luther never said,' p. 131. MacCulloch suggests this can stand as the motto of all Protestants, and perhaps of all western civilization.

[46]   *Westminster Confession of Faith*, Ch. 25, Section 6, "There is no other head of the Church but the Lord Jesus Christ; nor can the Pope of Rome in any sense be head thereof; but is that Antichrist, that man of sin, and son of perdition, that exalteth himself in the Church against Christ, and all that is called God."

ther,[47] and kept him in hiding in his castle at Wartburg
near Eisenach. Luther spent eight months there in disguise
as "Junker Georg." This was a very productive period for
Luther, when he worked on his German translation of the
Bible. The situation in Wittenberg was deteriorating, and
some of Luther's colleagues became dissatisfied with the
degree of reform Luther advocated and joined more radical
movements. Luther returned to Wittenberg March 6, 1522
to restore order, and produced a simplified liturgy. He discarded his monastic habit in 1524.[48]

### *Luther's Small Catechism as an Expression of Pastoral Vision*

Luther wrote famous commentaries on St. Paul's Epistles
to the Galatians and Romans, as well as on Deuteronomy,
which served to articulate his vision of the Christian life.
His *Small Catechism* elucidates his pastoral vision for his
people, and was considered by Luther to be his most important work. In his catechism Luther required an annual
auricular confession in the precincts of the church,[49] and
provided basic instruction on the Ten Commandments,
the Lord's Prayer, and the Apostles Creed, as well as the sacraments of baptism, confession, and eucharist. He provided

---

[47] Brecht (1981), pp. 470-476.
[48] Luther's works were being voraciously read at this time. In 1523 alone
there were 390 editions of various of Luther's writings published in Germany. MacCulloch (2003), p. 152.
[49] Oberman, p. 244.

forms for morning and evening prayers, blessings at table,[50] a small chart of Bible passages for use at home, and a simple marriage booklet for pastors. The *Small Catechism* became a cornerstone of evangelical doctrine, was the only official Lutheran document written solely by Luther himself, and was imitated on grand scale by both Protestants and Roman Catholics.[51]

### The German Reformation and Luther's 'Nationalism'

The word "Reformation" was as popular a word in the Middle Ages as "democracy" is today in our age.[52] It meant a return to original ideals, and had, especially in the early days of the Protestant revolution, a rather wide semantic range. In 1520 Luther wrote *An Address to the Nobility of the German Nation* in which he called upon the princes to reform the church themselves.[53] The Papacy was very afraid of the German-speaking Holy Roman Empire becoming a national/monarchist church, and also feared that France would make this step. England itself realized this papal fear under Henry VIII. Luther articulated a right of laity to summon a reforming German council without papal permission, asked princes to abolish taxes to Rome, and challenged clerical celibacy and masses for the dead. This

---

[50]  These forms appropriated the basic Orthodox forms and would be very familiar to Orthodox Christians.

[51]  MacCulloch (2003), p. 165.

[52]  *Ibid.*, p. 50.

[53]  Brecht (1981), pp. 369-379.

Wartburg Castle

work was followed by his *The Babylonian Captivity of the Church* in which Luther attacked communion in one kind and the doctrine of transubstantiation. In his *The Freedom of the Christian,* Luther posited his doctrine of justification as a "joyous exchange" between the sinner and Christ in which the righteousness of Christ is imputed to the sinner by faith. At this time there was a peasants' uprising and serious civil unrest in the Empire. In his treatise *Against the Raging Peasants,* Luther encouraged the princes to wage war against the peasants, and blessed their widespread slaughter.[54]

---

[54] Luther wrote this piece in May, 1525, after the Peasants' War had been in full force for over a year. Luther was later accused by the peasants of betraying them when he saw that their political cause would not succeed. Brecht (1990), pp. 178ff.

### Luther and Melanchthon

Philipp Melanchthon (1497-1560), Professor of Greek at the University in Wittenberg, was Luther's dear friend, closest collaborator, theological confidant, and counselor. There was a deep mutual respect between the two men, if not always theological agreement. Melanchthon's book on doctrine, *Loci Communes*,[55] became the early standard Lutheran theological summary.[56]

Philipp Melanchthon

### Luther's Personal and Family Life

Luther made his former monastery into his personal home. This, together with his marriage to a nun, did not take place until it was politically safe to effect. This required the death of Luther's main political benefactor, the Elector of Saxony, who was personally hostile to the marriage of Catholic priest-monks who had become Protestants. This hostility was doubled when, as was so often the case, the Catholic-become-Protestant clergy wanted to marry Catholic nuns. After the Elector's death, Luther was married to the nun Catherine von Bora on June 13, 1525, at the Black Monastery by Pastor Johannes Bugenhagen. The

---

[55] For an English translation see Manschreck (1965).

[56] *Loci communes rerum theologicarum seu hypotyposes theologicae* (Latin for *Common Places in Theology or Fundamental Doctrinal Themes*). Luther is reputed to have said concerning it, "Next to Holy Scripture, there is no better book." MacCulloch (2003), p. 140.

birth of the Luthers' first child was accompanied by great interest from both Protestants and Catholics, since many on the Catholic side thought the child would be born a many-headed monster.[57] Martin and Catherine raised six children, managed a large house constantly filled with runaway monks and nuns who needed shelter and were being encouraged to marry by Martin and Catherine, cared for Catherine's aged aunt, and used their home as a gathering place for Protestant causes.

### Controversies of the Final Years and Death
### Lutheran-Reformed-Anabaptist Conflicts

The Protestant Reformation was born in controversy, gave birth to controversy, and has continued to spawn irreconcilable controversies for the last five hundred years. Luther's last years were deeply scarred by unresolved controversies.[58] The greatest of these took place at the Colloquy of Marburg in 1529. This official gathering was designed to unify the Protestant theologians, but instead served to express the deepest of divisions between Luther and Swiss Reformer Ulrich Zwingli on the subject of the eucharist.[59] Zwingli denied that the eucharist was the true Body and

---

[57] Oberman, p. 278.

[58] It should be noted, however, that Luther's entire life was replete with theological controversy that threatened to shatter even his closest relationships with Melanchthon and other Lutheran theologians.

[59] Details on this controversy, and the conflicting teachings of the various Reformers on this most important subject, will follow in succeeding chapters.

Blood of Jesus Christ. Luther thought that his own teaching, known to the history of theology as consubstantiation,[60] was the clear teaching of Scripture, and neither could understand why the other was being so hardheaded and disobedient to the "clear teaching of Scripture." The Marburg Colloquy and Protestant eucharistic controversy revealed the greatest weakness of the Protestant embrace of the doctrine of *sola scriptura*, and proved the absurdity of any dependence on the clarity of Scripture alone to establish common doctrines. Luther felt very deeply on this matter, and said "Before I would have mere wine with the fanatics,[61] I would rather receive sheer blood with the pope."[62] Accomplished Protestant leaders like Carlstadt, Zwingli, Oecolampadius in Basel, and Bucer in Strasbourg disavowed Luther's teaching on the sacraments and church polity. We Orthodox Christians are led to ponder: where is the reality of *sola scriptura* and the perspicuity of Scripture[63] if even those bound by faculty, friendship, politics,

---

[60]  It should be noted, however, that consubstantiation is not the confessionally defined or accepted way that Lutherans generally speak about Holy Communion.

[61]  Fanatics here refers to those Protestants, most commonly known as Anabaptists, who, like Zwingli, denied that the eucharist was the Body and Blood of Jesus. This quote is assuredly devastating to contemporary Protestant Evangelicals, who universally deny that the eucharist is the very Body and Blood of Jesus, since Luther himself, their hero, disowns them as fanatics with whom he would have no fellowship.

[62]  Oberman, p. 232.

[63]  The doctrine of the perspicuity (from the Latin perspicare, to look through) of Scripture teaches that the meaning of the scriptural text is clear to the average person on essential matters.

and faith cannot agree on the meaning of the central Christian act of worship?

Luther's closest friend, Justus Jonas, was with him when he died at 3 am on February 18, 1546. Jonas recorded Luther's last twenty-four hours, and sent a copy to the Elector and to his university colleagues. Luther's body was accompanied by an honor guard from town to town and arrived at Wittenberg. Melanchthon heard of the death of his colleague and mentor while in the middle of class and cried out, "The charioteer of Israel has fallen." Luther was buried at Castle Church in Wittenberg. After Luther's death there was very little sign that the Reformation had a future. The papacy was striking back with the establishment of Ignatius of Loyola's Jesuit order, seeking to regain an educational edge over Protestantism. Additionally, the papacy, for the first time since the Fourth Lateran Council in 1215, convened a multinational papal council in Trent in 1545. On May 19, 1547, only 15 months after Luther's death, Wittenberg capitulated to the Holy Roman Emperor who was attempting to impose his Catholicism by force. The political conflict in Germany only ended after the Thirty Years War, which left Germany scourged in 1648, when Catholics, Lutherans, and Calvinists arranged to co-exist. Though the future looked bleak for Protestantism at the time of Luther's death, history is full of surprises.

Martin Luther

# 2

# *Lutheranism and Orthodoxy*

### *Is Martin Luther a Christian Hero?*[64]

Having examined the contours of Luther's life and teachings we shall attempt to make an evaluation. Does Luther deserve the adulation that is accorded him by Protestants of all persuasions? Is Luther truly a Christian hero? Martin Luther himself acknowledged that he had many vices that were quite incapable of being concealed from public view, including extreme irascibility and verbosity. He was deeply sarcastic, vulgar,[65] and harsh.[66] Many

[64] After his death in 1546 Luther became very much like a Medieval saint to Lutherans. His Saxon birthplace, Eisleben, was called by many a "New Jerusalem" and it became a place of pilgrimage. Pictures of Luther were said to have miraculous powers. MacCulloch (2003), p. 347. Though Protestants reject the notion that there are certain Christians uniquely set forth by the Church as "saints" to whom believers on the earth can and should turn to in prayer, they still seek Christian heroes. Martin Luther has often been set forth as one such hero as in the text by Kolb (1999) entitled, "Martin Luther as Prophet, Teacher and Hero: Images of the Reformer."

[65] Luther regularly employed vulgarities, and called his opponents by a variety of coarse names like "snot-nose." Brecht (1987), p. 70.

[66] Objects of Luther's ire and insult consistently for decades were the Jews, the Turks, the Pope, Anabaptists, the Muenzterites, the Antinomians, and just about any theologian who dared contradict Luther. Virtually all the 1st and 2nd generation Protestant Reformers acknowledged Luther's wrath,

over the centuries have questioned also his psychological stability. There are, however, more serious matters to address from an Orthodox Christian perspective.

### Luther's Moral Capitulation before Political Rulers

One of the great scandals of Luther's life has to do with the unethical counsels he gave to one of the leading politicians supporting the Reformation: Philip, Landgrave of Hesse.[67] Philip was an influential ruler at the time of the German Reformation, and Luther needed his support. As a young man, Philip came out in favor of the Reformers, but, despite his particular theological convictions, lived a licentious life. After being married three weeks he committed adultery, and lived in such lechery that he went without communion for a very long time. He conceived the idea of taking a second wife, which, after Philip threatened the Reformers with a cessation to his political support, was agreed upon by both Luther and Melanchthon. Rather than divorce his first wife, Christine of Saxony (reputed to be rather ugly and a heavy drinker), Philip, with the blessing of his spiritual directors, married also Margarethe von der Saale, becoming a bigamist on December 10, 1539.[68] It should be

---

and labored to co-exist with his temper. For example, John Calvin, wrote that Luther was "immoderately ardent and violent in character." Selderhuis (2009), p. 106.

[67] "Landgrave" is a political title used in the Holy Roman Empire to designate a count with immediate relation to the Holy Roman Emperor.

[68] In theory, Philip could have been put to death for bigamy at the hands of the Holy Roman Emperor, his sovereign, since an imperial law laid down

noted that Philip was captivated with the idea of procuring a second wife on the basis of the counsel that Melanchthon gave to King Henry VIII of England, who wished to divorce his first wife, Catherine of Aragon,[69] and marry Anne Boleyn. Melanchthon suggested to Henry VIII that he simply take a second wife instead of divorcing Catherine.[70]

Some scholars have suggested over the centuries that this was the greatest blot on the history of the Reformation, and evidence of the fact that Protestantism was entrenched in and subservient to politics to such a degree that morality on occasion took a second seat to political expedience. Philip of Hesse, the bigamist, ended up having ten children from the wife that he supposedly could barely look at, and the last three of his ten children with Christina were born after he had married his second wife, Margarethe. Luther's adversaries could, with some firm justification I think, call the Reformer the "toady of princes."[71]

---

in 1532 prescribed this penalty. In reality, Charles V gave Philip an imperial pardon. MacCulloch (2003), p. 229.

[69] Adding to the drama was the fact that Catherine was the aunt of the Holy Roman Emperor, Charles V, and that the Emperor had visited England and King Henry in 1520.

[70] It is ironic that the Wittenberg theologians, when all was said and done in the Anne Boleyn affair, considered themselves the only real advocates for Queen Catherine. Brecht (1987), p. 61.

[71] For more on this sordid affair, *Ibid.*, pp. 205-215. It should be noted, however, that the history of Christianity is full of ecclesiastical capitulation before political forces, and we Orthodox Christians certainly cannot claim innocence in our history. The point I am making here is not that Luther's

## *Luther's Theological Patrimony*

While Luther was a talented writer, the breadth of his theology is extremely limited from the Orthodox perspective. His exposure to the Holy Fathers was through very abbreviated editions, and usually through florilegia.[72] Luther's best attempt to place his theology in a patristic consensus[73] is through his appeal to St. Augustine of Hippo, from whom he claims to draw his teaching on justification by faith alone, his teaching on predestination, his disregard of monastic vows, and many more positions.[74] Though Luther appears to have had access to primary texts of Augustine in a respectable edition, and though he in his own words "devoured" Augustine's writings, he nevertheless appears to have exercised a great amount of selection in just what teachings of St. Augustine he embraced. Much of Reformation theology is an embrace of certain themes of Augustine pitted against certain other of Augustine's fundamental

---

moral compromise before a prince is unique to him or Lutheranism, but that it is not the action of a hero or moral model.

[72]    From the medieval Latin *flos* meaning "flower" and *legere* meaning "to gather." They were essentially patristic excerpts, collecting various quotes from the Holy Fathers on topics. In the Greek tradition anthologia /anthologies are the parallel.

[73]    The *consensus patrum*, the consensus of the Holy Fathers, is the traditional standard of infallible authority, the true magisterium, in the Holy Orthodox Church.

[74]    A good example of what patristic sources were available to Luther and his colleagues is found in the Catalogue of Testimonies appended to the Book of Concord. Much of the ignorance of the Greek tradition is simply a result of a cultural divide that became acute from the 5th century onwards.

convictions. Even the great Reformed Protestant stalwart and Princeton scholar B. B. Warfield acknowledged this, writing, "the Reformation, inwardly considered, was just the ultimate triumph of Augustine's doctrine of grace over Augustine's doctrine of the church."[75]

It is commonly argued by Protestant scholars that Luther was somehow continuing in the 16th century the legacy of St. Augustine, which had been overshadowed by Aquinas and Aristotelian philosophy. This is not tenable. Luther's use of St. Augustine was a misappropriation concerning which the saint of Hippo must assuredly be unhappy. Having said this, it should also be noted that such a heavy dependence upon the innovative St. Augustine himself, combined with the virtual neglect of the universal teachers of the Church like Saints Athanasius the Great, Basil the Great, Gregory the Theologian, John Chrysostom,[76] Maximos the Confessor, John of Damascus,[77] Symeon the New Theologian, and Gregory Palamas,[78] is one of the great

[75] Warfield (1956), 32.2.

[76] The accomplished 19th century Protestant church historian Philip Schaff (1889) writes of Luther's ignorance of Chrysostom in these words, "Of Chrysostom he must have read very little, or he could not have called him a 'rhetorician full of words and empty of matter.' He spoke well, however of Theodoret's commentaries on the Pauline Epistles, which is an indirect testimony in favor of Chrysostom's exegesis," p. 17.

[77] Though through Peter Lombard's Sentences, a standard theological textbook in the Latin West in the Middle Ages superseded only by Aquinas' *Summa Theologica*, there is some appropriation of the Damascene.

[78] It should be remembered that Palamas was a ferocious and articulate refuter of Latin heresies, which makes the Reformers' ignorance of Palamas all the more tragic.

weaknesses of post-schism Latin theology and reasons for its reductionism.[79]

## *Luther's Hermeneutical and Ethical Disconnect from Holy Tradition*

Just how far Luther strayed from the common inheritance of Christians in his reaction to papal heresies and innovations may be observed in his teaching on marriage and monasticism. Luther has many beautiful words to offer on the subject of marriage, and on the daily Christian family life. He was deeply convinced that the Roman Church had undercut the sanctity of marriage. Unfortunately, his teaching is as one-sided and heretical in his promotion of

---

[79] The early Lutherans were capable of producing an impressive array of patristic quotations at times. For instance, the *Catalogue of Testimonies* authored by Jakob Andreae and Martin Chemnitz, which was often appended to the 1580 publication of the *Book of Concord*, cited references from Eusebius, Athanasius, Epiphanius, Cyril of Alexandria, Theodoret of Cyrus, John of Damascus, Basil the Great, Ambrose, John Chrysostom, Theophylact, Oecumenius, Leo the Great, Vigilius, Nicephorus, Hilary of Potiers, Eusebius of Emesa, Gregory of Nyssa, Augustine of Hippo, Justin Martyr, Origen, as well as sacred canons of the Third and Fourth Ecumenical Councils. However, after quoting these venerable holy fathers, the authors of the catalogue explicitly affirm that only Scripture can be a source of dogma. Such a broad and authoritative citation of these holy fathers was made by these Lutheran scholars explicitly to affirm the traditional Christology of the Fourth Council, and the ubiquity of the glorified Body of Jesus Christ. If the Lutherans had sought to justify their doctrine of justification, ecclesiology, theology of marriage and monasticism, etc. with a similar list demonstrating the *consensus patrum,* they would have seen how full of innovations their theology was, for certainly just as impressive a catalogue of testimonies could be compiled demonstrating the Lutheran heresies in these areas.

marriage and disparagement of monastic life, as the anti-marriage Gnostic theology in the early centuries of the Church was one-sided and heretical in attacking marriage while promoting celibacy.[80]

In a complete reversal of scriptural and patristic teaching, Luther argues that marriage is the highest estate of life. Luther categorically refuses to recognize consecrated celibacy as scriptural and God-ordained. This erroneous presupposition demonstrates not just the vacuous reality of his teaching on *sola scriptura,*[81] but also manifests how much his own grievous circumstances and personal angst, as a late-medieval Latin monk, determined his reading and interpretation of the Scriptures.

---

[80] Perhaps the single most significant social change brought forth by the Reformation is the marriage of the clergy and abandonment of the paradigm and practice of celibate life. Western Europe had known centuries of clericalism, and forces undergirding the Reformation sought to close the gap between clergy and laity. The universal rejection of monastic life by the Reformers ought be viewed within this historical context. For more on Orthodoxy's teaching concerning the relationship between marriage and monasticism see Trenham (2013).

[81] For the supremacy of consecrated celibacy is one of the most obvious teachings of the New Testament. *cf.* 1 Cor. 7, Matt. 19. This supremacy of monasticism was not at all clear to those who embraced *sola scriptura* and the *perspicuity of scripture* and yet had theological and practical pre-commitments which influenced their reading of scripture to such a degree that no room for a scriptural monasticism whatsoever was found. Whole new interpretations of philo-monastic scriptural texts were propounded completely unheard of in the previous fifteen centuries of interpretation of the New Testament.

In his *Small Catechism* Luther calls marriage "one hundred times" more spiritual than the monastic estate. Yet to enter into the married estate himself Luther became an oath-breaker, as did his wife Catherine. As adults they had sworn oaths to serve Christ faithfully as celibate persons like St. Paul. Yet as adults they broke these oaths and encouraged hundreds of others to do likewise. In such a case of clear ethical violation Luther found it convenient to vilify the monastic estate in order to justify breaking his own vows.[82] Yet his own Protestant Prince, the Elector Frederick, who consorted with concubines himself, was so opposed to this offense that Luther was not able to marry as long as Frederick lived. Luther's colleague and friend Melanchthon was so opposed to Luther's oath-breaking and marriage to Catherine that he himself did not attend the wedding.[83]

Luther rejected the traditional distinction between natural necessary needs and natural needs. Marriage and sexual intercourse have been considered by the Fathers of the Church to be natural needs, but not natural *necessary* needs. Marriage is natural, but can be superseded without sin. Luther, on the other hand, taught that not one in one thousand persons, and that one only by a very special mir-

---

[82]   In his treatise in 1521, *Of Monastic Vows*, Luther argued that the monastic oath was not binding.

[83]   Some sources say that Melanchthon simply was not invited by Luther, but this begs the question as to why. MacCulloch (2003), p. 143.

acle, could faithfully live the monastic life.[84] As a result, though on principle Luther had to leave the door open for the one, all monasteries were dissolved in Lutheran lands.[85]

The Orthodox Church has always taught that monasticism is an essential ecclesiastical reality. There is no Church without monasticism. Luther's opposition to monasticism betrays a tragic eschatological eclipse in his vision.[86] In his self-justifying mania he quotes physicians of the day who said that if one does not pass reproductive fluids they will strike into the flesh and blood and become a poison and the body will become unhealthy, enervated, sweaty, and foul-smelling. Here Luther tries to affirm that intercourse

---

[84] Oberman, p. 272. Even with Luther's overly-pessimistic percentages one can still at 1/1000 see that monasteries would thrive in any Christian land. In America, where we have about 240,000,000 Christians, with Luther's percentages we would have 240,000 monastics! Almost 5,000 in every state!

[85] There were cases of monastic communities embracing the Reformation but wishing to remain in monastic community. Luther feared that such would lead to a relapse into the papacy and worked against such arrangements. Brecht (1987), p. 7. Luther was clear about how far from traditional asceticism he had strayed, "I now seek pleasure and take it wherever I can." *Ibid.*, p. 27. He should not have wondered, after such attack upon ascetical Christian practice, why he failed so bitterly to effect a moral improvement in Christian life amongst the Germans. Over this reality Luther was often terribly depressed. Ibid., p. 263.

[86] For a more thorough documentation and evaluation of the evolution of Luther's thought on monasticism, together with documentation of the cogent papal refutation of Luther's teaching, see the article entitled "Monasticism" in Forell and McCue (1982), pp. 286-321.

is biologically necessary.[87] What would Luther say about Jesus Christ? If men have to pass semen and be married as adults to be healthy, was Jesus less than human? Was he modeling an impossible life? For Luther marriage is God's alternative to the "false diabolical holiness" of monastic life.[88] Luther is not able to maintain his own consistency on the physical impossibility of celibacy and in one of his treatises on marriage he argues that a husband is lying if he says he can't remain continent while serving his invalid wife. In this case Luther affirms, at the cost of his own teaching elsewhere and his logical consistency, that celibacy is possible. We are to think that one can be celibate if he is married to an invalid wife, but not if he is married to Jesus Christ. In his treatise *On the Estate of Marriage* (1522) Luther argues that marriage is not a matter of free choice but of necessity. Persons are *"duty-bound* to forsake vows whenever they find that God's ordinance to produce seed and to multiply is powerful and strong within them."

---

[87]  See the underlying message in Luther's words: "I had to stop being a monk and get married. It was biologically necessary." Just how overly-dependent upon the marriage estate Luther and his followers became is evident in the life of one of Luther's closest friends and co-laborers, Justas Jonas. Reverend Jonas was widowed in 1542 at age 50, and was remarried to a 23 year-old within six months. *Ibid.*, p. 300.

[88]  Luther speciously argued that the monks were the real "Anabaptists" because of the traditional monastic practice of seeing tonsure as a second baptism. Brecht (1987), p. 70. Luther also thought that traditional priestly ordination devalued baptism. *Ibid.*, p. 76.

Besides his unbalanced and untraditional teaching on marriage, Luther also rejects the traditional rules of canon law, calling them papal.[89] He overturned the traditional laws of consanguinity and the canons which establish appropriate marital impediments. Hence, Luther criticizes canons which forbid the marriage of first cousins and many other close relatives. He produced novel interpretations of Old Testament marriage law (including levirate law). He permitted the marriage of spiritual relatives including the marriage of godparents with their godchildren, marriage with relatives by adoption, intermarriage with other religions. He castigated traditional censures as "money-seeking" and "foolish," rejected traditional canons on sexual fasting, taught that parents who encourage monasticism are taking their children to the devil, and criticized "St. Margaret legends."[90] His radical break with traditional Christian norms on the subject of marriage led him into consistent conflict with the jurists of Electoral Saxony, who protested Luther's innovations.[91] His demands for acquiescence by the jurists

---

[89]  Here again we see the Protestant mistake of failing to separate what is universal tradition/canon law of the undivided Church, and what is simply papal innovation. Canon law had become a universal code in Europe at a time when other legal systems in Europe were fragile. The reach of canon law into the everyday lives of Western Christians was deep, and the Protestant Reformers saw canon law as the cornerstone of papal power. MacCulloch (2003), p. 29.

[90]  Luther could not abide traditional examples of married holiness which were too other-worldly and ascetic for him.

[91]  Brecht (1987), p. 119.

to his novelties in marriage law, with the threat that if they did not comply he would leave Wittenberg, is just one of the many expressions of the reality that Luther established himself as the new Pope of Reformed Christendom.[92]

Despite all this unfortunate rejection of universal Christian tradition, Luther repeats the Augustinian teaching that even marital intercourse is never without sin, but God excuses it by his grace because the "estate of marriage" is at work. Here we see yet another incidence of the rejection of universal Christian tradition, with the maintenance of uniquely Augustinian notions that never garnered a patristic consensus. Luther made a bold and fantastic stand against many papal abuses, but provided no better alternative to his followers than papalism itself, when it comes to the issue of theological certainty. Where is the *tertium quid* between papalism and *sola scriptura*? By Luther's insistence on innovation in the teaching of marriage, encouraging not just secular priests to be married, but fanatically promoting the breaking of monastic vows and the marriage of monastics, Luther ended any possibility of reunion with Rome.

---

[92]  Luther was accused of this very thing not just by the Latins, but by his own colleagues and fellow Reformers. Despite his denials to the contrary, it is quite evident that this is exactly what had taken place. He argued that he had to insist on theological conformity to himself so that jurists (and other opponents) "would not split my (!) church!" Brecht (1987), pp. 119-121.

### Luther Not A Modern Protestant
### and Probably Not a Modern Lutheran

Though Martin Luther was a radical and forced a terrible breach in Western Christendom, he cannot so easily be appealed to by modern Protestants. Protestantism, starting with Luther, has become more and more radical over time, bearing the awful fruit of divisiveness and theological innovation that necessarily follows the dogma of *sola scriptura*. Would modern Protestants even recognize Luther as one of their number? Would Luther be comfortable in the Lutheran Church of the 21st century?[93] I think the answer to both questions is no.[94]

Luther taught the importance of making the sign of the Cross. He advocated for a yearly auricular confession in the Church sanctuary. He employed written prayers and a structured liturgy. He believed in and taught the perpetual virginity of the Most Holy Virgin Mary, the Theotokos. He completely rejected the idea of an invisible church as

[93]  2nd generation Reformer John Calvin did not think that Luther would have been happy with the Lutherans. Selderhuis (2009), p. 227. By the time that the last generation of Lutherans who actually remembered what it was like to be Roman Catholic passed, a devolution and radical mutation of Lutheranism began. Much of the vision of Luther and the original Lutherans was lost, and this devolution is true in all the Protestant traditions. None of the Reformers were able to create a movement that would sustain itself and its ecclesiological and cultural vision.

[94]  What has really sustained Lutheranism for the last four hundred years and has served as the hub of Lutheran piety has been Lutheran hymnody. For more on this see Brown (2005).

it is so commonly embraced by Protestants today. He considered those who rejected the miraculous nature of baptism and the real presence of Christ in the eucharist to be utter fanatics. He had no tolerance for Anabaptism, and castigated those who refused to baptize infants. He argued strongly against the so-called "Constantinopolitan fall" of the church. He had no affinity for Jews, and rejected any reading of Scripture that suggested that a return of Jewish people to the Holy Land was prophesied. He was deeply convinced of martyrdom as a mark of the church, and disavowed Christian triumphalism. Luther himself wished sincerely to be a martyr.[95] He severely criticized the Protestant iconoclasts who broke up holy images, and defended Christian art as "sermons for the eyes."

## The Augsburg Confession and Formation of Lutheranism

### Creeds and Confessions

The Nicene Creed is not the same as a confession. Writing detailed confessions is a particular characteristic of the Protestant Reformation. The literary and theological genre of "confession" came into its own in the 16th century Protestant West. Some church historians have termed the 16th to 17th centuries as the "confessional age." Even Protestant

---

[95] When Luther heard of the martyrdom of his fellow Augustinians J. von Essen and Heinrich Vos in Brussels he wept for jealousy.

churches known for being anti-creedal, such as the Mennonites and Anabaptists, wrote many confessions.

The rise in popularity of confessions paralleled the decline of popular confidence in church councils. Most of the
churches of the Reformation professed an allegiance to the
Nicene Creed, and often also to the Apostles Creed of the
West.[96] When Lutherans, Anglicans or Presbyterians use
the word "confessions" they usually refer to the doctrinal
statement of their own particular branch of the Reformation. Sometimes both the creeds and the confessions are
referred to by these bodies as "symbols."

The Roman Catholic Church also wrote "confessions" –
most famously the documents that came from the Counter
Reformation Council of Trent in 1545-1563. We will speak
more about the so-called *Counter Reformation* in the Roman Church, perhaps better called the *Catholic Reformation,* in an upcoming chapter. The Orthodox are not
famous for writing confessions, but we too had our own
confessions written in the 17th century such as *The Orthodox Confession of the Catholic and Apostolic Eastern Church
by Peter Mogila* in 1638, and the *Confession of Dositheos* of
1672, both of which follow the *Confession of Metrophanes
Critopoulos* of 1625. These "confessions" had, and perhaps
to some degree continue to have, an official authority in the
Church, though certainly not like the role of confessions

---

[96]  The Apostles Creed is usually the "creed" referred to in Protestant confessions and terminology by the word "creed."

The Augsburg Confession

in the Protestant communions. In fact, I doubt that most Orthodox have ever even heard of these confessions.

### The Augsburg Confession

The Diet of Augsburg assembled by Emperor Charles V in June 1530 was the occasion for the presentation of the Lutheran confession of faith that bears its name, *The Augsburg Confession*. Just a few months earlier the Turks had laid siege to Vienna, and the Emperor wished to root out heresy from his dominion, unify the faith of his lands, and secure the allegiance of all the German princes against the Turks.[97] The Augsburg Confession was written by Philipp Melanchthon, in consultation with Luther, to summarize and defend the *magnus consensus* of the churches in Germany following Luther and the other German Reformers.[98] It summarized the issues that Luther and his reforming colleagues wished to have discussed and resolved in a general council of the church that they sincerely hoped the Emperor would summon. The Augsburg Confession was presented to the Emperor in Latin and German by six German

---

[97]  The Turkish threat was central to Luther's success. If Charles V had not been so distracted in his efforts to stave off the Turks, he probably would have had the resources and willingness to crush Protestantism in its infancy. MacCulloch (2003), p. 57.

[98]  It was only after the Emperor refused the Augsburg Confession that the Lutherans began to conclude that a general council was not going to materialize. Hence, they then proceeded with local visitations and reforms of parish life on their own.

princes and the mayors and councils of two free cities, together with the Elector John of Saxony, Luther's lord and primary benefactor. In modern times the Augsburg Confession has been considered an ecumenical document, since it was so influential both on the Anglican Thirty-Nine Articles and on John Calvin

Emperor Charles V

and the Continental Reformed churches. In the 1970s, the Catholic Church even considered the possibility of recognizing the Augsburg Confession as an authentic presentation of Christian truth.[99]

Additional Lutheran confessions were written over a period of 50 years, between 1529-1577, and were joined together later in 1580 into the *Book of Concord*. It was assumed that these confessions would be studied together. Among the Lutheran confessions, the Augsburg Confession holds a pride of place. "Lutheran Confessionalism" became the foundational paradigm that influenced the creation of numerous confessions of the Protestant churches.

The Augsburg Confession is constructed of twenty-eight articles of faith. The first twenty-one present fun-

---

[99]  Joseph Burgess ed. (1980).

damental Lutheran doctrines, and the remaining articles address ecclesiastical abuses. One of the presuppositions of the Augsburg Confession is its claim to lay hold of traditional Catholic faith, asserting that the Reformers "dissent from the church catholic in no article of faith but only omit some few abuses which are new and have been adopted by the fault of the times although contrary to the intent of the canons."

The Augsburg Confession begins well by affirming strict adherence to the Nicene Creed. Perhaps in an attempt to distance themselves from more radical and fanatic reformers, the Augsburg Confession affirms the Nicene Creed and the Apostles Creed in its Article 1 on God (Nicene) and Article 3 on the Son of God (Apostles). Article 2 is on original sin. In Article 4 on Justification, Melanchthon, while affirming that justification is by faith, is careful to avoid the controversial word "alone" as Luther preferred. Further articles are entitled: the office of the ministry; the new obedience; the church (2 articles); baptism (including the condemnation of the Anabaptists who deny baptism to infants); the eucharist; confession (including private absolution); repentance; use of the sacraments; order in the church; church usages including the retention of holy days, etc.;[100] magistrates and civil government in which the

---

[100]  But, with the regular Lutheran refrain, criticizing monastic life and assuming that monastic vows and ascetical discipline are intended to satisfy God and atone for sins in contrast to faith.

temporal authority of the church is curtailed; the return of Christ and specific rejection of teachings called "Jewish" that before the second coming of Christ the godly will possess a worldly kingdom (forms of millennialism); the freedom of the will;[101] an affirmation that the perverted will is the cause of sin; an article entitled faith and good works affirming the essential connection between the two but ridiculing the cult of the saints, monasticism, pilgrimages, appointed fasts, holy days, and brotherhoods; an article (21) on the cult of the saints in which the lives of the saints are recommended as examples of how to live by faith, but an express denial that the Scriptures teach the church to invoke the saints by prayer or seek help from them. "He alone has promised to hear our prayers."[102]

Articles 22-28 are "Articles About Matters In Dispute In Which An Account Is Given Of The Abuses Which Have Been Corrected." Article 22 defends the practice of serving communion in both kinds. Here it is correctly pointed out that serving communion only in one kind is a papal innovation. Article 23 is on the marriage of priests in which the traditional practice of the marriage of priests is noted, but obscured by a failure to appreciate the traditional disciplines surrounding the marriage of clergy. Instead, a kind

---

[101] In which Luther's views are moderated and it is asserted that grace is necessary to perform any good work.

[102] Here the Lutherans, and Protestants in general who attempt this line of specious reasoning, have the problem of recommending imitation of the lives of the saints, who themselves *prayed to other saints*.

of reverse eschatology is used to justify the inability of practicing celibacy, i.e. since these are the last days and things are getting worse and worse we cannot expect priests to remain celibate. Here, while dealing with perhaps the most controversial of points between the Reformers and the Papacy, the Augsburg Confession both attempts to justify the abandonment of monastic vows and pleads for leniency at the same time. Article 24 is on the mass, in which it is denied that the mass is abolished, and it is claimed that the only change is that German hymns are sung as well as Latin.[103] "Mercenary" and "private" masses are also refuted. The article also opposes the "abominable error" which teaches that our Lord's death only atoned for original sin and that the mass is instituted as a sacrifice for other sins. Article 25 begins with the affirmation that "confession has not been abolished by the preachers on our side." Informed confessors should do away with an emphasis on man-made observances and long enumerations of sins, and focus on

---

[103] In fact, Lutheran hymnody was one of the major forces for theological reorientation and one of the major causes of the continuing success of the Lutheran Reformation. The very practice of hymn singing in the home and school was an expression of the Lutheran notion of the priesthood of all believers. Many Jesuits posited that Luther destroyed more souls by means of his hymnody than his preaching and writing combined. The first Wittenberg hymnal was published in 1529. In the 16th century, it is estimated that more than 2,000 editions of German Lutheran hymnals were published, and that more than 2,000,000 hymnals were in existence by the end of the 16th century. Lutheran or Catholic identities could often be determined by what hymns one sang. Boyd (2005), pp. 1, 4-5, 20, 170-171.

faith. Article 26 stresses that making a distinction of foods and "similar traditions" for earning grace and making satisfaction for sins is to be done away. Here, the authors are at a loss for how to recommend fasting and ascetical discipline without making it "mandatory" or a matter of sin.

Article 27 is on monastic vows. Among other things, this confused article asserts that monastic vows at the time of St. Augustine were voluntary;[104] documents abuses of young persons becoming monastics prior to reaching adulthood (it is actually claimed here that the majority of all monastics entered this way — yet Luther didn't); asserts that those in the monasteries learn little about Christ unlike ancient times when folks went to monasteries to learn the Scriptures; quotes St. Augustine to argue that even if the breaking of monastic vows is wrong, the new marriages of former monastics should not be dissolved; and dubs monastic life an "invented spiritual life" and an "improper and false ser-

---

[104] This may strike the contemporary reader as odd since monasticism on principle is to be voluntary as is marriage. However, just as there is a history of involuntary marriages that the Church labors to rectify, there is a history of involuntary monasticism. Monasticism was forced on the unwilling in some cases as criminal punishment, and in other cases for political objectives such as removing aristocracy from public discourse. History is also full of numerous cases of parents committing their under-aged children to monastic life. In this case, monastic tonsure is on principle to await a legal age. The service of monastic tonsure in the Orthodox Church emphasizes the voluntary nature of the vows in the rite itself by the abbot, hieromonk, or bishop throwing the shears for tonsure three times to the ground, and the aspirant then picking them up and placing them back into the hands of he who who will then tonsure.

vice of God." This way of life is asserted to be "an exaltation of works as a means of attaining justification."[105] Article 28 concerns the power of bishops, in which it is affirmed that bishops have no power of the sword, and that St. Augustine says to disobey a bishop who does not teach the truth. Lutheran teachers affirm that bishops can make disciplinary decisions for ensuring good order in the church, but not "as a means of obtaining God's grace or making satisfaction for sins, nor in order to bind men's consciences."

The Augsburg Confession concludes with a plea for leniency from the bishops toward clergy who affirm these things since they are "grounded clearly on the Holy Scriptures and are not contrary nor opposed to that teaching of the universal church."

Western Trinitarianism, unfortunately including the *filioque* heresy, is accepted wholeheartedly. This is a tragedy. While some aspects of universal Christian tradition were rejected, the most glaring error of the papacy was retained.[106]

---

[105] Pelikan (2003), *Creeds and Confessions of the Reformation Era*, Vol. 2, p. 102.

[106] The only exception of the complete embrace by Protestant churches of the Latin Trinitarianism and *filioque* heresy was in the confession of *The Easter Litany of the Moravian Church* of 1749. The Mennonite *Concept of Cologne* of 1591 reverts to the formula of the Council of Florence by its confession of the Holy Spirit as "proceeding from the Father through the Son." Pelikan (2003), p. 21.

*Lutheran Confessions to Confessional Scholasticism.*

The Protestant milieu at this time underwent a revival of Aristotelian philosophy and a subsequent stultification of various Protestant orthodoxies. The effort at detail and precision in these confessions necessarily led to the official endorsement of what had been considered *theologoumena*[107] (θεολογούμενα), and made the confessions themselves exist as only temporary and local theological standards.

One of the reasons that the Orthodox Church has spoken so carefully and in such a limited fashion as is expressed in the Nicene Creed is precisely because she believes this Nicene confession of faith to be the unalterable truth which must be confessed by all Christians, and expects this definition of faith to remain in force for all time unchanged since truth does not change. It is simply historical fact that even the most conservative Reformed churches have been unable to maintain a strict adherence to their confessions.[108]

*Lutheran - Orthodox Dialogue*

In his debate with the papal theologian J. Eck, Luther made reference to the Orthodox Church, and defended the

---

[107] Theological opinion.

[108] In my own experience, having been educated in the strictest and most historically-minded Presbyterianism, when I was examined on the floor of the Presbytery as a seminarian in order to be licensed to preach, I took numerous specific exceptions to portions of the Westminster standards and *this was expected*. The multiplication of Reformation confessions, besides over-articulating the Christian faith and relativizing themselves in so do-

Eastern Church against Eck's assertion that the Christian faith had been lost to the Orthodox at the fall of Constantinople. Luther asserted that "truth lies with the Greeks" as he affirmed that the Eastern Church did not recognize papal supremacy. Melanchthon wrote a personal letter to Patriarch Joasaph II in 1559. This was the first official Orthodox-Lutheran interaction. Patriarch Joasaph II sent Deacon Demetrios Mysos to meet the Lutheran leaders and study their teachings and the personalities behind the movement. Mysos spent six months as Melachthon's guest in Wittenberg, and they developed a sincere friendship. Melanchthon, no doubt with Mysos's help, translated the Augsburg Confession into Greek.

Between 1573-1581 fruitful contacts between Orthodox and Lutherans were made with an exchange of personal letters between Lutheran theologians at the University of Tübingen and the Ecumenical Patriarch of Constantinople, Jeremias II.[109] This correspondence was bilingual, being in Greek and Latin. The leading Tübingen theologian was Professor Jacob Andreae, who was provost of the university. Together with Martin Chemnitz he had unified the Lutheran movement. The German embassy in Constanti-

---

ing, also had the unfortunate effect of ensuring divisions amongst themselves, at least until the modern period, when whole new statements have been written and theological relativism has rendered confessions themselves irrelevant.

[109] Documentation of this correspondence cited in what follows comes from Mastrantonis (1982).

nople requested a theologian to come to the city. The goal of the Lutherans in complying was to win the Orthodox "over to the Gospel."[110] Patriarch Jeremias received personal letters from Andreae and other leading lights of Tübingen. Besides writing several letters in return, the Patriarch issued two formal *Answers* to the German theologians.

The Patriarch followed the format of the Augsburg Confession and answered its points in great details, noting agreements and disagreements. The Greek text was translated into German, and was received well by the Tübingen theologians. It was also read carefully by Pope Gregory XIII who sent a special envoy to congratulate the Ecumenical Patriarch on his answer to the Lutherans. The Lutheran theologians published all the correspondence in Greek and Latin in 1582 in Wittenberg. The correspondence was extremely respectful, with the Lutheran theologians calling the Patriarch "All-Holy Father" and the Patriarch calling them "esteemed spiritual sons."

### Common Beliefs, Adiaphora[111] and Matters in Dispute

The basic premise of the Patriarch was that he would say nothing new, but only what the Holy Fathers had always said. Disagreement was expressed regarding the *filioque*, the

---

[110] Here we see the Protestant arrogance in full bloom, and the discarding of the earlier opinion of Luther-Melanchthon.
[111] Adiaphora, Greek for "indifferent things," refers to theological opinions over which there is acceptable disagreement.

primacy of scripture over tradition, the state of man after the Fall (against the notion of a complete loss of free will), absolute predestination, justification by faith alone, and the number of sacraments. The Patriarch emphasized the Apostolic baptismal form by triune immersion and emersion versus the Lutheran practice at that time of single immersion. The Patriarch emphasized the miraculous change in the elements of the eucharist, saying he had heard many things from the Lutherans which had not pleased him and that the Augsburg Confession was not clear on this point. The Patriarch affirmed the communion of infants, and the use of leavened bread, and agreed with the Lutherans in rejecting indulgences as practiced in the Roman church, as well as purgatory, and the notion of a treasury of merits. The Patriarch disagreed with the Lutherans in their rejection of penance and affirmed the salutary nature of penances as healing remedies for the soul, and asserted the need for confession to a priest in detail versus the vague Lutheran confessional practice.

There were also differences on the subject of the priesthood. The Patriarch asserted that ordination required the presence of a bishop, whereas the Lutherans, who held a rather low view of the priesthood, maintained that in the absence of a bishop a priest could ordain. The nuances of the marriage of clergy were articulated by the Patriarch, and monasticism was defended. Both sides rejected the supremacy of the Pope, but the Patriarch insisted on the infallibility of the Church and the supreme authority of the conscience of the Church against the Protestant notion of *sola scriptura*. In discussing good works, the Patriarch noted that in Article 20 of their Augsburg Confession, the Lutherans affirm that they do not oppose good works, yet they characterize feasts, ceremonies, fasts, monastic life, etc. as useless! The Ecumenical Patriarch rightly points out this hypocrisy: "This is not good, nor does it agree with the Holy Fathers. For if you love all good works, as you say you do, you should love these also because they are good works." The Patriarch concludes his *First Answer* by quoting St. Basil the Great, "One who has the judgment of Christ before his eyes, who has seen the great danger that threatens those who dare to subtract from or add to those things which have been handed down by the Spirit, must not be ambitious to innovate, but must content himself with those things which have been proclaimed by the saints." After many years of dialogue, the Constantinople-Tübingen interaction fizzled out.

## Renunciations for a Lutheran
### upon Conversion to Holy Orthodoxy

For the reasons articulated by Patriarch Jeremias II and maintained in our dialogue with Lutheranism to this day, the Orthodox Church asks converts from Lutheranism to make certain public renunciations as part of the process of being received into Holy Orthodoxy. Those heresies that must be renounced include the *filioque* doctrine,[112] the inadequate Lutheran teaching on the change of the bread and wine into the body and blood of Jesus Christ in the eucharist, the erroneous belief that chrismation, marriage, anointing with oil, confession and the priesthood itself (without which there is no administration of the mysteries at all) are not sacraments, the rejection of apostolic succession, the erroneous belief which does not permit Lutherans to honor the saints or pray for the departed, and finally a general and irrevocable renunciation of all the Lutheran teachers deemed "false teachers" in the text of our service of renunciation, and of all their false teaching.[113]

### *Lutheranism Today*

Though Luther never intended to establish his own church, much less have it named after him, this is indeed what happened.[114] Throughout the 16th century, Lutheranism spread through much of Germany, Denmark, Norway, Sweden, Finland and parts of Eastern Europe such as Poland, Hungary, and Latvia. In some of these places, Roman Catholicism and/or Calvinism reversed some of these Lutheran inroads.

---

[112] The renunciation targets the illicit insertion of the *filioque* into the Nicene Creed.

[113] *Great Book of Needs* (1998), Vol. 1, pp. 75-77.

[114] Here is the beginning of Protestant denominationalism. Today there are tens of thousands of Protestant denominations in America alone, and new ones are registered with the government every week.

Lutheranism came to North America in the 17th century, but remained very small until after 1730 when German immigration became significant. The first Lutheran Synod in America was established in 1748, and through immigration a plethora of Lutheran bodies defined by ethnicities or nationalities developed. Today there are two major Lutheran bodies in America: the Evangelical Lutheran Church in America (ELCA), and the Lutheran Church—Missouri Synod.[115] Lutheran missionary activity has established Lutheran churches in many parts of the globe, and a Lutheran World Federation has been established to coordinate the world's Lutherans.

The Orthodox Church has interacted with Lutheranism through official bodies for theological dialogue on the international and national stages. Such dialogue is at a particularly low ebb today due to the ELCA's embrace of immorality by endorsing homosexual relations. Lutheranism has, together with all mainline Protestant bodies in America, been on a fast track to extinction. Many Lutherans have simply ceased practicing their Lutheran faith. In the last thirty years it should also be noted that many Lutheran laity, and not a few Lutheran clergymen, have been received into Holy Orthodoxy throughout the United States.

---

[115] The ability of America's Lutherans to eradicate their divisions along ethnic lines and to allow their common faith to bind them serves as an example to the Orthodox Church in America and indeed throughout the "diaspora."

Our All-holy Lady Eleousa (Merciful)

Ulrich Zwingli

# 3
# *The Life and*
# *Teachings of Ulrich Zwingli*[116]

## *The Background to the Swiss Reformation*

In the early 16th century, the Swiss Confederacy encompassed about the same geographical territory as it does today. It was composed of both rural districts and city-states. The various confederate states were in competition for land, and occasionally warred against each other. The population of the Swiss Confederacy was perhaps 800,000 persons, and the two largest cities were Zurich and Berne. During the 14th century the Swiss fought against the Habsburg House of Austria, and this military resistance in defense of "Swiss liberty" was a matter of pride for the Swiss in general and for the Swiss Reformer Ulrich Zwingli in particular.[117]

During the 15th century, the King of France attacked and was driven out of the Swiss lands, and later when Burgun-

---

[116] Gottfried Locher "The Message and Impact of Ulrich Zwingli: The Significance For His Time" in Furcha and Pipkin (1984a), p. 111. Though Zwingli is clearly the first Reformed theologian (in contrast to Lutheran theologian) he has been treated by history as a "distant third" in accounts of the Reformation, trailing far behind Luther and Calvin. Furcha and Pipkin (1984a), p. vii.

[117] Gäbler (1983), pp. 5ff.

dy attacked the Confederacy the French helped the Swiss defend themselves, establishing an enduring French-Swiss confluence in foreign policy that would last for centuries. The Swiss were German speakers, though their dialect was significantly different from Luther's. They were zealously *not* a part of the Holy Roman Empire. As such, they rejected many of the political decisions of the Empire, reserved judgment for themselves on religious matters, and the so-called "sovereignty of princes" was offensive to them. The Emperor Maximilian tried to attack them and was repulsed in 1499. The Swiss Confederacy treasured its independence. As a Roman Catholic priest, Zwingli told his Diocesan Bishop, the Bishop of Constance, that the Swiss should not be ranked with the Germans. For the Swiss the "fatherland" meant the Confederacy not the Empire.[118]

Our focus here is the city-state of Zurich. Zurich had a guild system that established laborers in an equality of sorts with knights and landed men. There was a Great Council with 12 representatives of each of 12 guilds plus 18 members of the Society of the Constabulary. Each representative chose his own successor. There was also a Small Council where real power was concentrated, headed by a Mayor. Zwingli was himself a formal advisor to the City Council.

Zurich and most of the northeast of the Confederacy belonged to the Diocese of Constance. It led all the Ger-

---

[118] William Tell, who legendarily shot an arrow off the head of his son, was the great hero of the Swiss, and was considered the founder of confederacy freedom.

man dioceses in the number of souls and in geographic size. At the time of the Reformation the diocese had about 1,800 parishes,[119] 350 monasteries, and over 15,000 priests.[120] After 1496, it was headed by Bishop Hugo von Hohenlandenberg (1457-1532), who was descended from a Zurich family. Bishop Hugo had sympathies with the reform movement in general at points, but his leadership was ineffective because he was himself compromised morally. Many of the priests in the diocese lived with lovers, and paid a penance tax to the diocese for violating their vows of celibacy. Most common folk respected their priests nevertheless, because many maintained a marriage-like lifestyle. In fact, Zwingli's famous successor as chief preacher in Zurich, Heinrich

Heinrich Bullinger

Bullinger, was the son of a priest father who lived for decades as priest and dean in Bremgarten, unmolested and respected, with his wife and children.[121] There were some 200 clergy in Zurich, who made up 15-20% of all employable men.[122] Swiss civil governments

---

[119] Essentially the number of all Orthodox parishes in America.

[120] Gäbler (1983), p. 13.

[121] Gäbler (1983), p. 13.

[122] *Ibid.*, p. 14.

sought to protect priests from impoverishment due to these diocesan penance taxes for having wives, and in general the political situation called for the city council and local government to involve itself in regulating church property ownership, monastery funds, the behavior of clergy, and marriage laws.

## The Life of the Swiss Reformer
## Ulrich Zwingli, 1484-1531

### *Early Life and Education*

Ulrich Zwingli was born in 1484 into a peasant family. His father was an administrator and small-time trader. He was one of at least ten children, and he had two brothers who were priests, and two sisters who were nuns. The rest worked in agriculture on the farms. When he was five, he went to stay with his uncle Bartholomew (a priest) to be educated. When he was ten, he was sent to Basel for secondary education, and then to Berne where he stayed with the famous humanist Henry Wolfflin. The Dominicans were trying to recruit him there, and his father moved him to do university studies in Vienna and Basel (1498-1506) where he studied under Thomas Wyttenbach.[123] His matriculation at the University is the first documentable date

---

[123] Wyttenbach studied at Tübingen, and emphasized the new philological method of biblical study. From 1507-1515 he was priest in Biel and then canon at Berne until 1519. He married in 1524 and was deposed.

of Zwingli's life. He graduated with a Master of Arts in 1506, with a focus on Latin, Aristotle, and the scholastics.

## Priesthood and Pastorate

Zwingli was ordained to the priesthood in the diocesan see of Constance, in September of 1506.[124] He served his first mass in his hometown. He was appointed to serve as parish priest in Glarus, and became immediately familiar with the work of office peddling (simony) since he had to pay 10 gulden a year for his pastorate. There were about 1300 persons in Glarus, and Zwingli had three or four assistant priests. No sooner had he been installed as pastor than he found himself in the midst of a political debate which forced him to take sides with either the French-leaning Swiss, the imperial-leaning Swiss, or the papal-leaning Swiss. He sided with the papal-leaning Swiss, and was rewarded by the Pope with 50 gulden annually. At this time, Zwingli considered the Swiss to be the Pope's special defenders. Later he would say the same thing about Zurich in relationship to the Swiss Confederation. In 1513, during this first pastorate, he took part in the Battle of Novarra, and in the summer of 1515 was part of the disastrous battle at Marignano where his five hundred men fared poorly. As a result of this poor performance on the battlefield, the political climate of Glarus turned decidedly toward the French, and Zwingli had to de-emphasize his advocacy of the papacy.

---

[124] Gäbler (1983), p. 29.

Soon thereafter in 1516, Zwingli left Glarus for Einsiedeln where he served in a less tense political climate until 1518. Einsiedeln was a pilgrimage center of Marian devotion. During these years, Zwingli gave himself to the study of classical, patristic, and scholastic materials, participated as an active member of the Swiss humanists, and devoured the writings of Erasmus, even interacting with him personally. During these years Zwingli was focused upon the supreme issue of church authority. Zwingli amassed a fine library of some 350 books, many with his handwritten comments in the margins. Scholars have been able to identify about 100 of those books, including editions of Ss. Athanasius, Augustine, Basil the Great, Chrysostom, Cyprian, Gregory of Nazianzus, Irenaeus, and others.[125] His collection included more texts by Erasmus than any other author.[126] During these years Zwingli has been described as an "unreserved Erasmian."[127] He gave himself to the study of Greek (especially Erasmus' New Testament *editio princeps* 1516), and is said to have memorized St. Paul's epistles in Greek.

### Zwingli's Appointment as People's Priest in Zurich

On January 1st, 1519, Zwingli took up his new and prestigious post as People's Priest of the Grossmünster in Zu-

---

[125] Gäbler (1983), p. 34.

[126] Erasmus and Zwingli had a major falling out as it became clear that Zwingli would reject traditional Christian teaching on the sacraments and church hierarchy. See Dorothy Clark, "Erasmus and Zwingli's *On True and False Religion*" in Furcha and Pipkin (1984a), pp. 23-42.

[127] Gabler, p. 35.

rich.[128] The political climate there was more in accord with Zwingli's anti-French sentiments. The Grossmünster in Zurich had a number of competent humanists associated with it, and Zwingli's humanism was the key to getting his pastoral post. He assumed office on his thirty-fifth birthday. Rumors of his immorality had been advanced just prior to his acceptance of the new post. He explained himself in a very candid letter in which he admitted to having acted immorally with women in the past, but affirming that he had ceased such behavior, and had renewed his commitment to celibacy. His honesty was appreciated and one week later he was offered the post which he accepted with great satisfaction.

Nothing survives of his preaching prior to 1522 when Zwingli launched a series of commentary-style homilies on the entire Gospel of Matthew, the Acts of the Apostles, and the Letters to Timothy. During these early Zurich years, he was basically calling for an Erasmian-type moral improvement and reform of the church. By 1520, Zwingli abandoned this measured approach to reform. Some have argued that this was due to Luther's influence, but this position is not tenable. Zwingli, with good justification, claimed that he had come to embrace the Gospel and teach a pure Scripture-based form of Christianity indepen-

---

[128] The *Grossmünster* was dedicated to Ss. Felix and Regula. A giant statue of Charlemagne looked forth from its south tower. MacCulloch (2003), p. 50.

dent of Luther's influence. Indeed, Luther was not pleased with Zwingli's positions on many matters, and thought he treated the Scriptures with violence. Zwingli did read Luther extensively, but only after he had committed himself to his fundamental theological positions, and primarily to acquire Luther's polemics and to check himself on issues of church politics and organization such as celibacy, indulgences, tithing, papal power, etc. Zwingli viewed Luther as a polemicist, and not above the typical reform of humanism which was unable to shed many Roman Catholic ideas. Essentially for Zwingli, Luther was not fully committed to the Reformation and was too conservative. Of interest to Orthodox Christians is the fact that Zwingli was also a voracious reader of the writings of St. Augustine. He claimed to have learned the Gospel from the writings of the Apostle and Evangelist John and St. Augustine, and yet he came to many different opinions than did Luther.[129]

By 1522, after a few years in Zurich, Zwingli resolved for himself the authority issue and rejected the humanist reform which kept intact the traditional Latin *loci* of authority: scripture, dogma, councils, and papal authority. Zwingli

---

[129] Neither Scripture nor the writings of St. Augustine can be properly understood without reference to the patristic consensus of the Church. This is demonstrated very clearly in the works of Luther and Zwingli who shared a mutual commitment to the texts. However, without the guardianship and patristic consensus of the Church, both men came to very different conclusions. To avoid this pitfall and avoid proof-texting, individual reading must be complemented with the greater exegetical tradition of the Church.

replaced this notion of Holy Tradition with the notion that Scripture is the sole basis of all authority. He articulated this view more decidedly and with far more radical consequences than did Martin Luther. Zwingli's hermeneutics are radically subjective and antinomian, and it is precisely this fact that set him apart from other more conservative Reformation voices and from the Roman Catholic Church itself.[130]

Zwingli also publicly denounced certain Zurich citizens by name, including immoral priests and monks,[131] for whom he reserved particular venom. As the corollary to his enthronement of the principle of *sola scriptura*, Zwingli also denied church authority, and the offices of bishop and priest according to the writings of scripture and tradition. He contested against the concept of apostolic succession and the tri-fold ministry of bishop-priest-deacon in his writings and preaching, something which had been articulated clearly and concisely by St. Ignatius of Antioch as early as the first years of the 2nd century. The traditional notion of the "power of the keys" was denied, and the power of binding and loosing sins was said to be the power of preaching, not priestly absolution and canonical authority. In fact, repudiation of the hierarchy of the Latin church became the hallmark of the Reformers, and the dividing line

---

[130] Furcha and Pipkin (1984a), p. 51.

[131] A case of removing the speck from another's eye while having a log in one's own.

between those who sought reform within the church and those who sought it without. Thus, Zwingli questioned the value of excommunication, and having completely stripped away the structure for such discipline, accommodated himself to a new polity in which civil government was enthroned as governor of the church. He rejected the veneration of saints, and called for a purgation of their so-called legends. His greatest explosive power was his attack on tithing. Tithing had already been desacralized because certain rights to tithes had been transferred from the church to secular institutions, and Zwingli attacked the whole concept.[132]

Zwingli's attack met with opposition from his superiors since the economy was threatened. There was opposition especially from Canon Hoffman (1454-1525), who had been People's Priest himself for some years and was highly respected. Throughout his years in Zurich, however, this opposition remained but a minority, and in 1521 a vacancy arose on the 24 canons and Zwingli was chosen to fill it. He now had political power as well as spiritual authority.

Zwingli's influence erupted into public controversy when he attacked the traditional Lenten fasting discipline. On the first Sunday of Lent, Zwingli participated in publicly eating cooked sausages to proclaim Christian liberty. Since there was no church authority that could legislate

---

[132] Ulrich Gäbler, "Zwingli in the Year of Decision – 1522" in Furcha and Pipkin (1984a), pp. 60ff.

and bind Christians to obedience in Zwingli's mind, all such fasting rules were impositions on proper Christian liberty. Two weeks after this incident, Zwingli expressed his opinion in a published sermon entitled, *Regarding the Choice and the Freedom of Foods*. He argued not only that all foods are clean but refuted the opposition's tenets: that specific times of fasting can be determined by the church, that if one could eat meat in a fast then no one will practice abstention, that even though the command to fast is a human commandment such a regulation of our pious ancestors cannot simply be abrogated, and that eating meat in Lent scandalizes the weak. Zwingli rejected all of these tenets, and supported fasting, but only in the private sphere. Zwingli had no tolerance for seeking patient change through the normal structures of church authority such as local and regional councils.

As Zwingli and his allies grew in boldness, they began to publicly interrupt sermons to oppose the teaching of priests that did not support the Reformation. Zwingli himself cried out "This is where you err!" when a traveling monk from Avignon, Franz Lambert, was preaching on Mary and the saints in Mary Minster.[133] The City Council appointed the monastic priests to preach scriptural sermons like Zwingli himself, and they were to drop references to traditional scholastic authorities like Aquinas and Scotus.

---

[133] *Ibid.*, p. 65. *cf.* Gäbler (1983), pp. 54ff.

To raise a public debate, Zwingli and his allies then sent a request to the bishop in Constance for abolition of celibacy and permission for "scriptural" preaching — meaning *their* preaching. Zwingli himself had been living in a secret union with a widow, Anna Reinhard, since the beginning of 1522.[134] On April 2, 1524, when his lover was pregnant with their first child, he married her and together they had four children: Regula, William, Ulrich, and Anna.

In November of 1522, Zwingli was released from his other duties so that he could commit himself to preaching. This was a sign of his growing influence in Zurich and the dependence of the leadership on his opinions. He articulated these opinions, claiming that they were based upon the clear and simple teaching of Scripture which needed no church authority or patristic support. The Holy Spirit is the teacher of the sincere Christian according to his treatise, *Regarding Clarity and Certainty of the Word of God.* Zwingli preached on Mary and affirmed her title "Mother of God" and her perpetual virginity, but rejected her role as mediator and religious adoration to her.

---

[134] This was a sin not just against chastity for living in intercourse outside of marriage, but against the canons of the Church which forbid a priest to marry, and which forbid a man who is to be a priest from marrying anyone but a virgin. These canons are based on scriptural law. Zwingli referenced such scriptural law and upheld it in many areas — especially in those that did not condemn Zwingli. The real theological father of much contemporary Protestant Evangelicalism was living in fornication while he was articulating evangelicalism.

All official ties were severed between Zurich and Bishop Hugo in the summer of 1524.[135] The Confederate states met in Diet on Jan 4, 1524, without Zurich, to decide about Zurich's actions. They concluded that Zurich was the seedbed of hatred and discord in the Confederacy, and Zwingli and his associates were the ringleaders. By the fall of 1524, there was fear of war in the Confederacy.

In 1524, all preaching was required to be strictly from the Bible, and pictures and statues were removed from churches and were called by Zwingli's allies "idols," while the veneration of saints was considered the "deification of creatures." The Baptism service was "purified," confession was eradicated and the priest's power of absolution denied. The monasteries, 350 of them, were dissolved, and their lands appropriated by the civil authority. Initially, these lands were dedicated to charitable causes, but eventually they were seized for secular purposes.[136]

In 1525, the mass was abolished, and Zwingli's new style of worship was enshrined, wherein one can see the radical nature of Zwinglianism. Zwingli caused great liturgical

---

[135] Erasmus reacted with horror to Zwingli's approach to his own bishop. Willingness to work with the Latin hierarchy was the key difference between those reformed-minded persons who went with the Reformation and those who remained in the Papal Church. Ulrich Gäbler, "Zwingli in the Year of Decision – 1522" in Furcha and Pipkin (1984a), p. 67.

[136] Here we see one of the innumerable cases of Protestant theft on a grand scale. The Protestant assumption appears to be that believing wrongly invalidates property rights.

confusion. Only after witnessing this did he attempt to regulate it with the support of the city council. He maintained the essential liturgy of the word or first half of the mass, but with no congregational singing, and with the sermon as the center of the entire service. The traditional teaching on the Eucharist, the sacrament of sacraments, was refuted, the real presence denied, and Zwingli taught that holy Communion should only be administered four times a year, at Christmas, Easter, Pentecost and in "the autumn" probably around the feast day of the Grossmünster. No Reformer so radically altered the Eucharistic practice of Christianity as did Zwingli. Zwingli's confidently described his newfangled Eucharistic service as an "apostolic celebration of the eucharist."[137] Zwingli's overconfident radicalism also is demonstrated by his nearly complete rejection of the traditional theology of Baptism and of the traditional rite itself, which the Reformer dubbed "magic." Reformation scholar Timothy George writes, "Zwingli concluded that all the teachers of the church since the days of the apostles had been in error on baptism."[138]

Zwingli's views were contested, and the Great Council of Zurich held two disputations in 1523 in which Zwingli's

---

[137] Fritz Büsser, "In Defence of Zwingli: 1536" in Furcha and Pipkin (1984a), p. 15.

[138] "The Presuppositions of Zwingli's Baptismal Thelogy" in Furcha and Pipkin (1984a), p. 71. Luther considered Zwingli's teaching on Baptism to be worse than the teaching of the Anabaptists.

opponents were allowed to debate him. In the first, some six hundred people gathered together to judge charges against Zwingli, and no one could prove him guilty of heresy. For this occasion, Zwingli hastily drew up his 67 Theses, which were essentially gleaned from his sermons of preceding years. Allow me to make a selection here.

Zwingli introduced his 67 Theses thus:

> the people of Zurich demanded that I defend the honor of God when my teaching was attacked...the clear word of God. These articles contain almost all of the major controversies which engage us today, such as the following... Therefore, wise, gracious, dear gentlemen, do not allow the teaching of Christ to be driven out from among you as if it were something new; for it really breaks forth loud and clear today, as it has not done since the time of the apostles. I commend to you...[here he lists four pastors, one of whom would later distance himself from Zwingli] who preach the gospel of Christ faithfully.[139]

---

[139] Furcha (1984), p. 5. Note the arrogance of affirming that his teaching has been unparalleled since the time of the Apostles! This is the great parenthesis presupposed by all the Protestant Reformers. From the death of the last of the twelve Apostles until the rise of truth in the teaching of this or that Reformer, there existed a great parenthesis when the truth was not clear. The opposition of this assumption to our Savior's promise that He would uphold the Church in the truth and the gates of Hades would not prevail against her is obvious.

*Excerpts from the 67 Theses*

1. Those who say the gospel is invalid without the confirmation of the church err and slander God.[140]

15. All truth is clear in Him.

16. Human doctrines and decrees are useless for salvation.

17. Christ is the only High Priest, and all who have called themselves high priests have completely rejected him.

18. Christ sacrificed himself once for all, and so it follows that the mass is not a sacrifice but a commemoration of Christ's sacrifice.

24. Christians only have to obey God, and fasting rules are a "Roman imposture."

25. Time and place are not binding either.

26. Vestments, tonsures, etc. are hypocrisy.

27. The title "Father" should not be given to anyone on earth.[141]

30. Those who promise chastity do wrong and foolishly take too much on themselves.

31. Excommunication can only be made by the congregation corporately.

32. Only those who give public offense should be excommunicated.

40. Only civil government can enact the death penalty.

---

[140] Here we see the false God-church dichotomy, so essential to the justification of Protestantism, established at the very outset.

[141] Despite the fact that it is used this way by the Scriptures themselves! *cf.* 2 Kings 2:12, Lk. 1:73, 16:24.

49. There is no greater scandal than that priests are not allowed to take lawful wives, but may keep mistresses if they pay a fine.

50. God alone remits sins.

51. To give this authority to men takes away God's honor and this is real idolatry.

52. Confession to a priest should be viewed just as seeking for advice.

57. The true holy Scriptures know nothing of purgatory.

58. The fate of the dead is known to God alone [no saints].

60. Prayer to God for the departed is not to be rejected, but to fix a time for this is demonic.

61. The Scriptures know nothing of the "indelible character" conferred in recent times on the priesthood.

Zwingli's most systematic theological statement is found in his 1525 book *On True and False Religion*, but his *oeuvre* comprises more than 13 volumes in critical edition in the *Corpus Reformatorum* (Vols 88-101). Although his work in the Reformation has been historically overshadowed by the influence of both Luther and Calvin, Zwingli's theological influence in America and in modern Evangelicalism trumps both Reformers.

The public theological disputation at which Zwingli articulated his 67 Theses was designed to clear Zwingli's name from any charge of heresy and to authorize a greater proclamation of his teachings. Bishop Hugo of Constance sent his official delegates representing the papacy, but it went poorly for these delegates. A second disputation gathered some nine hundred participants, including 350 priests. During these disputations, Zwingli happily allowed city councilmen to assume the traditional prerogatives of the ecclesiastical hierarchy, and to function as bishops and a clergy council in sitting in judgment upon dogma. This was a complete novelty, a confusion of competencies, and very typical of the statism of early Protestantism.

### The Closing Years of Zwingli's Life

Zwingli spent his remaining years in Zurich as the head of the Latin school, from where he launched his school of exegesis called *The Prophecy*. This school served to re-educate former Latin priests as well as train new Reformed clergy and educate the laity. During these years of political unrest throughout the Confederacy, Philip of Hesse sought to unite the Protestant powers at the infamous Marburg Colloquy in 1529. It was at this event that Zwingli entered into open conflict with Martin Luther. The Colloquy was convened by Philip in order to achieve unity between the Lutherans and the Zwinglians. Luther and Melanchthon were on one side, and Zwingli, J. Oecolampadius, and Martin Bucer were on the other. Fourteen of fifteen theological articles Luther had drawn up were agreed upon,[142] and Lu-

---

[142] One of these fourteen agreed-upon articles was on Baptism. How Zwingli, who denied all efficacy in water Baptism, could agree with Luther,

ther revised them shortly after this colloquy and published them as the *Articles of Schwabach,* which served as a precursor to the Augsburg Confession.

However, no agreement could be made on the fifteenth article on the subject of the Eucharist. Incredibly, the Reformers, following the principle of *sola scriptura*, could not come to an agreement about the significance of the most important sacrament in the Christian faith and the traditional center of divine worship. This irreconcilable theological difference on the very nature of the Eucharist, a subject the Reformers themselves considered of utmost importance, would be the very headwaters of a river of Protestant disagreement and theological disunity that would only morph into a dizzying number of Protestant denominations and conflicting confessions of faith right up until the present day.

The Latins accused Zwingli of Lutheranism, but Zwingli and Luther and their dogmas are quite distinct, as seen at Marburg. Besides the Lutheran teaching on the Eucharist, Zwingli rejected the Lutheran Law-Gospel distinction. He also believed, contrary to Luther, that the civil authorities could legislate in religious matters and acquiesced when

who affirmed baptismal regeneration, is difficult to fathom. In fact, Zwingli thoroughly disagreed with Luther's sacramental realism. Zwinglianism is thoroughly gnostic in its affirmation that God's grace does not come via physical means, something Luther considered heretical. There was and is an unbridgeable theological chasm between Zwinglian/Anabaptist theology and Lutheran theology on the subject of the sacraments.

the Council of Zurich condemned an Anabaptist leader to death by drowning in 1527.[143]

The political fallout of the Marburg debacle was a tenuous existence for Zurich. Zwingli convinced the Berne canton to join the reformed movement. The Five Forest Cantons fiercely resisted Zwinglianism, and war almost broke out in 1529 and finally did in 1531. The Forest Cantons made a sudden attack upon Zurich with some 7000 men, and were met by a small force of 3500 at Kappel, where Zwingli and 500 Zurichers were killed on October 11, 1531. Some historians have posited that Zwingli was the military chaplain and was killed carrying a banner and not weapons. This is a highly suspect assertion. Zwingli himself, and most of the twenty-five pastors killed with him on the field of battle,[144] were the leading proponents of war with the Catholics, and Zwingli himself even threatened the city council with resignation if they did not declare war. Zwingli's death was glorified as a martyrdom and miraculous events were attributed to his "blessed end" in the 1536 *Life of Zwingli* written by Zwingli's disciple Oswald Myconius.[145] After Zwingli's death Heinrich Bullinger (1504-75)

---

[143] Timothy George, "The Presuppositions of Zwingli's Baptismal Theology" in Furcha and Pipkin (1984a), p. 71.

[144] Zwingli's body was captured, drawn and quartered, and then burnt by his Papal adversaries. Robert Walton, "Let Zwingli be Zwingli" in Furcha and Pipkin (1984a), p. 172.

[145] *Ibid.*, p. 17. Luther, on the other hand, considered Zwingli's death on the battlefield to be the judgment of God against him, executed to protect

Zwingli's Death at Kappel

became Chief Pastor in Zurich. Bullinger was probably the most influential, next to John Calvin, of the second-generation Reformers.

### *The Connection between Zwingli and the Anabaptist Movement*

The great problem with this new church-state arrangement, among other things, was not only that it had no precedent in Christian history, but that the councilmen's lives were not always any better than the corrupt papal cler-

---

persons from Zwingli's heresy. Robert Walton, "Let Zwingli be Zwingli" in Furcha and Pipkin (1984a), p. 177. Some of Zwingli's followers praised Zwingli as a martyr and a saint to which Luther responded in disgust, "My God! The man a saint and a martyr!" *Ibid.*, p. 178.

gy, and so those who followed Zwingli's principles simply asked why their authority should not also be resisted by a "more thorough reformation." If church authority ought to be abolished why not civil authority? And why should not all simply rely upon the Holy Spirit's direct inspiration? The impatience of Zwingli's followers and their insistence on less compromise with the civil authority is part of the pre-history of Anabaptism. Zwingli attacked the traditional tithe as the economic fuel of the papacy, and the economy that tied church and society together. His more radical followers wanted abolition of the tithe altogether, and the Anabaptists wanted autonomy against having to pay either monastery *or* town council. Though Zwingli himself decried many of the Anabaptist teachings and their anarchy, he is nevertheless the main theological source for their beginnings.[146] Having affirmed Zwingli's contributions to Anabaptist theology and practice, it should be noted that Anabaptist groups emerged spontaneously in Switzerland, central and south Germany, north Germany, and the Netherlands. In our next chapter we will explore in detail how the so-called Radical Reformation or Anabaptist Reformation developed, and how Zwinglianism and Anabaptism came to dominate Protestant Evangelicalism in America.

---

[146] Gäbler (1983), "Anabaptists are without doubt indebted to Zwingli as far as theology is concerned; to that extent they can be considered his disciples," p. 127.

# 4

# *The Anabaptist Reformation and Its Triumph in America*

### *The Radical Reformation Emerges*

I n our chapter on the life and teachings of Ulrich Zwingli, the influential Swiss reformer, we concluded by noting that, although Zwingli himself opposed the Anabaptists, nevertheless Zwinglianism provided the fundamental tenets for Anabaptism and was its seedbed. Luther articulated the Protestant dogma of *sola scriptura,* but did not embrace this dogma in the fashion of Zwingli, maintaining instead a regard for sacred community, the visible church, and the necessity of hermeneutical continuity with the historic Church. Zwingli did not show such regard, and in his teachings, and in his unwanted offspring the Anabaptists, we see what the dogma of *sola scriptura* is capable of producing.

You will recall that Zwingli repudiated the entire structure of traditional ecclesiastical authority: bishops, dioceses, and councils. In place of traditional church governance Zwingli handed authority over the church to the political authorities—his benefactors. Yet some of Zwingli's closest

disciples began to ask why it was necessary to obey civil authorities in the church if it was not necessary to obey the
traditional church authorities? Adding fire to this query
was the fact that many of the civil authorities were no more
upstanding in moral concerns than were the corrupt papal
clergy. Inevitably, Zwingli's followers began to accuse him
of the very thing he himself had accused Martin Luther of:
*insufficient reformation*. Zwingli was styled as a compromised man with the civil authorities, and was criticized for
not being "biblical enough." Zwingli responded aggressively, but in vain.

This is the pre-history of the Anabaptist movement, and
it did not simply center around Zwingli. Anabaptist groups
emerged spontaneously in Switzerland, central and south
Germany, north Germany, and the Netherlands. What is
the history of this so-called *Anabaptist* or *Radical Reformation*?[147] And what are the tenets of this faith that has, more
than any other form of Protestantism, so deeply influenced
American religion?

### *Thomas Müntzer and the Peasants' War*

The first signs of the political radicalism that the bur-
geoning Reformation was capable of appeared in the spring

---

[147] For a substantial treatment of the Anabaptist movement, with an emphasis upon ideology, see Estep (1996). For an excellent translation of the
primary theological texts of the Anabaptist movement see Baylor (1991). *cf.*
Liechty (1994).

of 1525 in Lutheran-influenced areas of southern and central Germany, and spread to Switzerland, Austria and France. Angry peasants spontaneously joined together in marauding mobs intent on overthrowing the established order.[148] The peasant uprising struck great fear into the hearts of the ruling classes, and would lead the Holy Roman Empire in 1529[149] to declare Anabaptism a capital offense. It was the most widespread popular uprising in Europe prior to the French Revolution of 1789.[150]

Protestant preachers were commonly the leaders and spokespersons of these peasant groupings. Thomas Müntzer, an educated man and former Latin priest, joined Luther around 1518. By 1522, he was one of Luther's most bitter opponents, publishing tracts against what he saw as Luther's compromise of the Gospel with political authorities and shameful endorsement of antichristian social structures. He preached and wrote with venom, calling Dr. Martin Luther, "Dr. Liar."[151] He became increasingly apocalyptic, and in his *Sermon before the Princes* (July 13, 1524), preached on the prophecy of the second chapter of Daniel, arguing that the Kingdom of God was presently overthrowing the political structure. He also blessed the use of

---

[148] For an overview of the Peasants' War with a translation of primary texts documenting peasant grievances see Scott and Scribner (1991).

[149] Second Diet of Speyer.

[150] MacCulloch (2003), p. 158.

[151] Gritsch (1967), p. 31ff. Müntzer attacked Luther and honed in on the teaching of justification by faith alone which he dubbed "invented."

the sword for the destruction of the ungodly. Müntzer asserted in this sermon that his teaching was absolutely clear from the Bible saying, "This passage of Daniel is thus as clear as the sun, and the process of ending the fifth monarchy of the world is in full swing."[152] Bold absolute claims on the basis of novel interpretations of apocalyptic passages of Scripture became common fare for Protestant preachers and have been heard from their pulpits for five hundred years. This has been especially true since the middle of the 19th century when a great interest in prophecy and eschatology arose in Protestant circles. Numerous invented and detailed schemes of eschatological drama have been articulated including the pre-, mid-, and post-tribulation rapture theories, the 1000-year earthly millennium, the rebuilding of the Jewish temple, the return of the Jews to the Holy Land, and numerous other details that have spawned the creation of entire Protestant denominations and influenced American politics and foreign policy.

Müntzer began to call on various towns to rise up and effect social transformation by violence. In February 1525, conflicts erupted, and sometime in February or March a number of written documents were produced expressing the concerns of the peasants. The most widely distributed

---

[152]  Baylor (1991), pp. 11*ff.* It should be noted that eschatological speculation and overconfidence in prophetical interpretation was something quite consistently apparent in the work of most of the Reformers. Luther was certain that Daniel 2 referred to the Turks. Brecht (1987), p. 96.

12 Article Pamphlet

of these documents, *The Twelve Articles*,[153] was written by Sebastian Lotzer, a furrier, and Christoph Schappeler, a Lutheran pastor. The first of these articles demanded the right to appoint and dismiss the local pastor by decision of the congregation of peasants. The second article requested that the tithe be modified and collected by locally elected church elders. The third article rejected the commonly accepted notion that peasants were a lord's property. The fourth and fifth articles gave peasants the right to fish the streams and access the forest lumber. Among other articles were requests for decreased production demand, rent reduction, more community lands, and a final article pledging their willingness to be corrected by the Scriptures if they were in error.

Luther read these articles in early April and wrote two short replies. The first he wrote in April, and calling upon the peasants to be patient and civil, and upon the lords to address some of their reasonable grievances. Later when it appeared the peasants were taking up arms, Luther wrote a scathing attack of the peasants, and provided an endorse-

---

[153] *Ibid.*, pp. 231-238.

ment for aristocratic brutality in putting down the rebellion. "I will not oppose a ruler who, even though he does not tolerate the gospel, will smite and punish these peasants without first offering to submit the case to judgment." Luther thought the slaughter was spiritual.[154] On May 15, Müntzer's forces were slaughtered by the nobility at Frankenhausen. Some 6000 peasants were killed, with only some six casualties on the side of the princes. Müntzer was captured and beheaded twelve days later. In upper Germany alone, it is estimated that some 130,000 peasants were slaughtered. To put this in perspective, that is two and a half times the number of losses America suffered in Vietnam.[155] Luther was sharply criticized by many for his position, and was called "the hammer of the poor" by Hermann Mühlpfort, the mayor of Zwickau.[156]

Another strange expression, apparently on the fringe of Anabaptism, was a group of extremists who took over the city of Münster and proclaimed it the "New Jerusalem." The godless were to be slain, Old Testament polygamy was to be restored, all property was to be held in common,

---

[154] In the words of Diarmaid MacCulloch (2003) Luther became "an apologist for official savagery," p. 160. Commenting on Romans 13:1 Luther wrote, "Let everyone who can, smite, slay and stab, secretly or openly, remembering that nothing can be more poisonous, hurtful or devilish than a rebel." *Ibid.*, p. 160.

[155] One Protestant political principle was exceedingly clear: the Protestant Princes could steal land at will from the papacy, but the Protestant peasants better not.

[156] Gritsch (1991), p. 124.

and infant baptism and the Lord's Supper were described as rites of the Antichrist. "For fourteen hundred years the truth has been falsified and repressed" they articulated in the 1534 document *A Restitution of Christian Teaching* by Bernard Rothmann. Jan Mathijs served as the new "King David" for six weeks. Then he was killed by Catholic troops who besieged the city.

Such was the nature of political unrest and social confusion during the early years of the Reformation, and it is with this in mind that we turn to the Anabaptists.

### The Early Anabaptist Leaders and Their Principles

Two of Zwingli's compatriots, Conrad Grebel and Feliz Mantz, provided leadership for early Swiss Anabaptists. Mantz was the man mentioned in the preceding chapter, whom the Zurich authorities, with Zwingli's blessing, punished by drowning. Anabaptist histories criticize Zwingli for cowardice, suggesting that he agreed with the rejection of infant baptism but thought that it would lead to civil unrest. The first adult baptism of a man, George Cajacob, who had been previously baptized as an infant took place in January 1525. This "true Christian baptism" was the origin of the authentic separation of the faithful from the world in the Anabaptist mind. Soon the Anabaptist movement recruited its most able theologian and defender: Balthasar Hubmaier.[157]

---

[157] A good translation of Hubmaier's theological works together with a fine introduction to his life is Pipkin and Yoder (1989).

Balthasar Hubmaier (1480-1528) was a doctor of theology (having studied under J. Eck), professor at Ingolstadt, and a Latin priest ordained in 1510. In 1516 he was appointed preacher of Regensberg Cathedral. He was deeply influenced by Zwingli, and quickly joined the Anabaptists by 1525. He wrote an impassioned plea for religious tolerance entitled, *Concerning Heretics and Those Who Burn Them*.[158] In this treatise Hubmaier blamed the "unwatchful bishops" as the cause of heresies. He also asserted that the inquisitors were the greatest heretics of all. His most influential work is his *Christian Catechism*,[159] written at the height of his leadership in the Anabaptist movement. During this time he lived safely in Moravia without fear of punishment. In this work, he affirms the sole authority of the Bible, rejects pilgrimages and purgatory, affirms justification by faith alone, and forbids images. Significantly, Hubmaier also affirms that correct Baptism had been "lost for a thousand years," that true Christian Baptism was of adult believers only,[160] and that infant baptism is "no baptism," but rather, idolatry, because the child knows neither good nor evil. This affirmation itself denied the Baptism of virtually every Christian in the Western world at this time.[161] Hubmaier

---

[158] Pipkin and Yoder (1989), pp. 58-66.

[159] *Ibid.*, pp. 339-365.

[160] His *On The Christian Baptism of Believers* was written in 1525.

[161] Contemporary Baptists continue this rejection of infant baptism, and regularly baptize adult Christians who were already baptized as infants. This Baptist rejection of the validity of infant baptism should enable the Baptists

insisted that a person must know the catechism prior to Baptism. In the *Catechism*, Hubmaier also maintained that "the bread and wine [of the Eucharist] are nothing but memorial symbols,"[162] and explicitly asserted that Christ only instituted the sacraments of Baptism and Eucharist, both of which are merely outward signs. Hubmaier posited that the Latin mass was the idol and abomination spoken of by the Prophet Daniel. Interestingly, Hubmaier affirmed the virginity of the Theotokos, "before, during, and after giving birth,"[163] as did nearly all the Protestant Reformers. Nevertheless, the faithful were forbidden from offering prayer to the Mother of God, which he calls "blaspheming Christ." He also denied that the saints can do miracles.

Hubmaier was involved in the Peasant's War (which set him apart from the majority of Anabaptists who forsook military service, war, and the sword), and may himself have been the author of the *Twelve Articles* although this is not certain. He fled his pastorate in Waldshut[164] in December of 1525 when the Austrians invaded, fled to Zurich, and recanted his Anabaptist views under pressure from Zwingli. Early in the next year, he fled Zurich, and renounced his recantation. He spent the next two years writing pamphlets

---

to understand better and accept the Orthodox rejection of the validity of Baptist baptism.

[162] Pelikan and Hotchkiss (2003), *Creeds and Confessions*, Vol. 2, p. 684.

[163] *Ibid.*, p. 686.

[164] Just over the Swiss border in the province of Austria.

for the Anabaptist cause, and engaging in heated disputes
with other Anabaptists. Between 1524-1528, he wrote twenty-five works, ending each of them with the words, "Truth
is Unkillable." This was an accurate statement about the
truth, but not about Balthasar Hubmaier. The Austrians
finally extradited him, and burned him at the stake in Vienna on March 10, 1528. His wife had a stone tied around
her neck and was thrown into the Danube a few days later.
Those Anabaptists in and around Zurich organized themselves as the Swiss Brethren. In contrast to the Münster
extremists, these Anabaptists practiced non-resistance.
This group has survived in the mountains of the Canton
of Berne, however the majority migrated to Germany, the
Netherlands, and the United States of America where they
form a significant part of the Mennonites.

### *Menno Simons*

Menno Simons was born in 1496 in Holland, and ordained a Latin priest in 1524. In 1536, he joined the Anabaptist movement. Simons guided Dutch Anabaptism
away from its more radical elements, and led the movement
until his death in 1561. Over time, certain segments of the
Mennonites in the Netherlands embraced heretical views
of the Holy Trinity. John Smyth (1570-1612), the reputed
founder of the General Baptists, who had been ordained
in the Church of England, later became a Puritan preacher,
and then led a group of separatists to Amsterdam where he

Menno Simons

was in increasingly intimate contact with the Mennonites. After baptizing himself in 1609, he established the first modern "Baptist Church." Not all Baptists accept a historiography that traces Baptist roots to John Smyth, some tracing their roots to Zwingli and some of his followers.

## Anabaptist Confessions

An Anabaptist confession of faith stands in opposition both to the Lutheran and to the Reformed confessions (of which you will hear more in successive chapters). The more extreme wing of the Reformation that is being referred to as the Radical or Anabaptist Reformation was considered fanatic or enthusiast by the Lutherans and Reformed because they appealed to spiritual experience or an "inner light" as the key to interpreting the Scriptures and properly confessing the Christian faith, and because they rejected much of what was considered common Christian teaching. This appeal to experience as central to articulating faith would become a hallmark for their spiritual descendants, and remains fundamental to many expressions of Protestant Christianity today. Since experience is so variable, it is extremely difficult to arrive at any consensus of theological opinion. This lack of consensus even set individual reform groups against one another. For example, the Swiss Brethren called the German

Anabaptists in southern Germany "false brethren." Anabaptists in general considered themselves anti-creedal,[165] though ironically they produced as many confessions as Calvinism, and many more than the Lutheran movement, during the first 100 years of their history.[166] It also makes extremely difficult any consensus of theological opinion since experience is so variable.

What sets the Radical Reformation apart from what is called in modern times the Magisterial Reformation is the fact that these believers not only were not supported by political entities, but most eschewed politics on principle. All of the various confessions of faith articulated by Anabaptist thinkers express more radical definitions of separation from traditional Christian belief and practice.

### The Schleitheim Confession of 1527

This confession was the first major expression of theological consensus for the Anabaptists, and is named for a town in which Anabaptist leaders met in February of 1527. The meeting was presided over by Michael Sattler (1490-1527), a former prior of a Benedictine monastery, who joined the movement in 1525,[167] and the *Confession* was penned at a

---

[165] Popular Anabaptist lingo includes statements such as, "No creed but the New Testament," or "No creed but Jesus." One might point out that these are both simplistic *creeds.*

[166] Pelikan and Hotchkiss (2003), *Creeds and Confessions,* Vol. 2, p. 749.

[167] Sattler was himself very shortly thereafter arrested in Austria and executed. In his confession prior to his execution he affirmed that the body of

time when some of the leaders had been executed and many Anabaptists were in flight for their lives. Sattler probably drafted the seven articles of the Schleitheim Confession.[168]

The Schleitheim Confession presents the beliefs of the Swiss Brethren. Other groups identified as Anabaptists by historians of the Reformation include: Thomas Müntzer's followers and the Zwickau Prophets, the Hutterites, the Melchiorites, the Mennonites, and the radical Münster community. Common to Anabaptist belief was an anti-sacramental worldview, a rejection of infant baptism, opposition to bear arms or take oaths, congregational church polity and an emphasis on the ban. There was a divergence of views amongst the Anabaptists on the legitimacy of civic government, polygamy, and the principle of private or communal property.

There are definite links between the Anabaptists and the rise of Unitarianism in Poland and elsewhere. This connection ought not to surprise the reader since the Anabaptists embraced a view of *sola scriptura* that allowed virtually no hermeneutical accountability to tradition or any Church

---

Christ is not present in the Eucharist, that infant baptism does not save an infant, that no priest can bless oil and make it holy, that the Mother of God does not intercede for us, and that the saints are present believers, and that if the Turks should come, they ought not to be resisted. Here we see an expression of the Anabaptist commitment to pacifism. For more on Sattler see John H. Yoder (1973) *The Legacy of Michael Sattler*, Scottdale, PA: Herald Press.

[168] Baylor (1991), pp. 172-180.

Fathers. As such, the Anabaptist theological method in general is firmly a-historical, as though the pious labors of previous generations were irrelevant. On these principles extra-biblical words like "Trinity" and "hypostatic union" could be judged inappropriate by the rather naïve biblicism and disregard for traditional dogma of the Anabaptists.

The tenets of this first Anabaptist Confession include the following: First and foremost the confession affirms that baptism is to be administered to adult believers only (Article 1). Infant baptism is called "the greatest and first abomination of the pope." Article 2 affirms the use of church discipline/ the ban in local congregations. This commitment to the use of the ban would become a great center of Anabaptist division as different groups agreed to use the ban in differing measures of severity. Article 3 affirms that the "breaking of bread" (Anabaptist preferred language for the eucharist) is a remembrance and is to be shared only by Anabaptists, since it is wrong to partake of the table of the Lord and the table of demons. Article 4 affirms that all Roman Catholic ecclesiastical life is an abomination to God and separation from it must be definite. Article 5 affirms the leadership of the local congregation is to be under "shepherds" according to scriptural standards. Article 6 concerns the sword and affirms pacifism, excluding the faithful from use of the secular courts, from wielding punishment, or participating in civil government. Article 7, the last, concerns oath-taking and forbids it strictly.

Both Zwingli and Calvin formally refuted this Anabaptist Confession in treatises of their own. Calvin called the Anabaptists by the pejorative: catabaptists.

### *The Concept of Cologne 1591*

In 1591, a synod of Dutch and High German ministers met to heal the splintered movement and produced the *Concept of Cologne* designed to unify the Mennonite churches. This confession is noteworthy to Orthodox Christians since it is virtually the only Protestant statement of faith *not* to embrace the *filioque* heresy. On the contrary, the confession reproduces the language of the Council of Ferrara-Florence (1439) affirming that the Holy Spirit proceeds from the Father through the Son. This statement of faith also restricts marriage to within the Anabaptist movement, and affirms the practice of foot-washing. The central confession of the Mennonite churches summarizing these fundamental tenets is the *Dordrecht Confession* 1632.

### *Anabaptists Today*

**The Mennonites.** Today the largest group of direct Anabaptist descendants, the Mennonites, take their name from Menno Simons. There are some one million Mennonites today, of which the largest number live in America. Mennonite communities in America have endured immense internal divisions and factions over the years, and exist as many divided groups.

**The Amish.** The Amish, sometimes called the Amish Mennonites, originated from a division among the Swiss Brethren under the leadership of Jakob Ammann. They differed from other Swiss Brethren by their more frequent reception of the Lord's Supper, their practice of frequent foot-washing, and their plain-style dressing. Most migrated to the U.S.A. in the 18th and the 19th century. They have concentrated numbers in Ohio, Pennsylvania, Indiana, and Iowa, and are well known for their rejection of much modern technology, insurance, etc. They are also famous for their handicrafts. They have in some cases been granted special civil and political dispensations, and opt out of social security taxes and benefits. Presently, there are approximately 281,000 Amish in America, and the Amish population is consistently growing. Most of the Amish who remained in Europe rejoined their mother churches.

**The Baptists.** From the mid-17th century Baptist churches existed in the American colonies. The settlement of Roger Williams at Providence, Rhode Island, and the church formed there in 1639 on Baptist principles is generally regarded as the beginning of American Baptist history. The oldest Baptist church in the South is First Baptist Church of Charleston, South Carolina, which was organized in 1682. The first Baptist Church of Virginia was founded in 1715, and another in North Carolina in 1727. Most of the churches founded in the colonies were Anglican, Presbyterian, or Congregational,[169] and all shared a general antipathy toward the Baptist movement. Baptist preachers were often prosecuted for preaching without a license, and Baptists consider the early defense of these Baptist preachers by the likes of Patrick Henry and James Madison as a Baptist contribution to the American principle of religious freedom.

The Baptists are one of the largest Protestant and Free Church communions in the world with a membership of over 35 million persons. The Southern Baptist Convention is the world's largest Baptist denomination, and the largest Protestant denomination by far in America with some 16 million adherents in 42,000 churches. The word *Southern* reflects that the Convention became a separate denomination in 1845 in Augusta, Georgia. The Convention's churches are still most concentrated in the South, but there are 42 state conventions throughout the US. The issue of slavery divided the various Baptist churches, and the SBC actually formed itself in order to defend white supremacy and the validity of slavery. In 1995, the SBC adopted a resolution to renounce its racist roots. The SBC is famous for its theological controversy and disagreement within the Convention. The *Baptist Faith and Message* is the basic confession of the SBC. The SBC self-identity includes, besides classic Anabaptist emphases, also a strong emphasis upon missionary

---

[169] Colonial Congregational Churches were usually pastored by Reformed Puritan pastors.

work. On many moral issues of concern to all traditional Christians, the SBC has taken a courageous leadership role.

About two-thirds of all black American Protestants are Baptist. Protestant Evangelicals, who share many fundamental Anabaptist tenets, whether or not they belong to a denomination formally called "Baptist," number approximately 70 million persons in America. Baptist churches are congregational in church polity, having rejected the traditional ecclesiastical polity of diocese and bishop, which is rooted in the New Testament and conspicuously present throughout Church history. They express their unity by voluntary associations or conventions which continue to play a large part in Baptist church life. Baptists align in distinct conventions and associations based on varying and unique theologies such as the Seventh Day Baptists (who are Sabbatarians), or the various Baptist groups coming down on one side or other of the Calvinist-Arminian debates.[170]

Famous Baptists in history include John Bunyan, Charles Spurgeon (the great London preacher), William Carey (the father of modern Protestant missions), Dr. Martin Luther King, Dr. Billy Graham, Dr. Charles Stanley of Atlanta, Rev. Rick Warren of Saddleback Church in Orange

John Bunyan

---

[170] The chapter on the Reformed churches will elaborate on these debates.

County, California, Hon. Duncan Hunter, a US Congressman from San Diego, and, at one time, former President Jimmy Carter (who broke in 2000 with the SBC for "gender discrimination"), former President Bill Clinton and Vice-President Al Gore–both of whom left the SBC, and Bill Moyers, the well-known journalist and television commentator.

*Theological Reflections on*
*the Anabaptist Rejection of Infant Baptism*

Since I will be reserving our last chapter for a more extended Orthodox critique of the Reformation theological slogans common to all of its branches, I will not here comment upon them. Rather, I will conclude this chapter by addressing the central tenet of Anabaptism, which is the rejection of infant baptism in favor of adult baptism alone (so-called "believer's baptism"). Infant baptism remains a controversial topic, especially in the United States, which has been profoundly shaped by individualistic Baptist culture. America has never been an Orthodox nor Roman Catholic nation, though there are some 70 million Roman Catholics in America today.[171] Whether or not we American Christians have ever been officially associated with

---

[171] The Roman Catholic Church attained to its zenith of power and cultural influence in the first fifty years of the twentieth century when some six million American children were being educated in their parochial schools. Since that time its influence has waned immensely due to its internal disorder and innumerable moral scandals.

the "Baptist" movement, we have been deeply affected by this movement and its world-view in more ways than any of us know. The theology and practice of infant baptism is the heart of the "Baptist" milieu and American individualism. The name "Baptist" comes from the belief that infants should **not** be baptized, and that only individuals who are mentally mature and developed "enough"[172] to make a reasonable and conscious decision should be baptized.

One short anecdote about the relevance of this issue within American society today comes from an Orthodox priest whom I know. He held a European doctorate with extensive experience in higher education and was an administrator at an Evangelical Protestant university. His high position in the University provoked a response by numbers of concerned alumni. A letter was written to the Provost to document their concerns. At the top of their list of concerns was this: "It has been reported that this Dean believes in, practices, and has not repented of baptizing babies."

What is the Orthodox Christian response to those who refuse to baptize infants, and stigmatize our Church's practice as sinful? Our answer is this: The baptism of infants is both a biblical practice and one that has a great measure of unanimity in church history and tradition.

---

[172] There is no consistent age affirmed as appropriate for baptism: is it five years old? ten? fifteen?

## *The Structure of God's Covenants*

Abraham, our forefather in the faith, lived about 2000 years before the Incarnation of our Savior, the Lord Jesus Christ. God appeared to Abraham while he was living in Ur of the Chaldeans (Babylonia), and told Abraham to set out on a journey. Almighty God entered into a covenant with Abraham by promising to be his God and the God of his descendants, who in turn would be His chosen people.[173] The sign and seal of God's relationship with Abraham was circumcision. It served to show that those who possessed it belonged to God.[174]

St. Paul posits that, in the Church, circumcision has been done away with as the sign of the covenant. "For neither is circumcision anything, nor uncircumcision, but a new creation" (Gal. 6:15). While God no longer employs circumcision as before, he continues to be the God of the covenant. He has not changed the way in which He deals with His people, even though the covenant with Abraham has come to fulfillment in the New Covenant (Gal. 3-4). God still uses physical means to establish His covenant relationship with His people, and to communicate His grace, and this sign distinguishes His people from the world, marks them as His own. In the Church today, Christian baptism is the new covenantal sign which conveys God's grace to His peo-

---

[173] The history of the Patriarch Abraham is recorded in Genesis 12-17.

[174] Gen. 17, Rom. 4:11

ple. Baptism has replaced circumcision. St. Paul writes, "In Him you were also circumcised with a circumcision made without hands, in the removal of the body of the flesh by the circumcision of Christ; having been buried with Him in baptism, in which you were also raised up with Him" (Col. 2:11-12). St. Paul says that Christian believers have, in baptism, the fulfillment of circumcision. What circumcision was to Abraham and his descendants until the coming of the Christ in the flesh, baptism is for Christians. It is the mark of God's ownership and of our salvation (Rom. 4:11).

Reflecting on the moment when God instituted the covenant of circumcision with Abraham, we see that God not only established the sign of circumcision, but told Abraham very clearly *who* should receive this Old Testament sacrament. The God-Seer and Prophet Moses writes, "And every male among you who is eight days old shall be circumcised throughout your generations, a servant who is born in the house or who is bought with money from any foreigner" (Gen. 17:12). Infant circumcision was mandated by God.

Infant circumcision is the biblical precedent for infant baptism. Circumcision was given to the infants of one or more believing parents, and the same is true today for baptism. Indeed, as St. Peter said on the day of Pentecost about the forgiveness God promises in baptism, "For the promise is for you and your children, and for as many who are far off, as many as the Lord our God shall call to himself" (Ac. 2:39). Theological criticism of infant baptism could be equally applied to infant circumcision, and thus be a criticism of God's ancient institutions.

### The New Testament 'Oikos Formula'

The second major thread of biblical teaching which makes plain the divine character of infant baptism is the "*oikos* formula." The New Testament use of this "*oikos* formula" allows us to answer this question, "Was baptism administered in the New Testament according to the Abrahamic household model or according to the modern Baptist model which insists that baptism is an individual and adult decision"?

Repeatedly throughout the New Testament we come across incidents in which whole households were saved and baptized. So common is it that there is a clearly repeated formula about the "whole house" being saved or baptized. This is the "*oikos* formula."[175] Here are some examples,

"And Jesus said to him, 'Today salvation has come to this house, because he, too, is a son of Abraham'" (Lk. 19:9). This is found in the story about Zacchaeus the tax-gatherer. No other member of Zacchaeus's family is mentioned in the story, yet Jesus doesn't say that salvation had come to just Zacchaeus for his repentance, but that salvation had come to Zacchaeus' household.

---

[175] Oikos (οἶκος) is a Greek word meaning "house, household, or family." Liddell and Scott, *Greek-English Lexicon*, p. 546.

Consider St. Paul's words, "Now I did baptize the household of Stephanas" (1 Cor. 1:16). And again concerning Lydia and her family, "And when she and her household had been baptized..." (Ac. 16:15). And again concerning the Philippian jailer and his family, "And immediately he was baptized, he and all his household" (Ac. 16:33). And again, "The Lord grant mercy to the house of Onesiphorus for he often refreshed me, and was not ashamed of my chains" (1 Tim. 1:16). Onesiphorus had served Paul, so the Apostle invoked a blessing upon his entire household. There are numerous texts throughout the New Testament which relate the salvation of whole households at the same time. The salvation of the household is the usual New Testament pattern, not the salvation of independent individuals (Jn. 4:53, Ac. 10:2; Heb. 11:7-9, Matt. 10:12-14).

This household formula of baptism is conspicuously present in the data of the New Testament, and leads to the undeniable conclusion that the general practice was the baptism of an entire household at one time. The baptism of individuals one by one as is practiced and emphasized by the Baptist movement was not the practice of the first Christians.

These references to receiving the covenant sign of baptism are couched in the exact same language as the references to Abraham's reception of the covenant sign of circumcision. The Old Testament pattern of giving God's salvation and the sign thereof to the whole household, including infants (remember Isaac), carries right over into the New Testament. As a matter of fact, there is not one reference in the New Testament to any person being baptized who had been raised in a Christian home and had finally become an adult and able to exercise reason, believe, and be baptized. It simply did not happen. Infants were baptized together with the whole household, and those infants who were born into a Christian family were given the grace of baptism as infants after the pattern of Abraham.

### The Historical Practice of Infant Baptism.

The testimony of Church history is of no small importance in the matter of infant baptism, because it demonstrates that believers and their children were baptized together. This has been affirmed by the Orthodox Church, the Roman Catholic Church, and indeed the Magisterial Reformers. Infant baptism has remained the standard practice for the vast majority of Protestant communions including the Church of England, the Reformed Churches (Presbyterianism), the Methodist and Wesleyan Churches, and the Lutheran Churches.

### The Reversal of Our Savior's Teaching that to Children Belong the Kingdom of God

The Lord Jesus Christ taught saying, "Truly I say to you, unless you are converted and become like children, you shall not enter the kingdom of heaven" (St. Matt. 18:3). Far from being "unbaptized Christians" and second-class citizens in the Church, Orthodox Christian children are both fully baptized, chrismated, and communing members of the Body of Christ, and the models for adults. It is not the children who must grow up and become like adults in order for them to be baptized and saved as the Baptists would have us believe, but, on the contrary, it is the adults who must be converted and become like children if they hope to be saved.

The Baptism of the Lord

# 5
# *The Life and Teachings of John Calvin*

### *The Life of John Calvin*

The greatest of all the second generation Protestant Reformers, John Calvin, was born in 1509 in Noyon, France,[176] into an aristocratic family. He was intended by his family for an ecclesiastical career, and at the age of twelve received the tonsure at the hands of the Bishop of Noyon. At the age of fourteen, having finished his studies in his hometown, he went to study the arts in Paris. During this period, he was deeply influenced by the humanists, and studied theology under the leading Catholic theologians fighting Protestantism. Calvin wrote of this period of his life that he was "obstinately addicted to the superstitions of the papacy."[177] There is no evidence that Calvin was detaching himself from Rome until 1533, when he was in his mid-20s.

---

[176] Calvin's relationship with his hometown was not always pleasant. In 1551, the inhabitants of Noyon held a big celebration when they heard a false rumor that Calvin had died. A year later Calvin wrote that he had outlived Noyon for it had been sacked by Habsburg troops and only his parent's house was left still standing. Selderhuis (2009), p. 9.

[177] Wendel, p. 20. The outline of Calvin's life here is taken from Wendel's excellent text.

By his twentieth year, Calvin had given up his ambition to study for the priesthood, and took his Master of Arts. At this point, he turned his attention to the study of law. Calvin gave himself to extreme discipline in study, and acquired a thorough understanding of the Greek language. Upon the death of his father,[178] Calvin was free to determine his own course and returned to Paris to study literature as well as to pursue his legal interests. He published his first book, a translation of and commentary on Seneca's *De Clementia.*[179] In Paris, Calvin added a competence in Hebrew to his newly acquired Greek, as well as his already perfect Latin and French.

By the time he was twenty-four, Calvin had embraced the Reform movement and separated himself from the Papacy. In the future, he would write that by a "sudden conversion" his heart was softened toward God, and he became completely taken by a desire to study piety and theology.[180] He was deeply influenced by the writings of Martin Luther, whom he called "an apostle."[181] Calvin's cousin, Robert

---

[178] Calvin's fallout with the papacy was generational. His father Gerard was a successful lawyer and accountant of sorts for the church. He was accused of corruption in regard to the estates of two priests, and was excommunicated in 1528. He died in that state in 1531. Calvin's brother, Charles, was a Catholic priest. He was excommunicated for insulting a colleague and striking a parishioner, and, though offered absolution and last rites on his deathbed in 1537, he refused both and died excommunicate. Selderhuis (2009), p. 10.

[179] He published the book at his own expense. *Ibid.*, p. 26.

[180] *Ibid.*, p. 37.

[181] Luther himself acknowledged Calvin's scholarship, but remained suspicious of Calvin due to the latter's doctrine of the Eucharist. Brecht (1987),

d'Olivetan, with whom he was very close, was a confirmed Lutheran. In November 1533, he fled Paris after an outcry provoked by a pro-Reformation address given by the Rector of the University of Paris, Nicholas Cop. It is thought that Calvin himself wrote the address. Besides this controversial address, pro-Lutheran placards had been posted in Paris, and even successfully posted onto the bedroom door of King Francis himself.[182] In 1534, Calvin resigned his scholarships from the church,[183] and fled to Basel in 1535. For the next thirty years he would give his heart and mind to advancing the cause of the Protestant Reformation, and to synthesizing and perfecting the theology of Luther, Melanchthon, Bucer, and others.

In passing through Geneva in July 1536 Calvin was persuaded by Guillaume Farel,[184] the early French Reformer who first brought Protestant teachings to Geneva, to remain there in the city. In order to keep him from departing Geneva, Farel uttered a curse upon Calvin should he leave.[185] The latter began his career in Geneva with an ap-

---

p. 328.

[182] Selderhuis (2009), pp. 26-27.

[183] Calvin was well cared for by the Roman Church. He held three ministry positions: chaplain at La Gesine Chapel in the cathedral of Lyon [he paid another to care for it at a lower wage]; a position at the church of St. Martin de Marteville; and pastor of Pont-l'Eveque.

[184] Farel became something of a spiritual father to Calvin. Over the course of twenty years, Calvin wrote Farel on average once per month. Their relationship was seriously damaged when Farel, at age 69, decided to marry a 17 year-old girl. Selderhuis (2009), p. 186.

[185] Wendel (1950), pp. 48-49.

pointment as Reader in the Holy Scripture to the church in Geneva. During this time, Calvin and Farel drew up regulations of church government and worship for the church of Geneva. Calvin drafted a confession of faith, which became incumbent upon all Genevans to affirm in order to retain citizenship. The Genevan milieu, however, was still unsettled, with Catholic and various Reform movements in conflict. As in other places where the Protestant Reform was breaking out, the civil government had no wish to see a strong Protestant ecclesiology and authority established that would replace the obedience that these civil authorities had previously owed the papacy. Calvin would struggle his entire life in Geneva to free the church from the control of the civil powers, and he would fail. On Easter 1538, Calvin was asked to leave the city when he refused to obey the city council and confirm the Zwinglian ecclesiastical usages of Geneva's sister city Berne.[186]

Fleeing Geneva, Calvin accepted an invitation of Martin Bucer to pastor the French immigrants in Strasbourg.[187] For the next three years, Calvin worked exceedingly closely with Bucer, with whom he would maintain the closest links of personal friendship and theological sympathy. He sought to pastor the French Protestants in Strasbourg on his new principles of church polity, and he also assumed

---

[186] Wendel, p. 56.
[187] The Lutherans eventually closed the French refugee church in Strasbourg. Selderhuis (2009), p. 227.

Martin Bucer

a chair of exegesis at the new college of Sturm.[188] From this chair, he began to publish his extensive commentaries. During these years, Calvin participated with Martin Bucer in a series of important conferences designed to attempt to overcome the divisions between Protestants and Catholics in the Holy Roman Empire. During these conferences, he

[188] *Ibid.*, p. 61.

became acquainted with Melanchthon, and established his reputation as the leading mind of the second wave of the Reform.

Idelette de Bure

In August 1540, he married the widow, Idelette de Bure. She had been the wife of an Anabaptist, who had been one of Calvin's own converts. His only child with Idelette would die in infancy, and Idelette herself reposed in 1549. Calvin would raise her two children from her previous marriage. In September of 1541, the council of Geneva, in a state of civic and religious turmoil, begged Calvin to return to the city and help settle its internal problems. He was thirty-two, and would spend the next twenty-three years producing a massive literary corpus and endeavoring to establish the church of Geneva upon his principles.

*Geneva Under Calvin*[189]

The city council accepted his work on *Ecclesiastical Ordinances* in 1541,[190] and he established a consistory of

---

[189] Cross and Livingstone (1997), p. 266.

[190] Calvin wrote, "We know that each church is free to set up its own church order as it sees fitting and useful, because the Lord has not given us

pastors and elders to oversee church discipline and public morality.[191] This body of elders was to have the power of excommunication, which was the cornerstone of his entire system of church polity. Through the police force, the power of this consistory extended into every aspect of personal life in Geneva, and would be the basis for much resistance by its citizens and grounds for the charge that Calvin created a theocracy in Geneva. The consistory censured anyone regardless of age or sex.[192] It examined one's religious knowledge, criticism of ministers, absences from sermons, use of charms, and family quarrels. It exercised discipline against a widow who prayed requiem prayers at the grave of her departed husband, a goldsmith for making a chalice, a barber who tonsured a priest;[193] against someone for saying the pope was a good man; against one who criticized Geneva for executing a heretic; and against someone who

---

any specific directions in this regard." This radical and unsubstantiated presupposition, so at variance with traditional Christian ecclesiology, is what lies behind both the confidence Calvin possessed to innovate and the general undeveloped nature of Protestant ecclesiology. Selderhuis (2009), p. 63.

[191] Calvin was far more interested in the external organization of the reformed church than was Luther. Calvin's work in Geneva was his chance to flesh out what a Reformed community ought to look like. MacCulloch (2003), pp. 238-247. Geneva, a city of about 10,000 people in 1536, had had 400 Roman priests. After committing to the Reformation, it retained only about 10 pastors. Here we have a prism through which to see the anticlericalism of the Protestant Reformation—a 97.5% reduction in ordained clergy. Selderhuis (2009), p. 55.

[192] Wendel (1950), pp. 84-85.

[193] Latin monks wore a form of hair style that required regular trimming unlike Orthodox monks who generally do not trim their hair and beards.

sang a song critical of Calvin.[194] The consistory forbade card and ball games, regulated how much cutlery and how many plates were allowed to be used at the table, prescribed the clothing that could be worn, abolished Christmas day and made it a normal workday, and forbade brides from adorning their hair on their wedding day.[195] Calvin's hand was intimately involved in almost all matters of the consistory, and it took its cues from him. There was great public resistance to his moral oversight, and almost continuous political opposition from anti-Calvin parties until the last five years of his ministry.[196]

Calvin himself was not known for his humility, and thus reacted poorly to the public's resistance to his measures. In 1546, a member of the Little Council, Pierre Ameaux, called Calvin a wicked man and a preacher of false doctrine. Calvin felt that the Bible itself was being attacked since he, the chief interpreter of the Bible, was being so. The civil authorities offered to make Pierre beg Calvin's pardon on bended knees before the large Council of the 200. Calvin considered this insufficient, and declared that he would not enter the pulpit again until he had been given satisfaction. Pierre was sentenced to walk around the town only in his

---

[194] *Ibid.*, p. 84.
[195] Selderhuis (2009), p. 159.
[196] It ought to be noted as well that, astonishingly, between the 1540s and 1594 the clerical ministry in Geneva did not include a single Genevan. Mac-Culloch (2003), p. 239.

Michael Servetus

shirt, bareheaded and carrying a lighted torch, and then to present himself before the tribunal and cry to God for mercy. This Pierre was not a peasant, but a member of the civil government.[197] A country pastor later criticized Calvin's attitude in this case, and was immediately defrocked. Pastor Jerome Bolsec criticized Calvin's teaching on predestination and was arrested and banished forever from Geneva.[198] Geneva was typical of its time in its practice of burning heretics, the most famous being Michael Servetus, the physician who attacked the doctrine of the Trinity as unbiblical. Though Calvin petitioned for Servetus to die by a more humane method, he nevertheless was the one who revealed Servetus to the Inquisition and pressed their work.[199]

Calvin was supplied with a very large salary by the city, which was a symbol of their support, but was not able to

---

[197] Wendel, pp. 86-87.
[198] Bolsec returned to Catholicism and wrote a nasty book against Calvin in 1577. Selderhuis (2009), p. 191.
[199] Janz (2008), pp. 265-268.

obtain everything he wanted for the Genevan church. He failed to secure the administration of holy communion every month as he wished, but only once a quarter, nor was he able to direct the installation of pastors to be made with the laying on of hands as it was done in Strasbourg, but only with a simple prayer of installation. Calvin considered these failures to be of minor concern and acquiesced.

### The Theology of John Calvin

Calvin was an exceptional scholar. His most enduring work was his *Institutes of the Christian Religion*. He published the first edition in March, 1536, in Basel. He greatly expanded and revised the text in a new edition in 1539, and produced a massive revision and republication in 1559. The *Institutes* was a life-long project for Calvin,[200] a work of art that he developed and continuously improved throughout his life. The *Institutes* in English translation is almost 2000 pages in length. It was designed to provide a basic summary of the faith, a Reformed catechism, a systematic theology. It was designed to serve as a theological schema through which to read and properly interpret the Holy Scriptures.

Calvin authored not only his famous *Institutes of the Christian Religion*, but also commentaries on twenty-four books of the Old Testament and all of the New Testament except for 2 John, 3 John and Revelation. These classic com-

---

[200] See Wendel, pp. 111-126 on the successive editions of the *Institutes*.

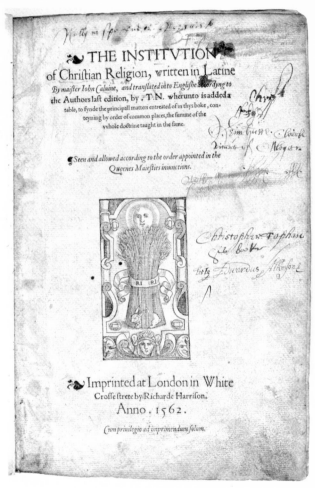

Cover page of an early English edition of
the *Institutes of the Christian Religion* by John Calvin

mentaries continue to be valued exegetical reference works for pastors and serious students of the Bible. The most prevalent English translation of Calvin's *Commentaries* consists of twenty-two large volumes. It is rightly asserted that Calvin himself took the tools of humanism and applied them to the study of the New Testament, and in so doing founded the modern science of scriptural exegesis. Calvin also oversaw the Genevan Academy, which provided an international forum for the propagation of his theology. The Academy could be said to be Calvin's crowning work.

What are the contours of Calvin's theology? Here a distinction must be made, as it was between Luther and Lutheranism, between Calvin himself and Calvinism per se as it has been embraced and taught for the last five hundred years. The theological system of John Calvin, chiefly expressed in his *Institutes,* and formulated by his successor, Theodore Beza, has many sources.

Calvinism is dependent upon Lutheranism for its commitment to *sola scriptura*, justification by grace through faith, the denial of free will, and many other points. Calvin immersed himself in the Scriptures more thoroughly than did Luther, and considered Luther to have been too conservative in his hermeneutic.[201]

Calvinism departs from agreement with Lutheranism in its more radical use of Scripture as a criterion for doctrine and practice, its great stress upon predestination and the

---

[201] For Lutheran influence on Calvin see Wendel, pp. 131-135.

importance of personal assurance of election and the perseverance of the elect, its rejection of the Lutheran teaching on the sacraments, and its general hermeneutic relating the Old and New Testaments.

### On the Holy Fathers and Patristic Authority

Calvin read and quoted many Holy Fathers. He admired St. John Chrysostom's biblical commentaries and once had resolved to translate them into French. He was a devotee of St. Augustine, and quoted Ss. Cyprian and Athanasius and others frequently. However, his attitude towards them was not an Orthodox one. Here are his words,

> Certainly, Origen, Tertullian, Basil, Chrysostom and others like them would never have spoken as they do, if they had followed what judgment God had given them. But from desire to please the wise of the world, or at least from fear of annoying them, they mixed the earthly with the heavenly. That was a hateful thing, totally to cast man down, and repugnant to the common judgment of the flesh. These good persons seek a means more in conformity with human understanding: that is to concede I know not what to free will, and allow some natural virtue to man; but meanwhile the purity of the doctrine is profaned.[202]

---

[202]  Wendel, p. 125.

Here is Calvin in all his arrogance and theological overconfidence. His accusations against the likes of Ss. Chrysostom and Basil the Great are that they were too worldly, too submissive to worldly powers, and not willing enough to defy merely human judgments.

These charges are ironic in that they apply far more to Calvin himself and the Protestant Reformers than to the Holy Fathers he attacks. Chrysostom and Basil were ascetic monks who were other-worldly, and show Calvin as still quite fixed to the earth by comparison. Who was the one who rejected his tonsure and married? And that a widow? Who was the one so irascible that he could not bear to be contradicted? Who was the one who determined eucharistic practice by the judgment of the civil powers? Who was the one who received a large salary from the state? Who was the one complicit in the execution of heretics? Who was the one who died in the comfort of his own home with the approbation of the wise of Geneva, instead of in harsh exile with the opposition of the emperor? That the Holy Fathers refused to articulate Calvin's doctrine of predestination is hardly a sign of complicity with worldly men, but rather a refusal to articulate what does not have the support of the Holy Scriptures and the *consensus patrum*.

On the issue of authority Calvin, as the other Reformers, posited a vacuous doctrine of *sola scriptura* which provided insufficient hermeneutical authority to insure even the agreement of those who claimed to believe the same things. Calvin fought with the Anabaptists, the Zwinglians, the Lutherans, and with the Roman Catholics, while claiming that the Scriptures were clear. And, though he read the Holy Fathers extensively, Calvin judged them all by their level of agreement with him, imputing moral depravity where none objectively existed in order to justify their universal disagreement with him. This is self-serving and contradictory theology.

Early on in his theological career Calvin was accused of Arian sympathies and a deficient Trinitarianism. He adamantly defended his adherence to the Trinitarian and Christological positions of the first Four Ecumenical Councils. How is it that Calvin, and the other Reformers who maintained a similar position, could embrace the intricate theology of the Holy Fathers of the First Four Ecumenical Councils (which he affirms is a pure and natural interpretation of Holy Scripture) yet which went well beyond *sola scriptura* in its terminology, when these same Holy Fathers taught universally and with common agreement clear doctrine on the Church and its polity and sacraments which tenets were wholly at odds with Protestant convictions? Were not the 318 Nicene Fathers bishops? Did they not believe that the Eucharist was the very Body and Blood of Jesus Christ? Did they not celebrate the liturgy, honor monasticism, venerate relics, make holy pilgrimage, express devotion to the Holy Theotokos and Ever-Virgin Mary, pray for the departed, invoke the saints, obey sacred canons, and read Scripture in accord with the tradition? The answer, of course, to these questions is "Yes."

And so, the Reformers and their descendants have this question to answer: Why do they demand adherence to the Trinitarian positions of the Holy Fathers while explicitly or implicitly degrading these same Holy Fathers by their Protestant criticisms? How can Protestant teachers be consistent in demanding an adherence to the dogmas of the Fathers of the early councils when these same Fathers believed the Holy Eucharist to be the very Body and Blood of Christ, worshipped liturgically, prayed to saints, venerated the Mother of God, insisted on the governance of the Church by bishops, and interceded for the repose of departed souls? Why accept the creeds of these four councils but reject their canons, something that the Fathers of the councils themselves explicitly forbade? This dilemma remains unsolved even for Protestants today. Protestants say they wish to preserve the fundamental teachings of Christianity, yet denigrate the lives of those Christians who articulated these fundamental teachings.

## On the Doctrine of God

Calvin affirmed his strict adherence to the classical Christian teaching on the Holy Trinity, the Incarnation of Jesus Christ, and the hypostatic union. Calvin is best known for his exaltation of the majesty and sovereignty of the living God, and the first book of his *Institutes* is duly famous for its august description of the living God, its beautiful emphasis upon revelation, and its Christocentricity. Calvin is at his best when he is describing the overarching providence of the living God and His intimate involvement in every aspect of existence. Unfortunately, Calvin joined his teaching on providence to his unique doctrine of double predestination, which he set forth very clearly. God elected both those who would be saved and also those who would be damned apart from any merit or fault of their own. Here Calvin took Luther's teaching and expanded it, much to the consternation of Melanchthon, who thought that the subject of predestination was a mystery that should not be discussed much, and that free will certainly existed.

In subsequent years, as Calvin's teaching was systematized into Calvinism, this emphasis on predestination grew in importance and prominence, yet many of his followers, including his immediate successor in Geneva, Theodore Beza, abandoned Calvin's teaching on double predestination. Calvin's doctrine of man and the Fall is quite bleak, and explicitly denies the postlapsarian ability of man to respond to God in any way or to do any good. Calvin rejected on principle the use of the term "free will." The doctrine of predestination is developed in Calvin in such a way as to suggest that the glory of God is the center of God's work, not the salvation of mankind. A false dichotomy enters, wherein the glory of God is defended as an end in itself (hence a justification for double predestination) apart from the good of mankind.[203] Such a dichotomy is rejected by the Orthodox, who affirm that the glory of God and the salvation of mankind are not dichotomous, and hence God is not willing that a single soul perish.

## On the Doctrine of Salvation

Calvin embraced the Reformation slogan *sola fidei*, and defined justification largely in the Lutheran sense. His understanding of Christ's redemptive work on the cross is fashioned largely according to the satisfaction theory. Calvin paid special attention to arguing, against the opponents of the Reformation, that man's justification does not lead to his passivity in seeking sanctification, thus placing special emphasis upon the work of the Holy Spirit in the sanctification of the believer. Calvin greatly emphasized the Christian's spiritual union with Jesus Christ.

## On the Doctrine of the Church

Calvin rejected the traditional hierarchy of the church. He argued that, instead of the patristic triple ministry of bishops, priests and deacons, there were four orders of offices in the church: pastors, teachers, elders, and deacons.

---

[203] For more on this see the former Calvinist Fischer (2014), *Young, Restless, No Longer Reformed: Black Holes, Love, and a Journey In and Out of Calvinism.*

Calvin learned this from Martin Bucer. Each week the pastors and teachers were required to meet to discuss the Scriptures. During this interaction, they were to agree on any doctrinal differences, and could appeal to the elders, and the elders could ultimately appeal to the civil government. The Genevan council considered itself as delegating authority to the consistory, and so the clergy functioned as a subsidiary of the state.

Calvin's position on the ordination of the clergy was a far cry from traditional notions, and even his position requiring the laying on of hands was rejected by Genevans. It is a particular irony, and illustrative of what a low view of the church and ordination Calvin had, that he himself *never appears to have been ordained by anyone.*[204] How *sola scriptura* justifies ordination without a laying on of hands by a person in appropriate ecclesiastical authority, when that same *scriptura* everywhere witnesses to this reality, is illogical. It is also sad that Calvin seemed to have no confidence in the role of the church as the guardian and support of the truth, to use St. Paul's language in 1 Tim. 3:15.

Unlike St. Augustine, who affirmed that he believed in the Scriptures precisely because of the authority of the Holy Church, Calvin taught that the Scriptures have their

---

[204] MacCulloch (2003), p. 238. One of Calvin's friends, Louis de Tillet, a one-time Protestant who returned to the Roman communion, wrote Calvin and pointed out that he was not called by God or ordained, but only called by men. Selderhuis (2009), p. 66.

authority confirmed by the internal testimony of the Holy
Spirit. He fails, however, to anchor this appeal to personal
experience to some objective criterion, and so rails against
Luther himself, who on the basis of such subjectivism, argued that the Epistle of St. James should be removed from
the canon of Holy Scripture. Here we see Calvin, in fact,
living off the tradition of the Church while denying he was
doing so. There is nothing in Holy Scripture that proves
that the Church's canonical collection is infallible.

Calvin also took up the classical teaching on the Church
as a Mother, and insisted on participation in the visible
body of Christ outside of which no one may hope for salvation. While maintaining this classical doctrine, so beautifully expressed by St. Cyprian of Carthage, Calvin nevertheless failed to explain how the Church maintains itself
after so much rejection of its substance and the severance of
apostolic succession. Calvin simply asserted that where the
Word is faithfully preached and the sacraments faithfully
administered, there is the Church. Yet since none of the
major Reformed traditions could agree on the sacraments,
what are we to think about their constitution as a "church"
according to Calvin's own principles?

## On Liturgy and Worship

Calvin was never a priest, and held the Roman Mass in
disdain. He thought the Mass was the greatest idolatry, and
said the priests performed "magical mumblings" and the

people gazed on in "stupid amazement."[205] In 1542, Calvin published a new liturgical compilation entitled *Form of the Ecclesiastical Prayers and Hymns.* The service began with a written prayer of confession. This is followed by the singing of the first half of the Ten Commandments, then Psalm singing. He utilized the Psalms primarily, even creating a French Psalter for congregational singing, and the forms he had perfected in Strasbourg. Then there was a prayer for illumination, the reading of the Scripture lection and a sermon. This prayer for illumination was lengthy, longer than our Orthodox anaphoras. On days when Holy Communion was served, there followed the recitation of the institution of the Eucharist, distribution, and prayers of thanksgiving and a dismissal.

Essentially, Calvin invented his own liturgical rites based, he claimed, upon Holy Scripture and the customs of the "ancient Church." It should be noted that, though he made it up, he expected his new liturgical form to be carefully adhered to. The idea that worship should be "spontaneous" and not employ written prayers and structured liturgical form, which is so common today amongst America's Protestant Evangelicals, is not a tenet adhered to by the Magisterial Reformers. Calvin's liturgy was entirely written. Calvin wished for a weekly celebration of Holy Communion, of which he said there was nothing more useful, but had no success accomplishing this vision. His liturgy sought

---

[205] Thompson, *Liturgies of the Western Church*, p. 185.

to preserve the union of word and sacrament, so that on days when the Communion would not be made, the service could be viewed as ante-Eucharistic. Calvin suggested that the Church ought not add human inventions in the liturgy to what the Scriptures taught. Such external ceremonies Calvin considered to be stumbling blocks to spiritual worship. He set preaching over against outward adornment and embellishment, in what is judged by the Orthodox to be yet another Protestant false dichotomy, leading in this instance to very ugly Reformed church buildings.

## Sacraments

Calvin agreed with Luther and other Reformers in his acceptance of only two primary sacraments: Baptism and Holy Communion. Defining these realities, however, was a different story. He engaged in a very hostile debate with the Lutheran theologian Westphal on the subject of the Eucharist. Calvin rejected the Lutheran affirmation of the real presence of Christ, and tried to forge a middle ground between Luther and Zwingli. Rejecting the notion of the ubiquity of the resurrected Body of Jesus Christ assumed by Luther and all traditional Christianity,[206] Calvin argued for a "spiritual presence" of Christ's Body and Blood. The elements were not changed in any way, and the physical

---

[206] Ubiquity is synonymous with omnipresence. Calvin went so far as to suggest that the unusual ability of Jesus' resurrected body to pass through doors etc. was not a necessary conclusion from the text of Scripture.

Body of Jesus was not received, yet somehow His Body and Blood were spiritually present. It should be noted that this rejection by Calvin of the ubiquity of the glorified Body of Christ determines also Calvin's rejection of the traditional notions of real union with Christ and theosis.

Calvin rejected Zwingli's teaching that the elements of the Eucharist are only bare signs and empty symbols. Calvin considered them to be much more, but virtually no one, including his own followers for the last five hundred years, have been able to understand what receiving Jesus' Body and Blood *spiritually* means. The Lutherans accused Calvin of Zwinglianism, much to his dismay and anger, yet despite all his protestations, it is very difficult to refute the Lutheran accusation.

### Creed and Confession

Besides his own *Institutes,* Calvin wrote a catechism for the Genevan church that would serve as the basis for the later Heidelberg Catechism, the standard catechism of the Reformed Churches. Calvin denied the reality of Christ's descent into Hell, while attempting to affirm the validity of the Apostles' Creed. He argued that this phrase was simply an image for the sufferings Christ endured on the Cross and of his death in the body. Here is yet one more instance in which Calvin rejects a universal Christian belief, and one which lies at the heart of the Church's Gospel. By denying

Christ's descent into Hell, Calvin has attacked the Gospel and damaged the saving message of Jesus Christ.[207]

### Hermeneutics and Covenants

Calvin is especially good in his interpretation of the covenants, and his articulation of the relationship between the Old and New Testaments. Calvin was more thoroughly educated in the Old Testament than any other Reformer, and maintained a brilliant Christocentric hermeneutic.[208] The Old Testament people of God lived according to the same promises we have, but by anticipation and as though seeing Christ dimly and in promises. The Scriptures can only be rightly understood in their relationship to Jesus Christ Himself. Calvin also set forth a very positive view of the divine law, arguing against Luther that the Law not only revealed sin and evoked condemnation in order to drive the sinner to Christ the Savior, but also glorified God by revealing his righteousness, hindered the wicked by its constraints, furthered peace in society, and contributed to the sanctification of the faithful by guiding them.[209] Calvin's doctrine of the last things is where he may be most traditional. He showed careful reserve, not writing a commentary upon the Revelation, and affirming only a basic and

---

[207] For more on the central Gospel affirmation of the descent into and plundering of Hades by Jesus Christ see Alfeyev (2009).

[208] Wendel, pp. 208-216.

[209] *Ibid.*, pp. 196-208.

creedal eschatology. One might wish that he had shown such reserve in his teaching on predestination.

The year 2009 marked the five hundredth anniversary of the birth of John Calvin, and memorials and celebrative symposia were held throughout the western Christian world in honor of his birth. Calvin's influence today continues not just upon those churches that are his direct legacy, but also upon many forms of Protestantism which, to one degree or another, have embraced aspects of Calvinist soteriology and so self-identify as Calvinistic. In our next chapter we will examine more closely the subject of the history of Calvinism in the Reformed Churches of the Continent, the Church of Scotland, and American Presbyterianism, and even speak about an Orthodox Patriarch of Constantinople whom some believe came under the sway of Calvin.

John Calvin

# 6

# *Calvinism and Orthodoxy*

John Calvin has exercised the greatest influence of any of the Protestant Reformers, and is considered the father of the Reformed churches. It is difficult to overestimate how influential John Calvin has been on virtually all branches of Protestantism. Though his most thorough influence was on those churches we call Reformed, which adopted virtually his entire agenda, even those branches of Protestantism that are not directly dependent upon him have been at times deeply influenced by Calvin's articulation of the Protestant tenets that they share with him, and by his general approach to the Scriptures.

The designation 'reformed' (with a lowercase 'r') applies to and has been used by confessions of churches of the Reformation that define themselves in contradistinction to Roman Catholicism. The Lutheran *Formula of Concord* refers to the Augsburg Confession as the "common confession of the reformed churches." The slogan, *ecclesia reformata et semper reformanda*[210] is articulated by all the churches of

---

[210] "The reformed and ever-reforming Church." This was Calvin's response to the Latin accusation that he and the other Protestants were innovating. He articulated in his *The Necessity of Reforming the Church* that this process

the Reformation. But 'Reformed' with a capital 'R' quickly acquired a more specific reference to identify those Reformation statements of faith and churches that depended directly upon Zwingli and Calvin rather than Luther. Unlike the Lutheran faith, the Reformed confessions arose separately from each other, and were embraced and passed on in a more de-centralized process, without anything like the Lutheran *Book of Concord*.

### French Huguenots

Calvin's influence upon the French Protestants, called Huguenots, was great. The name is thought to be derived from a German word referring to those admitted to the Swiss Confederation. Calvin himself is considered the ultimate founder of French Protestantism. Though he fled France in 1534, he dedicated his first edition of the *Institutes* to King Francis I of France. Geneva was the chief source of pastors for the French Protestants, and it was decided at the first Synod of the French Protestants in 1539 that their church would be organized on Calvin's principles. Calvin

---

of reform is the work of God in the Church at all times, and is to be done "according to the Word of God." In the last five hundred years of Reformed history it has served as a door to justify innovations that Calvin himself could never have dreamed of. It is also of interest to note that Calvin, in his final sermons and addresses prior to his death, called upon the Reformed pastors to leave all things as they were, and to change nothing because "change brought about little good." Here is a classic case of "Do as I say, not as I do." Selderhuis (2009), p. 256.

translated the *Institutes* and many of his works from Latin into French, and these works had a tremendous influence, not only upon the theological scene in France at the time, but upon the development of the French language itself. The influence of the *Institutes* upon French is comparable to the influence of Luther's *German Bible* on the German language. It should also be noted that the *Genevan Catechism* was composed by John Calvin for Geneva in 1536 originally in French. This was the catechism that, under Calvin's influence in Geneva, was set forth as fundamental to establish one in communion and in full citizenship. In 1541, Calvin greatly expanded this catechism in the form of questions and answers covering the *Apostles' Creed* (Questions 1-130), the *Ten Commandments* (Questions 131-232), the importance of prayer and an exposition of the Lord's Prayer (Questions 233-95), and God's relationship with man through His Word and sacraments (Questions 296-373). This final version of the *Genevan Catechism* became a type for later Reformed catechisms throughout Europe. The use of the catechism in Protestant Christian pedagogy was to replace the Latin practice of confirmation, which was held by Calvin to be "without foundation" and "without edification."

The Huguenots became a significant minority in France, and subscribed to the Calvinist *French Confession* of 1559/71. It is estimated that by 1562, after a decade of rapid growth, there may have been two million Huguenots in one thousand congregations.[211] Eventually, they were deemed by the royal house to be a threat to the stability of the state. Religious wars erupted in 1562 and continued until 1594. The most terrible of these conflicts was the Massacre of St. Bartholomew's Day in 1572 during which some five to ten thousand Huguenots were put to death in numerous large French cities at the instigation of the Queen Mother, Catherine de Medici.

### Calvinists in Geneva and Switzerland, Northern Germany, and the Netherlands

The First (1536) and Second (1566) Helvetic Confessions were the authoritative profession of faith of the Swiss Reformed Churches, and served as a basis for many later Reformed confessions. Until the Wars of Religion, Calvinism vied mightily to win France. In 1622, Calvinism became the state religion of the Netherlands. The Netherlands was subjected to tremendous internal conflict over predestination and free will, and was the site of the Calvinist-Arminian debates. Parts of Germany, Hungary, and Romania embraced Calvinism.[212] Calvinism had some influence upon the Church of England, and Calvin dialogued with the English Protestant boy-king Edward VI about church polity.

---

[211]  MacCulloch (2003), p. 307.
[212]  *Ibid.*, pp. 442-463. *cf.* Brecht (1987), pp. 318-319.

## *Church of Scotland and the Presbyterians*

In 1560, the Scottish Parliament commissioned Scottish Reformer John Knox (1513-1572), who had traveled in England, Frankfurt, and Geneva, and five other ministers to compose a confession of the Reformed faith for Scotland. Within just a few days, a confession was presented and accepted by Parliament almost unanimously. The 25 articles of the Scots Confession draws on Calvin, the French Confession, the First Helvetic Confession, and the Augsburg Confession. It remained the Scottish standard until it was superseded by the Westminster Confession in 1647. The Genevan *Book of Church Order* was adopted in Scotland, and within 20 years formal geographic presbyteries were established to replace the traditional dioceses. The Reformed Church polity was established throughout the country, but was to co-exist with the old Roman system preserved for the sake of its old leadership. The Reformation in Scotland was uniquely thorough.[213] It also demonstrated a remarkable genius for compromise, even allowing the old guard to continue to draw two-thirds of their former revenues if they agreed to step aside and not involve themselves in the new church.[214]

The name "Presbyterian" comes from the Greek word *presbyter* meaning "priest" or "elder." The latter definition

---

[213] Ryrie (2006), p. 3.
[214] MacCulloch (2003), p. 379.

is the one embraced by Presbyterians. The Scottish erection of geographic presbyteries was the first of its kind on a national scale. Martin Bucer in Strasbourg had articulated a presbyterian polity for his city, and Calvin had established such in Geneva. Scotland, however, gave it national expression, and did not have to simply disestablish the diocese of one bishop, but essentially ended episcopacy in Scotland altogether. To this day, Scotland remains the mother country of Presbyterian churches.

Scottish ecclesiastical history has witnessed the divisions that always follow the embrace of Protestantism. Today there are a number of Presbyterian denominations in Scotland including the Church of Scotland, the Free Church of Scotland, the United Free Church of Scotland, the Free Church of Scotland (Continuing), the Free Presbyterian Church of Scotland, the Associated Presbyterian Church, and the Reformed Presbyterian Church of Scotland.

Presbyterianism existed quietly and illegally in England from the time of Thomas Cartwright in 1572.[215] The advance of more radical elements of the Reformation in England in the 17th century established for some time the prevalence of Puritan clergy[216] and teaching, and the ascendancy of

---

[215] Cartwright was Lady Margaret Professor of Divinity at Cambridge. His views against episcopacy led to the loss of his professorship, then emigration to Geneva. MacCulloch (2003), p. 383.

[216] A "Puritan" was initially an Anglican clergyman who considered the Anglican Reformation to be insufficient, and agitated for a more thorough

Presbyterianism at the Westminster Assembly in 1643-1649. In 1660, when the monarchy was re-established,[217] the Presbyterians remained in non-conformity, outside the established Church of England. By the 19th century, most English Presbyterians had jettisoned the Christian faith and become Unitarians, a foreshadowing of the wholesale detachment from traditional faith that would take place in all mainline Protestant churches in the 20th century. In 1972, the Presbyterian Church of England joined the Congregational Church in England and Wales to form the United Reformed Church.

Puritanism, so important to the founding of the American colonies, was primarily a Calvinistic and Presbyterian movement. Most of the churches in the early colonial times were established upon a Presbyterian model, though some were congregational. Virtually all were Calvinistic in doctrine and Puritan in disposition. Calvinism was the faith of the great American preacher of the 18th century Great Awakening, Jonathan Edwards.

There are numerous Presbyterian denominations in America today including: the Presbyterian Church (USA)

---

rejection of episcopal government and traditional sacramental practice. "Puritan" is not an antonym of "hedonist."

[217] The English Civil War (1642-51) began under the reign of King Charles I. It was a conflict between the Parliamentarians led by Oliver Cromwell and the Royalists, faithful to the King. King Charles I was executed on January 30, 1649, and England was without a monarch until the Restoration in 1660.

with about 2 million members; the Presbyterian Church in America (PCA) with about 300,000 members, the Cumberland Presbyterian Church, the Evangelical Presbyterian Church, and the Reformed Presbyterian Church. There are at least 20 additional smaller Presbyterian denominations. Presbyterians have zealously evangelized the nation of Korea, and there is a significant and growing number of Korean Presbyterians in America.

In general, Reformed denominations in the USA that do not self-identify with the Presbyterian name are also manifold: Dutch Reformed denominations include the Reformed Church in America with some 300,000 members, the Christian Reformed Church with some 300,000 members, and the United Reformed Churches in North America. Much of the United Church of Christ traces its roots to the German Reformed, and claims about 1.1 million members.

## *Modern Day Resurgence of Calvinism*

Amongst more conservative Protestants in recent decades there has been a resurgence of Calvinism across denominational lines. This may be attributed to the attraction, in an age of shoddy thinking and the embrace of relativism amongst so many Christians of the West, of a rigorous intellectual system in which theology is taken very seriously. There are also a good number of exceedingly talented Reformed teachers and professors in America who are using modern technology and their impressive rhetorical skills to spread the Reformed faith amongst America's Protestants and throughout the world.

It is not unusual today to hear Protestants in traditions not historically associated in any formal way with the Reformed Churches to identify themselves as Calvinist. This self-identification refers primarily to the issue of soteriology, and not necessarily to larger Calvinist concerns like covenant, culture, infant baptism, etc. On the popular level, Calvinism is often associated with what is known as "the five points of Calvinism."

## The Five Points of Calvinism

The five points of Calvinism were first concisely articulated in the midst of a conflict between Protestants in the Netherlands over the teaching of John Calvin on predestination. One of the leading Dutch Protestants was a man named Jacob Arminius. He was a man of great intellect, and had studied many places, including Geneva under Calvin's successor, Theodore Beza. While studying the Epistle to the Romans he came to disbelieve the Calvinist doctrine of predestination. It is ironic that the study of the same Epistle by different Reformers led them to such differing conclusions despite their affirmation that Scripture is clear and interprets itself without the necessity of the Holy Fathers. Arminius set as his goal the revision of the Reformed Confessions to purge them of what he considered false teaching on predestination. Those who adhered to his teaching in Holland were called Remonstrants, and they published a document of their beliefs called *The Remonstrance of 1610.* A special synod was called in 1618 to address this subject, not just of Dutch ministers and theologians but including voting representation from all the Reformed lands. As such it was the most representative gathering ever seen in the Protestant Reformation.[218] This was the Synod of Dort and the canons it issued would put forth the five points of Calvinism, which history has given a life of its own as an independent soteriological system.

The Remonstrants at this synod put forth their own fundamental theological assertions, which were that divine sovereignty is compatible with human free will, that Jesus Christ died for all and not only for the elect, and that both double and single predestination as the Calvinists articulated them were unbiblical. In response to these assertions, the Synod of Dort affirmed Calvinist teaching, and expressed it in five points together with addenda refuting specific Arminian alternatives.

These five points have been popularly expressed through the mnemonic device: TULIP.

T= Total Depravity. Since the Fall, all men are born dead in sin, and unable even to dispose themselves toward salvation, being without free will.[219]

---

[218] MacCulloch (2003), p. 378.
[219] Calvin opposed the term "free will" on principle.

U= Unconditional Election. The explanation for the conversion of some and not of others lies not in anything the individuals did to merit election, but solely in the grace of God and His predetermined counsel to elect some to demonstrate His love, and to pass by others justly to demonstrate His wrath.

L= Limited Atonement. Jesus Christ's death is an effectual satisfaction of the wrath of God, and as such was intended and accomplished only for those who are really and truly saved, that is, the elect.

I=Irresistible Grace. Those who are called by God are regenerated by His grace, and by the rejuvenation of their will, will certainly follow God.

P= Perseverance of the Saints. Those whom God has predestined and called will certainly persevere in faith until the end. True believers can obtain an assurance of salvation that they will persevere and be saved.

The teaching of Jacob Arminius became known as Arminianism, and the Calvinist-Arminian debates have continued unabated in Protestant circles from the early 1600s until today. Arminian theology was popularized in America by such great preachers as John and Charles Wesley, and their Methodist movement.

Those who embraced Calvinism as a soteriological system, without its ecclesiastical polity or cultural worldview, self-identify as Calvinists today. Properly speaking these modern-day Calvinists are those who embrace the five points of Calvinism as articulated at the Synod of Dort. Some contemporary Protestants who identify as Calvinists, however, confess themselves to be "four-point" Calvinists and reject the notion of limited atonement.

## Orthodoxy and Calvinism

The history of dialogue between Orthodox Christianity and the Reformed Churches is not so extensive or colorful as that between Orthodoxy and Lutheranism. There is, however, one historical figure whose supposed admiration and embrace of many Calvinistic principles provoked a thorough theological response to Calvinism. This historical figure is Cyril Lucaris, Patriarch of Constantinople.[220] Cyril was born in Crete in 1572, traveled extensively in his youth, studying at Venice, Padua, Wittenberg, and Geneva. In Geneva, he encountered many of Calvinism's most articulate theologians. In 1596 he was sent by the Patriarch of Alexandria to Poland to work against any Orthodox union with Rome, and for six years served as professor of the Orthodox academy in Vilnius (in modern day Lithuania). He was a zealous opponent of the Latins, and particularly of the Jesuit effort to Romanize the Orthodox Churches. He

---

[220] Hadjiantoniou, George A. (1961), provides the only full-length treatment of Patriarch Cyril Lucaris written in English in the last fifty years. It is written from a decidedly Protestant perspective, and assumes that the supposed Calvinist sympathies of the Patriarch were authentic. This position is assumed by the article on 'Lucar, Cyril' in the *Oxford Dictionary of the Christian Church*, p. 1001.

became the Patriarch of Alexandria (as Cyrill III) from 1602-1620, and later the Patriarch of Constantinople.

Patriarch Cyril Lucaris was revered by the Orthodox clergy and laity and is best known for his violent opposition to the Unia. As Patriarch of Constantinople he was pressed between the Jesuits, who were constantly scheming against him, and the Protestant ambassadors, who wished to secure the endorsement of the Patriarch for their own purposes. He sent many young Greek theologians and seminarians to study at universities in Switzerland, the Netherlands, and England. In 1629 in Geneva, a *Confession of Faith* under his name was published, which was decidedly Calvinistic. In the same year it was published in two Latin editions, four French, one German, and one English.[221]

### *The Eastern Confession of the Christian Faith, Cyril Lucaris 1629 (1633 Greek)*

The Calvinist stamp on this confession is revealed in many places: Ch. 2 on the Holy Scriptures states "the witness of the Holy Scripture is of higher authority than that of the Church." Ch. 3 affirms double predestination. Ch. 8 affirms that Christ alone rules from heaven and protects and cares for His Church. Ch. 13 affirms the imputation of Christ's righteousness. Ch. 14 denies free will in the unregenerate. Ch. 15 affirms only Baptism and Eucharist as sacraments of the Gospel. Ch. 17 affirms the "real presence" of

---

[221] Pelikan (2003), pp. 549-550.

Jesus in the Eucharist, rejects transubstantiation, but denies that the real presence is the elements themselves.

Historians have differed on the authenticity of this confession, some affirming the authorship of Lucaris, and others noting that we have a large body of books and letters from the Patriarch in which he does not advocate Calvinist positions and is a defender of Holy Orthodoxy.[222] There is no doubt that the Jesuits were seeking to undermine Lucaris and to brand him as a Calvinist and a betrayer to Holy Orthodoxy so that his valiant opposition to Latin intrigues would be weakened. The French and Austrian Catholic Ambassadors were pressuring the Sultan to dethrone Lucaris. It is also true that the Reformed countries were anxious to publish something associated with the Orthodox Church that would lend credence to their views. Though Patriarch Lucaris is said to have disavowed authorship of the *Confession* orally on several occasions, this was never done in writing. We may never know the exact relationship between Patriarch Cyril Lucaris and the Calvinist *Confession* published in Geneva under his name.

Lucaris was deposed and banished from his patriarchal throne only later to be restored six times, and, at the order of the Ottoman Sultan, was eventually strangled by janis-

---

[222] For more on the supposed Protestant convictions of the Patriarch see Hadjiantoniou, George A. (1961), *Protestant Patriarch: The Life of Cyril Lukaris* (1572-1638), *Patriarch of Constantinople*, Richmond, VA: John Knox Press.

saries while on a ship in the Bosporus on June 27, 1638.[223] This demonstrates how tenuous was the position of the Ecumenical Patriarch under the Ottomans. His body was thrown into the sea, but recovered and buried outside the capital and only brought back to Constantinople after many years. The life of Patriarch Cyril Lucaris was a great tragedy not only because of his association with Calvinist teachings and the many sufferings he endured, but because Cyril was an exceptionally brilliant man whose gifts were not able to be fully enjoyed by the Church. Metropolitan Kallistos Ware in his *The Orthodox Church* suggests that Lucaris was perhaps the most brilliant Patriarch of Constantinople since St. Photios the Great in the 9th century.[224]

It was this churchman and the deviant *Confession* published in his name that provoked a serious controversy in the Orthodox Church. No less than six local councils between 1638 and 1691 condemned Lucaris's *Confession*. In reaction to Lucaris, two Orthodox bishops, Peter of Moghila and Dositheos of Jerusalem, produced *Confessions* of their own making. Peter Moghila's *Confession* was written in 1640, and depended heavily upon Jesuit templates. It was revised and its Latin influences reduced in the following years, and it was approved by the Council of Jassy in Romania in 1642 and remains the most Latinized theological statement ever adopted by an official local synod/council of the Orthodox

---

[223] Davey (1987), p. 98.
[224] Ware (1963, 1997 revised), p. 96.

Church. The anti-Calvinist statements culminated in 1672 at the Synod of Jerusalem (sometimes called the Council of Bethlehem) where Orthodox hierarchs gathered under the chairmanship of Dositheos, Patriarch of Jerusalem (1669-1707), to formally refute Calvinist teachings. This was done in the *Confession of Dositheos and the Synod of Jerusalem* which refutes Lucaris' *Confession* point by point.

### The 'Confession of Dositheos' and the Synod of Jerusalem 1672

John Meyendorff has called this *Confession* the most important Orthodox dogmatic text of this period.[225] Its table of contents reflects exactly that of the so-called *Confession of Faith of Lucaris*, which demonstrates that it was intended as a specific rejection of this previous confession.

The Confession in Chapter Two affirms the authority of Holy Scripture, but requires that it be interpreted as the Church has always interpreted and believed it, noting that every foul heresy receives the Holy Scripture but interprets it perversely. The authority of the Church is not inferior to the Scriptures. Like the Scriptures, the Church is infallible and has perpetual authority, and it is one and the same thing to be taught by the Scriptures and to be taught by the Church.[226] Calvin is specifically named as a heretic in

---

[225] (1986), p. 86.

[226] In the questions and answers section Dositheos says that believers should not read all the parts of the Scriptures, which is too dangerous, especially the Old Testament. He also says that the Longer Canon is fully Scripture.

this chapter and rebuked for shamelessly learning from the Church only to wickedly repudiate her. Chapter Three affirms predestination to justification and condemnation, but not in the Calvinist sense of predestination, without cause except in the will of God, but rather by foresight into how each would use his own free will. Chapter Eight affirms that Christ is the only mediator between God and men, having reconciled us to God by His blood, but affirms at the same time that saints, angels, and above all the Most Pure Theotokos are heavenly intercessors. Besides the saints, we also number amongst our mediators God, the bishops, and priests around the altar, and righteous Christians eminent in virtue, for Scripture tells us the prayer of the righteous man accomplishes much. We know that the prophets, while they were in a body with the perception of the senses, knew what was done in heaven, and throughout the earth, and foretold the future, so we know that the saints in the light of the Holy Trinity know what concerns us. Chapter Nine affirms that we are saved by faith, the correct Orthodox faith, which works in us by love expressed in keeping God's commandments. Chapter Ten on the Church affirms that Christ is the sole head of the Church, but adds that he governs "through the holy fathers." Additionally it is posited that the Holy Spirit appoints bishops over parish churches, and that only bishops can ordain priests and not other priests as the Calvinists "wickedly affirm." Without the dignity of a bishop, neither a Christian nor the Church could exist. The bishop is as necessary to the Church as breath is to man. Chapter Fourteen affirms that the Fall of man did not eclipse his nature, which has free will as an essential element. A man before he is regenerated is able by nature to incline to what is good, and to choose and work moral good; but this is not directed to blessedness, for a natural action has a natural end, not a divine and blessed one. For the regenerated to do spiritual good, the guidance and providence of grace is necessary, so that he is not able of himself to do any work worthy of a Christian life, although he has it in his power to will, or not to will, and to cooperate with grace. Chapter Fifteen affirms the sacraments refuted by the Protestants, notes their origin in Scripture, and denies that the sacraments are simply signs but affirms that they are efficacious means of grace. It is also rejected that the nature of the sacrament changes based on the presence of faith, as though the faith of the recipient makes the spiritual presence of the Body and Blood of Christ present as "the irreligious Calvin" postulates. The presence of Christ posited by Calvin in the Eucharist is not true and firm, but a fantasy and a figment of the imagination, not truly real and factual. The Body of Christ is the Body of Christ even for those who receive it in unbelief, which is why a sinful reception according to St. Paul may result in severe chastisement and even death.[227] Neither is, as Luther in his madness claimed, the presence of Christ present by impanation rather than a change.[228]

Though the tenets of Calvinism were given a stern rebuke and refutation, the person of Lucaris himself was not referenced by Patriarch Dositheos and the *Confession*. Whether this omission was in the interests of the peace of the Church, or whether Lucaris himself was not thought to be the actual author of the *Confession* that went by his name as some more recent Greek scholars have suggested, I am uncertain.[229] The Ecumenical Patriarchate today maintains on its website an article on Patriarch Cyril Lucaris, in which it is suggested that the *Confession of Lucaris* was a forgery.[230] The *Confession of Dositheos* effectively halted

---

[227] Of interest is that Dositheos quotes St. Augustine more than once in his section on the sacraments. He also argues for the "indelible character" of the priesthood.

[228] Impanation refers to the teaching which affirms that there exists the real presence of Jesus Christ in the Eucharist, but without any change of the bread and wine into the body and blood of Jesus Christ. The historic origin of the term appears to be in the controversies against the disciples of Berengarius of Tours at the end of the eleventh century. The term was used by the Reformed theologians who described the Lutheran teaching with this language. Though many non-Lutherans understand impanation to be similar to consubstantiation, the Formula of Concord explicitly rejects impanation.

[229] See "The Myth of the Calvinist Patriarch," http://www.orthodoxinfo. com/inquirers/ca4_loukaris.aspx. For further reflection on propaganda from the West at the time of Loukaris see Yannaras (2006), pp. 59-84.

[230] http://www.ec-patr.org/list/index.php?lang=en&id=202

the influence of Calvinism in Orthodox lands, after having made some headway into Romania, mostly among ethnic Germans and Hungarians, who form a sizeable minority in the Transylvanian region of Romania to this day.

Though Holy Orthodoxy has not made as much headway into the Reformed Churches in America as it has into the Lutheran and Anglican traditions, a new and steadily increasing stream of Reformed converts are finding their way to the Orthodox faith – where the grandeur and majesty of God, with which they were nourished in their Reformed upbringing, is not only thought of and preached about, but is expressed and lived in the magnificent and theocentric divine services of the Orthodox Church.

Sts. Cyril and Methodios
presenting the Glagolitic alphabet to the Slavs

# 7
## The Church of England

Having examined at length Lutheranism and the Reformed Churches of the Continent, we turn our attention in this chapter to the Reformation in England. By the 11th century England had produced a glorious Christian history on its own soil. The Celts of Brittania had been initially evangelized during its Roman period. Britannia was a Roman province, and evidence of Roman rule in England dots the landscape to this day, from Hadrian's wall in the North marking the furthest northern reach of the Romans, to the great walls around towns like York, to the Roman baths in Bath, etc.

The evangelization of England was furthered by the missionary work of St. Gregory the Great, Pope of Rome (590-604), who sent St. Augustine of Canterbury to preach the Gospel from the south northwards, especially among the pagan Saxons. The Irish missionaries at the same time were evangelizing the Picts in Scotland and Northumbria. In 664 at the Synod of Whitby these two elements were fused, while the Angles, Saxons and Jutes who had invaded the British Isles were being Christianized extensively. From this period until the time of the Norman invasion in 1066, the Anglo-Saxon Orthodox Catholic Church grew and prospered, and monasteries were established throughout the land.

The Normans brought with them their own Norman-Roman ways, and Roman Catholic England continued producing notable Latin saints[231] and scholars right up until the early 16th century and the reign of Henry VIII. No cursory examination of the English Reformation is possible without the central figure of Henry VIII. Though he was no Protestant,[232] he was key to the success of the Protestant movement in England. Though he was no theologian, a book on the seven sacraments was published under his name (probably ghost-written) that obtained for him the title from the Pope of "defender of the faith."[233] Such papal efforts to nurture a connection with Henry failed, however, and he compelled England to break with the papacy.

---

[231] The Norman invasion of England in 1066 A.D. is a standard demarcation or terminus date in the recognition of saints in Britain by the Orthodox Church. With the coming of the Normans, Britain becomes fundamentally identified with the heretical and schismatic papacy, and therefore it is no longer possible to recognize the English Church as a member of the one, holy, catholic and apostolic church or her great ones as saints of the same.

[232] The term "Protestant" in England remained well into the mid-sixteenth century a foreign word to describe the actions of foreigners much like glasnost or perestroika in England and America in the 1980s. MacCulloch (2002), p. 2.

[233] *Fidei defensor*. This is a formal title, given by popes of that time to many monarchs who defended Catholicism against the Protestants. The English kings liked it very much and kept it even after joining the other side. It persists to this day on coins of Britain and the Commonwealth as "F. D."

Unlike the Reformation in Germany, Switzerland, and the Netherlands, where the theologians led the move to Reformation with the support of Protestant political powers, England was not driven to the Reformation by its theologians, but rather by the immoral wishes of a corrupt and vile king: Henry VIII. This is not to say that there was not significant anticlericalism (in response to lax moral standards among clergy) or theological unrest. There indeed was, as we noted when we spoke of John Wycliffe and the Lollard movement.[234] English churchmen maintained extensive communication and personal contact with the major continental Reformers. Lutheranism reached England about 1520, and on May 12, 1521, Cardinal Wolsey, in the company of leading prelates and nobility at St. Paul's Cathedral in London, pronounced Luther's excommunication and burned his books. However, there was no Luther, Calvin, or Zwingli in England to lead the civic power into the Reformation. Rather, the firecracker for a break with Rome was a king's wish for an immoral divorce. In England's case, the politicians were leading the churchmen, not vice versa.[235] Each of four successive English monarchs,

---

[234] The Lollards remained in existence in well-defined areas of England's lowlands, the very place where mid-Tudor evangelicals blossomed. *Ibid.*, p. 112.

[235] Archbishop Cranmer reserved no function from the secular magistrate. He was a thorough-going Erastian who believed that the Royal power was supreme over all ecclesiastical appointments. Loades (1991), p. 12. Cranmer rejected the traditional doctrine of apostolic succession writing, "A bishop

beginning with Henry VIII, would establish England in a different religious commitment:

King Henry VIII: Ecclesiastical independence from Rome, but basic Latin doctrinal conservatism.

King Edward VI: Ecclesiastical independence from Rome, with the thorough embrace of Protestant dogma.

Queen Mary Tudor: Ecclesiastical reunification with Rome, strict Latin dogma, and intolerance of Protestantism.

Queen Elizabeth I: Ecclesiastical independence from Rome, ambiguous union of Catholic and Protestant tenets, intolerance of either traditional Roman Catholicism or zealous Protestantism.

## *King Henry VIII*

King Henry VIII is an infamous figure in Western history. He was the second monarch of the Tudor dynasty, who had reigned supreme in England since the Battle of Bosworth Field in 1485. Henry had married the Spanish princess, Catherine of Aragon, but had not successfully obtained a male heir through her. Unsatisfied with this situation and unable to control his wandering lusts, he wished to marry his favorite lover, Anne Boleyn. Pope Clement VII

---

may make a priest by the scriptures, and so may princes, and governors also, and that by the authority of God committed to them." MacCulloch (1996), p. 279. Again we see, even in the branch of Protestantism that claims to maintain apostolic succession, a complete rejection of traditional Church hierarchy and apostolic succession, and this in the teaching of the foundational English reformed theologian.

Henry VIII of England

would not bless it for several reasons. First, Henry VIII's father, Henry VII, had obtained a special dispensation from the Pope for his younger son (Henry VIII) to marry Catherine of Aragon in the first place. Catherine had been married to Henry's older brother Arthur, who had died after only a few months of marriage. Not wanting to lose the connection to the Spanish royal house, Henry VII sought permission for his younger son Henry (VIII) to marry his brother's widow. Pope Julius II granted this dispensation, which was in direct contradiction to scriptural injunction and canon law. Christians are not to marry their sisters-in-law. For Clement VII to nullify the dispensation of Pope Julius II would not speak well of papal authority, especially when it was under attack from the Lutherans.

Additionally, Pope Clement was living as a virtual prisoner of the Holy Roman Emperor, Charles V, whose soldiers had sacked Rome. Charles V was the nephew of Catherine of Aragon. Henry VIII was not going to get any clemency out of Clement VII. So, Henry had his theologians write various Reformers in order to obtain additional opinions. When he recognized that he would not succeed in getting the papacy to bow, he pressed the theory of absolute monarchy to extremes, and incited his Parliament to declare him head of the Church of England on Earth. He got his new ecclesiology–and his divorce. His unsavory personal life would lead him through six wives, two of whom died at his hands.

Henry's conflict with the Pope was well received, however, by certain leading churchmen, who had already been deeply influenced by Protestant ideas.[236] Chief among these personalities was Thomas Cranmer, Archbishop of Canterbury. Even at the time that Wolsey burned Luther's books and sought to confiscate them in England, a small group of Lutheran sympathizers were meeting at the White Horse Inn in Cambridge.[237] Cambridge University produced most of England's Protestant leaders, and almost all of them were martyred for their Protestant faith. Some of these figures included classical scholar Robert Barnes; future archbishops Cranmer, Heath, Parker, and May; and future bishops Latimer, Ridley, and Foxe. The Protestant movement spread to Oxford, where the great scholar William Tyndale, a master linguist who spoke fluently in Hebrew, Greek, Latin, Italian, Spanish, French, and English, fled to Germany and carried out his ambition to publish an English Bible.[238]

Tyndale used his translation to further Protestant ideas, and upset the Catholic establishment in England by translating the Greek word *presbyter* as "elder" rather

---

[236] Henry VIII drew more than 160 scholars and 23 European universities into the discussion of the affair of his marriage. MacCulloch (1996), p. 41. Thomas Cranmer was dispatched to Europe to solicit opinions.

[237] *Ibid.*, p. 25.

[238] Tyndale was the first biblical translator of the Reformation to die, executed by the officials of the Holy Roman Emperor with the support of King Henry VIII and the Bishop of London. MacCulloch (2003), p. 203.

William Tyndale

than "priest" or "presbyter", and the word *ecclesia* as "congregation" or "community" rather than "church." By Tyndale's crafty translation, the New Testament existed for the first time in Church history *without the words "church" or "priest."*[239] Tyndale published Luther's tracts in his New Testament and separately *without authorial attribution.* Tyndale snuck Luther's theology even into the so-called Matthew Bible, which was issued by royal permission. Cranmer convinced Henry VIII to put this Bible in all English churches.[240]

---

[239] Translations inevitably reflect theology and hermeneutics, but some Protestant translations advance the cause of Protestant ideology more than they provide accurate translation. A good example of this is the New International Version (NIV), so exceedingly popular amongst Protestant Evangelicals today. The theological agenda of its translators is all too clear. Take, for instance, the word in the New Testament for tradition, in Greek, paradosis (παράδοσις). The New Testament refers to apostolic tradition, ecclesiastical tradition, which is to be embraced by all Christians, as well as man-made tradition, unholy tradition, which nullifies God's word and is to be avoided by Christians. Conveniently, but not honestly, the NIV translates all references to apostolic "tradition" by the word "teaching" or "teachings" and all references to man-made "tradition" by the word "tradition." Hence, the innocent reader of the NIV will come to the conclusion that the only tradition that exists is man-made and unholy, and will never know that there is such a reality in the New Testament as apostolic tradition.

[240] Cranmer was quite capable of trickery. Henry VIII was concerned by the popular enthusiasm for the Bible and convinced Parliament to order that only the upper class be allowed to read it. MacCulloch (2003), p. 203.

For divorcing Catherine, Henry was excommunicated by the Pope in 1538, and became estranged from Catholic France and from Charles V, the Holy Roman Emperor. The Pope called upon King Francis and Charles V to wage a crusade against England and Henry. For these reasons Henry was particularly keen on entering into a political union with the Lutheran and Reformed princes of Germany and Switzerland. When the political danger decreased for Henry, he dropped his interest in Lutheranism and attempted to effect religious unity in England through his *Six Articles Act* of 1539. These six articles were an affirmation of traditional Roman Catholic teaching on the Eucharist, confession, celibate clergy, etc. Anyone who denied transubstantiation was to be burned and forfeit his possessions. We see clearly that the initial break with the papacy was purely a political matter, and a matter of Henry's personal wish to divorce and remarry. At this time Henry had three leading English Lutherans burned at the stake, and three Catholic theologians also burned. The latter had defended Catherine in the divorce proceedings. It was all about Henry's lust for supreme power, and in that quest he was, in the words of one scholar, "an equal opportunity executioner."[241]

In the 1530s, Henry also pursued a policy of almost complete dissolution of the hundreds of monasteries in England, stealing all their treasure, and essentially ending mo-

[241] Carter Lindberg (1996) *The European Reformations*, Oxford: Blackwell Publishers, p. 313.

nasticism in England.[242] Again, this was not so much from
Protestant conviction, as to enrich himself and eradicate the
papacy's greatest supporters, the monastics. In his last years,
Henry retreated more fully to his Roman Catholicism.[243]
However, after he died in 1547 and his young son Edward
VI came to the throne, the Protestant leaders formed Ed-
ward in a more thorough-going Protestant frame.

After Henry's death the throne would pass successive-
ly to three of his children: Edward VI, then Mary, then
Elizabeth.

## Edward VI

Edward VI reigned as a boy king for six years.[244] The
persecution of Protestants ended immediately after his ac-
cession, and the Six Articles were nullified. English Protestant theologians who had fled abroad returned home, and
famous Protestants from the continent like Martin Bucer
(who had been expelled from his city of Strasbourg) were
invited to lecture at Oxford and Cambridge, and Bucer
took up a post as professor at Cambridge until his death
in 1549.

---

[242] For an excellent account of the dissolution see Eamon Duffy (1992) *The
Stripping of the Altars: Traditional Religion in England c. 1400-c. 1580*, New
Haven and London: Yale University Press.

[243] In Henry's will, numerous requiem masses were required to be said for
the repose of his soul. Loades (1991), p. 14. There is some debate on the question of Henry's faith at the time of his demise since he also had provided a
very Protestant education for his young son.

[244] For a thorough account of Edward VI and his religious environment see
MacCulloch (2002).

## *Thomas Cranmer*

Thomas Cranmer, Archbishop of Canterbury, was the most influential architect of English Protestantism.[245] Cranmer had been secretly married to Margaret Osiander, niece of the famous German Lutheran theologian Andreas Osiander, in 1532.[246] During these years, Cranmer produced his prayer books (the first in 1549, and the second

in 1552) that brought the Protestant faith into full expression in worship and liturgy. In 1553, he produced a confession of faith that sought to compromise between Lutheran and Calvinist theologies. This confession of faith was called *The Forty-Two Articles* and was the foundation for the official Church of England confession adopted un-

Thomas Cranmer

---

[245] For the most thorough contemporary account of Cranmer see MacCulloch (1996). For two critical assessments of Cranmer by Papal scholars see Belloc (1931) and Maynard (1956).

[246] This was the second rash marriage of Cranmer. His first wife, Joan, died giving birth to their first child. This second marriage required the setting aside of his priestly vow of celibacy. MacCulloch (1996), pp. 21, 72. He showed little conscience with vows throughout his life, especially in affirming the nullity of King Henry's successive marriages. *Ibid.*, p. 158. He was a true puppet, declaring that Henry's marriages to Catherine of Aragon, Anne Boleyn and Anne of Cleves never existed. MacCulloch (2002), p. 5. For England's greatest Reformer, the ends often justified the means.

der Queen Elizabeth I called *The Thirty-Nine Articles.* The third major effort of Cranmer was to revise papal canon law. It was while engaged in this project that King Edward VI, the Protestant king, died as a boy, and Mary Tudor, a Catholic queen known to history as Bloody Mary, came to the throne.

### Mary Tudor

Mary Tudor was the daughter of Catherine of Aragon. Her great concern for restoring the Catholic faith in England radically contributed, in reality, to the establishment of Protestantism. She married Philip of Spain, which cemented the notion that Catholicism was associated with foreign powers, and unpopular foreign powers at that. She relied on her cousin, Reginald Cardinal Pole, to introduce the tenets of the Catholic Counter Reformation. She attempted to restore monastic lands, and alienated the nobility who had assumed title to these lands. She persecuted Protestant teachers, and filled John Foxe's famous Protestant *Book of Martyrs* with personalities.

Queen Mary I

Foxe's *Book of Martyrs* is essentially a Protestant martyrology designed to give the impression that the Protestant martyrs were one with the early martyrs of the Church, and dying for the same cause. Hence, Foxe begins his work recording several martyrdoms in the early church, including an account of the martyrdom of St. Polycarp, Bishop of Smyrna. Having mentioned a few early martyrs, Foxe skips to the Protestants in a classically Protestant sense—a few patristic references, the big parenthesis, then the 16th century. By such literary form it is possible for many readers to miss the fact that the early martyrs would not have recognized as authentically Christian and Orthodox the confession of faith for which the later Protestant martyrs were dying.

Mary obtained the sobriquet "Bloody Mary" by having more than 300 Protestant leaders burned at the stake. Based upon her father's invention that the sovereign was head of the Church, she also exiled some 800 leading Protestants to continental cities. Most were exiled for the sin of breaking their monastic vows. She separated some 2,000 married clergy from their wives.[247] Mary's actions inadvertently created an army of zealous educated Protestants who were eager to avenge her and win their native country. Queen Mary reigned only five years, but her short reign instilled, in English minds, a deep contempt for all things Catholic. Though Archbishop Cranmer recanted many things, eventually he was burned at the stake. In defiance, he thrust the

---

[247] MacCulloch (2003), p. 283.

hand that had signed his recantations into the fire as the flames engulfed him. In 1555, Philip returned to Spain, leaving Mary childless. In 1558, Mary died.[248]

### Elizabeth Tudor

Mary was succeeded by Elizabeth Tudor, whom she called "the little bastard." Queen Elizabeth I would reign from 1558-1603, a 45-year era of English pride and peace in which England was formally established in Protestantism, and would become a great world empire. Elizabeth sought a middle way, or *via media,* between the policies of her immediate predecessors Edward VI and Mary. She sought to hold back and tame both Catholics and radical Protestants. In order to do this, Anglicanism under Elizabeth was designed to be ambiguous, and capable of a broad interpretation. Catholic-style vestments and liturgy were retained, together with altars and the crucifix. Saints' days were retained in part. Words were used in liturgy, particularly for the Eucharist, that would reflect both a real

Elizabeth I

---

[248] Mary had hopes of a pregnancy which turned out to be stomach cancer. Coincidently, Cardinal Pole died on the same day as Mary in November 1558. MacCulloch (2003), pp. 285-6.

presence of Christ and a Zwinglian memorial meal. Bishops were maintained, together with a claim to apostolic succession. *The Forty-Two Articles* were altered and published as the *Thirty-Nine Articles*, containing remarkably ambiguous statements, such as that on predestination. This large umbrella approach, under which many divergences of opinion might dwell, became known as the "Elizabethan settlement." Despite the popular notion of a settlement and of English tolerance, it is a fact that England judicially executed more Roman Catholics than any other country in Europe. Hundreds of Latin priests and laypeople were executed under Queen Elizabeth.[249] The theologian *par excellence* of this new Anglican way, the *via media,* was Bishop Richard Hooker (1554-1600).[250]

## The Anglican Faith

### *The Anglican Catechism 1549/1662*

The theological content of the Anglican confession is expressed historically in the Anglican Catechism first published in the *Book of Common Prayer* in 1549 issued under the Protestant boy-king Edward VI, and placed in the sec-

---

[249] MacCulloch (2003), p. 392.

[250] Hooker's *magnum opus* was his *Laws of Ecclesiastical Polity.* He opposed the Puritan movement in the Church of England, but did not reject the holy orders of continental Protestants who had no bishops. In Hooker we see how inauthentic the Anglican affirmation of the necessity of apostolic succession really is.

tion on confirmation. It was revised under Queen Elizabeth and republished in its present form in 1662. The catechism, which has been revised by several Anglican churches in various parts of the world, remains technically in force today. This catechism is a brief statement of the nature and duty of a Christian, the Apostles Creed, the Ten Commandments, the Lord's Prayer, and the Sacraments of Baptism and Eucharist. The essential Protestantism of the catechism resides in its Reformed explanations of the sacraments. Apart from this, it is technically unobjectionable.

The official confession of the Church of England is the *Thirty-Nine Articles*. This confession has its roots in the *Forty-Two Articles* of Archbishop Thomas Cranmer, and represents the fusing of Lutheran, Calvinist, and Zwinglian theologies. Cranmer's *Forty-Two Articles* was short lived because King Edward VI died only one month after publishing them. Queen Mary I quickly negated all the doctrinal

legislation of Edward VI. When Elizabeth I came to the throne in 1558, she commissioned Matthew Parker, Archbishop of Canterbury, to revise the *Forty-Two Articles,* which he did, reducing them to thirty-nine. From 1571, when Elizabeth I decided to stop tampering with Article 29 "On the Wicked which do not eat the Body of

Matthew Parker

Christ in the use of the Lord's Supper" (which offended Roman Catholics and could hurt her negotiations with Lutherans), the *Thirty-Nine Articles* have been the required faith of Anglican clergy. Since 1975, Anglican clergy are no longer required to "subscribe to" but to "acknowledge" the *Thirty-Nine Articles*. The Episcopal Church in the USA (the American offspring of the Church of England) has, since 1977, relegated the articles to an addendum at the end of the *Book of Common Prayer* entitled, "Historical Documents of the Church."

*Content of the 'Thirty-Nine Articles'*

The Articles start with an affirmation of faith in the Holy Trinity, including in Article 5 a confession of belief in the *filioque* heresy. Article 3 affirms Christ's Descent into Hell, thus precluding the Calvinist understanding. Article 6 is on the sufficiency of Holy Scripture, and is a tame and more ambiguous statement of the Protestant belief in the sole authority of Scripture to establish dogma and Church practice. The so-called "Apocrypha," known to Orthodox simply as the Longer Canon of the Old Testament, is recommended for reading but not to "establish any doctrine." This last note is very important because the books of the Longer Canon contain teachings and practices not acceptable to Protestant convictions. This includes the Maccabean history, which contain examples of sacrifice and prayer for the departed. Article 8 affirms three creeds:

Nicene, Athanasian, and Apostles. The 1801 American revision removed reference to the Athanasian Creed. Article 11 is a simple affirmation of justification by faith alone. Article 17, "Of Predestination and Election," is the largest of all the articles of faith, but is written in such a way as to allow a large swath of understandings of predestination.[251]

Article 19, "Of the Church," is a simple Reformed definition of the Church as a congregation of the faithful where the Word of God is rightly preached and the sacraments are duly ministered, however there is added, "As the Church of Jerusalem, Alexandria, and Antioch have erred, so also the Church of Rome hath erred, not only in their living and manner of ceremonies, but also in matters of faith." This is an interesting article, which is capable of an Orthodox interpretation if we understand it to mean that, while the Church itself is infallible and indefectible, nevertheless local churches and synods themselves are capable of error and heresy and, in such, can cease to be part of the Church. This is, however, not the Anglican intent. Rather, the intent is to negate infallibility in the Church as a whole, in order to locate it solely in the Scriptures. Article 21, "Of the Authority of General Councils," begins by an assertion that such councils cannot be convened without the sanction of princes. Here we see an expression of the Erastian nature of the Church of England, and its statism. The article contin-

---

[251]  It is not correct to call the English Church, at least at this time, Calvinist since Calvin was at the time only a mildly popular theologian and in no way central to English ecclesiastical thinking. MacCulloch (1996), p. 428.

ues by affirming that since not all participants in the General Councils are governed by the Holy Spirit and Word of God, they may err, and have erred. Only those councils and decisions which may be declared as taking their authority from Scripture are to be accepted.

Article 22 forbids veneration of relics and images, and the invocation of saints. This rejection of the invocation of saints while maintaining the feasts of saints in the liturgical calendar has created a unique Anglican ceremonial in which God alone is addressed in prayer, and never the saint. The call in Orthodox services for a particular saint to "come and stand with us" is *verboten*[252] in Anglican worship. Article 25 rejects confirmation, penance, orders, matrimony, and unction as sacraments. Article 26 affirms that sacraments are valid and efficacious despite the unworthiness of ministers.[253] Article 27 gives a Calvinistic understanding of Baptism, but affirms the conveyance of what Baptism signifies in the act itself "as by an instrument."

### The Great Umbrella

Though the preface to the Articles reads that the confession was written "for the avoiding of the diversities of opinions and for the establishing of consent concerning true

---

[252] Forbidden.

[253] Here is an interesting affirmation. The Anglicans affirm that God-ordained sacraments are not injured by the unworthiness of the ministers, but do not apply such confidence in the working of divine grace to God-ordained ecumenical councils. These, in the Anglican view, because they are made up of men who are sinners and err, cannot be infallible.

religion,"²⁵⁴ it has not succeeded in accomplishing such. Historically, believers of many stripes and convictions have found themselves under the large tent of Anglicanism. High Church Anglicanism, sometimes called Anglo-Catholicism, has attempted throughout Anglican history to keep belief and practice as close to Roman Catholicism as possible, and Anglicans of this persuasion have seen themselves often as Catholics without the Pope, or sometimes even as "Western Orthodox." This Anglo-Catholic tradition in

John Henry Newman

---

²⁵⁴ Pelikan (2003), *Creeds and Confessions*, Vol. 2, p. 528.

Anglicanism found its high water mark in the 19th century Oxford Movement, and in the writings of theologians like Edward Pusey and John Henry Newman. Newman, a great scholar, became the most famous convert from Anglicanism to Roman Catholicism, and is currently in the process of canonization in the Roman Church. For years, however, as an Anglican, he, with his like-minded colleagues, wrote tracts on the 39 Articles and Anglican theology in which they attempted to interpret and put forth an Anglicanism more in line with traditional Christian faith.

In the same communion with the Anglo-Catholics, however, we find the "Low Church" evangelicals, who have a Zwinglian understanding of sacraments and Church life, and who consider the Anglican forms of episcopal government, vestments, etc. as unscriptural vestiges of the papacy. This group has consistently attempted to interpret Anglican faith in a more anti-Catholic direction. In the 17th century, Anglican clergy of this stripe became known as Puritans, and in the 18th century this sub-tradition in Anglicanism produced the famous preachers of the Great Awakening: Charles Wesley and George Whitefield. They found themselves much more akin to Reformed Churches than to anything Roman Catholic.

*Orthodox-Anglican Dialogue*

Over the centuries the Anglican Church has, at times, felt special closeness to Holy Orthodoxy, and has even fancied herself as the "Western Orthodox" Church. The great architect of English Protestantism, Thomas Cranmer, in his extensive corpus often quoted Eastern Fathers with great fondness. In his famous *preface* to the Great Bible he quoted from each of the Three Holy Hierarchs: Ss. John Chrysostom, Basil the Great, and Gregory the Theologian.[255] In the 17th century, the Non-Juror bishops[256] of the Church of England entered into a formal dialogue with the Orthodox Church, and substantial theological agreement was obtained. The Non-Jurors, however, were deficient in faith by not accepting the teaching of the 7th Ecumenical Council on the necessity of iconography.[257]

In more recent times, there was extensive Orthodox-Anglican dialogue at the turn of the 20th century.[258] In fact,

---

[255] In the words of the K. J. Walsh, Cranmer had "a somewhat retarded and fragmentary interest in Eastern patristic writing." Quoted in MacCulloch (1996), p. 416.

[256] Non-jurors were members of the Church of England who refused to take the oaths of allegiance and supremacy to William and Mary, considering themselves oath-bound to the Roman Catholic, King James II. They numbered nine bishops and 400 priests. These bishops were deprived of their sees and livelihood by an Act of Parliament. Between 1716 and 1725, the non-jurors carried on negotiations for union with the Orthodox Church, which came to nothing. Details of the Non-Juror interaction with the Orthodox Church may be obtained in the paper of Rev. H. W. Langford (1965).

[257] Iconography is affirmed by the 7th Ecumenical Council to be sacred tradition of the Church, and as such something that is not free to be embraced or discarded.

[258] For an extensive historical account of the extensive Orthodox–Anglican relations in the first half of the 20th century see Geffert (2010).

the great boast of our land, the Good Shepherd of the Lost Sheep of America, and the first Orthodox bishop consecrated in America, St. Raphael of Brooklyn, upon arriving in America in 1895, took up a formal post in an Anglican-Eastern Orthodox Churches Union. The Anglicans at this time were being exceptionally helpful to Orthodox immigrants, and the Anglican leadership wished to forge a formal union and mutual recognition between the Orthodox and themselves. Over the years in which St. Raphael developed deep friendships with many Anglican leaders, he also had the opportunity to more thoroughly evaluate their Anglican faith. In time, St. Raphael ceased his formal dialogue with the Episcopal Church and issued a formal judgment about their faith:

> I am convinced that the doctrinal teaching and practices, as well as the discipline, of the whole Anglican Church are unacceptable to the Holy Orthodox Church. I make this apology for the Anglicans whom as Christian gentlemen I greatly revere, that the loose teaching of a great many of the prominent Anglican theologians are so hazy in their definitions of truth, and so inclined toward pet heresies that it is hard to tell what they believe. The Anglican Church as a whole has not spoken authoritatively on her doctrine....The Holy Orthodox Church has never perceptibly changed from

Apostolic times, and, therefore, no one can go astray in finding out what She teaches. Like Her Lord and Master, though at times surrounded with human malaria–which He in His mercy pardons–She is the same yesterday, and today, and forever the mother and safe deposit of the truth as it is in Jesus. The Orthodox Church differs absolutely with the Anglican communion in reference to the number of Sacraments and in reference to the doctrinal explanation of the same....[here St. Raphael details the differences between Orthodox and Anglican understanding of each of the sacraments and demonstrates how un-apostolic the Anglican belief and practice is on all accounts]...besides all this, the Anglican Communion ignores the Orthodox Church's dogmas and teachings, such as the invocation of saints, prayers for the departed, special honor to the blessed Virgin Mary the Mother of God, and reverence for sacred relics, holy pictures and icons. They say of such teaching that it is 'a foul thing, vainly invented, and grounded upon no warranty of Scripture, but rather repugnant to the word of God' (Article of Religion, XXII). There is a striking variance between their wording of the Nicene Creed and that of the Holy Orthodox Church;

but sadder still, it contains the heresy of the *fil-ioque*. I do not deem it necessary to mention all the striking differences between the Holy Orthodox Church and the Anglican Communion in reference to the authority of holy tradition, the number of Ecumenical Councils, etc. Enough has already been said and pointed out to show that the Anglican Communion differs but little from all other Protestant bodies, and therefore, there cannot be any intercommunion until they return to the ancient Holy Orthodox Faith and practices, and reject Protestant omissions and commissions."[259]

St. Raphael's judgment is that of Holy Orthodoxy since the creation of the Protestant Anglican Communion until this day.

### *The Radical Deviance of Modern Anglicanism*

The tendency of the Anglican communion in the 20th century, which continues into the 21st, has not been good in any way. The history of modern Anglicanism may be summarized as an aggressive departure from traditional Christian faith and practice, and a bold disregard even for its own roots. One might note that many of the fundamental Protestant theological tenets were departures from tra-

---

[259] For a copy of two very important statements by St. Raphael concerning Anglicanism see the appendices.

ditional Christian faith themselves, and certainly there is an essential connection between the radicalism of the Protestant Reformation and its tenets on the one hand, and on the other, the progressive radicalization and secularization of all mainline Protestant Churches in the last 100 years. However, no Protestant communion of any substantial size and cultural influence has wandered so feverishly and fervently away from traditional Christianity as the Anglican Church in England and America.

The Anglican world communion is in mega-crisis. The mother church of England itself has become spiritually vacuous and its constituency has dissipated. In a country that used to rule half of the world, and today has some 55 million citizens, approximately 1 million self-identify as members of the Church of England, their nation's official church. The state church has lost the country. There are now more Muslims in English mosques each Friday than there are Anglicans in English churches on Sunday.[260] The church attendance rate is about two percent. Seventy percent of English children are born outside of wedlock. Secularism has won the day, and the country stands in radical need of re-evangelization. Such re-evangelization ought to be done by the Orthodox in England. St. Arsenios the Cappadocian[261] beautifully

---

[260] There are many texts being written on the Islamicization of the West, but of particular interest for England is Melanie Philips (2006).
[261] St. Arsenios the Cappadocian (1840-1924) was the spiritual father of the family of Elder Paisios the Athonite. Elder Paisios wrote his life. St. Arsenios

wrote in the 20th century that the English will return to the Christian faith when they begin again to honor their saints. Orthodox saints fill the annals of English history, and are waiting to be re-embraced by English people and to show their fellows once again the path to the Kingdom of God.

The Episcopal Church in America is in even worse shape than the Church in England, and has virtually driven out of its fold all traditional believers.[262] The progressive apostasy of the Anglicans in the West had several distinct turning points. The Lambeth Conference in 1930 was the first Christian body—Orthodox, Catholic, or Protestant—to formally endorse artificial birth control. Its grasp of traditional marriage and sexuality has been in an out of control spiral ever since. In 1977, the Episcopal Church in America approved the ordination of women to the priesthood and episcopate. In 2003, the Episcopal Church in America consecrated a practicing homosexual as a bishop. The consecration of divorced and openly homosexual and non-celibate Gene Robinson as an Anglican bishop has provoked scan-

---

was glorified by the Patriarchate of Constantinople in 1986, and his feast day is November 10th.

[262] As I write, there is featured in the *Los Angeles Times* the story of an Episcopal Church in La Cañada, California, which has just completed litigation with the mainline Episcopal authorities. Rather than accept the secularized and lifeless shell of Christianity, which is the faith of the Episcopal Church in the United States, this parish community and its pastor have forfeited their beautiful church and property and are starting anew. This story has been repeated dozens of times in America.

dal and division throughout the Anglican communion.[263] Neither the Roman Catholic nor Orthodox Churches have ever officially recognized the Anglican priesthood as authentic or apostolic, and as such have always judged the Anglican claim to apostolic succession to be spurious. The developments of the last 35 years only confirm the correctness of this judgment.

Today, to be Anglican in the West means virtually nothing with regard to traditional Christian dogma. One can belong to the Episcopal Cathedral of St. John the Divine in New York and see communion given to ducks. One can belong to Grace Cathedral in San Francisco and venerate the "icons" of Harvey Milk[264] and Martin Luther King which adorn two eastern end pillars. Anything goes with regard to explicit Christian faith. But to be a member of the Episcopal Church USA today means your faith is secularist, your church is radically feminist, and you endorse and support homosexuality.

### Conversions of Anglicans to Holy Orthodoxy in Modern Times

In this quick descent into secularism and unbelief, many believing Anglican clergy and laity have left their church ei-

---

[263] As an interesting side note, our current President Barack Obama, during his campaign for President, consulted Bishop Gene Robinson for spiritual counsel and wisdom more than any other clergyman.

[264] A rather unaccomplished homosexual San Francisco Supervisor killed in 1978, who has since become an icon for the homosexual activist movement in America.

ther to form one of the many "continuing Anglican churches" in America, or in more recent days to put themselves
under an Anglican bishop from Africa, where the majority of Anglicans live. These "flying bishops" from Africa,
who do not endorse the perversions of faith and practice
so common in America and England, are setting up their
own churches in America in a process called the Anglican
Realignment. So today there are numerous Anglican juris-
dictions in America, with a grand total of maybe 2 million
adherents nationally.

Disaffected Anglicans, especially clergy, have also fled
in large number to the Roman Catholic Church. The late
Pope John Paul II set up a special order for receiving Anglican clergy, most of whom were married, and for their
ordination as priests with non-parochial assignments. Disaffected Anglicans have also fled in large numbers to the
Orthodox Church. It is my estimate that there is no heterodox body in America from which more Orthodox clergy
have come than the Anglican communion. The number of
Orthodox priests in this country that were previously Episcopal clergy is certainly in the hundreds.

In my own pastorate, my oldest convert was a faithful
laywoman of the Episcopal Church whose family had been
faithful Anglicans in America going back to colonial times.
At 88 years of age she wrote a strong letter to the ruling
bishop of the Episcopal Church in the United States vocif-

erously protesting the Church's apostasy from traditional Christian faith and life, and entered into Orthodox catechism. She was received into the Orthodox Church and remained a faithful parishioner until her death ten years later. Her grandson is an accomplished Orthodox scholar active in Orthodox theological circles in America.

In 2005, in response to the reckless abandonment of the traditional Christian faith and practice and to the zealous Episcopal endorsement of immorality in our culture, the Antiochian Orthodox Christian Archdiocese of North America made a formal commitment to cease all dialogue with the Episcopal Church, then withdrew from said dialogue and membership in the National Council of Churches.[265]

---

[265] See Trenham (2005), "The Antiochian Withdrawal from the NCC" in *Faith and Freedom*, Institute on Religion and Democracy, Vol. 24, No. 4, p. 22.

# 8

# *The Catholic Counter-Reformation*

In the previous seven chapters we have examined the lives, teaching, and influence of the leading Protestant Reformers. In each chapter we have touched upon various Roman Catholic doctrines and customs against which the Reformers were reacting. The ecclesiastical upheaval which is the Reformation was not expressed only by those who articulated a Protestant theology and left Roman Catholicism. The upheaval and unrest took place *within* the Latin Church, and provoked what is sometimes called a Counter Reformation, or more often than not these days, a Catholic Reformation.[266]

### *15th century Impulses for Reform*

The post-Schism Roman Church was riddled with scandal and corruption. The Catholic Reformation was the culmination of internal reform movements that were underway as early as the beginning of the Lutheran uprising, and flowered as an answer to the Protestant aggression. The early 15th century Council of Constance (1414-1418)

---

[266] For a good overview of the Counter Reformation see Jones (1995) and, from a papal publisher, Wicks (1978).

Francisco Ximénez de Cisneros      Girolamo Savonarola

issued calls to reform the church and address the rampant simony, nepotism, and clerical immorality. Two reforming movements were afoot shortly before the time of the Protestant Reformation. They involved such colorful humanist figures as Francisco Ximénez de Cisneros (1436-1517), an anchorite who became the most powerful churchman in Spain, and the famous and charismatic Italian Dominican, Girolamo Savonarola (1452-1498). Such Catholic reformers protested against the abuses of the Latin church, and the lax morality of clergy.[267]

## Counter-Reformation Popes

The first fifty years of the Protestant Reformation and the subsequent Catholic Reformation took place under the

---

[267] Janz (2008), pp. 377ff.

pallia of numerous Popes: Leo X (1513-1521), Hadrian VI (1522-23), Clement VII (1523-1534), Paul III (1534-1549), Julius III (1550-1555), Marcellus II (April 9 1555-May 1, 1555), Paul IV (1555-1559), and Pius IV (1559-1565). I have concluded with Pius IV because the reforming Council of Trent adjourned in the last year of his papacy. These figures exercised tremendous influence on the Catholic response to the Protestant movement.[268]

Pope Leo X (1513-1521), the Medici Pope, was from an influential Florentine family, and was a politician, in charge of the papal army and an effective ruler of Florence even while Pope. He was made a cleric at seven years of age, and a cardinal at thirteen.[269] He was, in the words of J. N. D. Kelly, a "polished Renaissance prince," a "devious and double-tongued politician and an inveterate nepotist."[270] Under Leo X, reforming legislation

Pope Leo X

---

[268] Most of the information that follows on the Counter Reformation popes comes from Kelly (1986).

[269] Duffy (1997), p. 177.

[270] *Ibid.*, p. 257.

was passed by the Roman curia but no structure for enforcement established. He evinced no sense of the urgency of the day, and his life of personal extravagance often found him in need of money to fund his wars, his crusade against the Turks, and his building of St. Peter's Basilica. For such causes Leo pawned his own palace furniture and plate, sold church positions to the highest bidders, sold cardinals' hats, and authorized the aggressive sale of indulgences which provoked Luther so tremendously. In 1518, when Luther's tracts reached Rome, Leo ordered the general of Luther's Augustinian order to silence him. He attempted to win over Luther's protector, Frederick, the Elector of Saxony, which effort failed. Leo is the one who published the bull we examined in our chapters on Luther, entitled *Exsurge Domine* (1520), which condemned Luther on forty-one counts. After Luther publicly burned the bull, Leo excommunicated him in 1521. Leo failed to appreciate the significance of the revolution taking place in the church, and left it in disarray when he died suddenly of malaria at the end of 1521.

Pope Hadrian VI (January 9, 1522-September 14, 1523) was a carpenter's son from the Netherlands, the former tutor of Emperor Charles V, and a pious cleric who as pope shocked many by celebrating mass every day.[271] He was of high moral and intellectual reputation, having been a

---

[271] Duffy (1997), p. 203.

Pope Hadrian VI

Professor and eventually the Rector of the University of Louvain. He had been an inquisitor in Spain, and was zealously committed to checking the spread of the Reformation. During his tenure, the papal representative at the Diet of Nuremberg (December 1522) made the frank admission that disorder in the church was due to the corrupt Roman curia itself. Listen to the words of Pope Hadrian VI to the Diet of Nuremberg,

> God has allowed this punishment [the fall of Belgrade and Rhodes to the Turks] to overtake his church because of the sins of men, especially those of priests and prelates...There have been great spiritual abominations and abuses in the holy see for many years. Perversion has grown everywhere and it is hardly surprising that the sickness has spread from the head to the members...we will do everything in our power to reform first this see, from which the powerful evil advanced so that, even as corruption passed from Rome to every other part, so healing will spread from Rome. The whole world eagerly desires reform and we are

> definitely responsible...Be patient. Every error
> and abuse will not be swept away at once; the
> disease is well established. Therefore progress
> must be made step by step...lest everything be-
> come still more chaotic.[272]

His efforts and vision for reform were cut short by his
untimely death after just 18 months in office. Most of the
Roman clergy rejoiced at his demise, and it would be another four hundred and fifty years before the cardinals
would elect another non-Italian pope.

Pope Clement VII (1523-1534) was the bastard son of
a famous Medici,[273] and his father was murdered when
Clement was in the womb. He was nephew to Pope Leo
X, who made him Cardinal Archbishop of Florence. Clement was chiefly responsible for Leo's policies against Luther,
and continued them. He found himself in great political
turmoil, and, having offended the Holy Roman Emperor
Charles V by making an alliance with the King of France,
found himself invaded by Charles and a prisoner under
house arrest for six months.[274] His continuing conflict

---

[272] Janz, pp. 332-333.

[273] The Medici family was a famous Florentine family reputed to be the
wealthiest in Europe in the 15th-16th century. The family gave the papacy
four popes, and established the Medici Bank, one of the most respected European institutions.

[274] Amongst the Imperial armies were many zealous Lutheran soldiers.
For eight days the armies rampaged through Rome committing all sorts of
atrocities. Horses were stabled in St. Peter's itself and the Sistine Chapel.

with Charles V hampered a collaborative effort to stop the spread of Protestantism in Germany. Though the Emperor asked the Pope to summon a general council, something even Luther wished for and which might have contained the explosiveness of the Reformation, Clement VII missed an opportunity for constructive action. He was the Pope who excommunicated King Henry VIII of England, which action precipitated the creation of the Church of England. He was, however, a patron of Machiavelli and Michelangelo, and commissioned the "Last Judgment" in the Sistine Chapel just before his death, having accomplished nothing positive in addressing the Reformation.

Pope Paul III (1534-1549) was from a famous Italian family, and received a fine humanist education. He was Cardinal Deacon under Pope Alexander VI and was nicknamed "cardinal petticoat" because his sister was the Pope's mistress. Paul III himself had a Roman mistress with whom he had three sons and a daughter before his late ordination at 51 years of age.[275] At the time of his ordination he went through a personal reform, and became identified with the reform party in the Roman curia. At 67 he was the oldest cardinal and was unanimously elected Pope after a conclave

---

Graffiti of Luther's name was written on a painting of Raphael. A group of Lutheran soldiers assembled under the Pope's window screaming that they were going to eat him. Some 4,000 citizens were murdered, and many treasures stolen. The sack of Rome by Charles V would remain a blotch on the Emperor's reputation. Duffy (1997), p. 206.

[275] Duffy (1997), p. 209.

of only two days. He named two of his grandsons, aged only 14 and 16, to be cardinals. Paul III discerned the need to address the challenges of Protestantism constructively, and placed the calling of a general council at the head of his agenda. In 1536, he set up a commission to appraise the internal condition of the church, and this commission submitted a penetrating report in 1537 that would serve as the basis for the upcoming Council of Trent. This report documented the fact that the pope was selling clerical offices, that no proper care was being taken in approving candidates for ordination, that reverence for the divine services was virtually extinct, that most bishops were absentee and even most priests had deserted their flocks, that monks were not disciplined, and that prostitutes filled Rome and consorted with noblemen, cardinals, and priests in broad daylight.[276]

Paul III made three exceedingly important decisions that helped define the Catholic Counter Reformation. The first was the establishment of the Jesuit Order in 1540. The second was the establishment of the Roman Inquisition in 1542 as the main authority for stamping out Protestant heresy. Lastly, he convened the General Council of Trent on December 13th, 1545, and was represented by three papal legates. While blessing these three endeavors designed to counter Protestant influence, Paul III actively encouraged the Holy Roman Emperor in his battles against Protestant princes, and the French king to persecute the Huguenots.

---

[276] Janz, pp. 346-7.

Pope Paul III

Pope Julius III (1550-1555) had been governor of Rome. The Englishman, Cardinal Reginald Pole, missed election by one vote.[277] Julius III was a typical Renaissance pontiff, who loved his pleasures which he intermixed with occasional bursts of energy and work. He carried through piecemeal reforms, encouraged the Jesuits, and was the Pope under whom England temporarily returned to Catholicism under Queen Mary. He sent Cardinal Morone, at the request of Charles V, to the Diet of Augsburg (1555) in the vain hope of recovering Germany to Roman Catholicism on the model of England.

Pope Marcellus II (9 Apr – 1 May 1555) was one of the three Presidents of the Council of Trent, a member of Pope Paul III's reform commission, and an outspoken critic of the Pope's nepotism and luxurious lifestyle. He was installed as Pope with expectation heavy in the air that this was the Pope for the moment of the church's crisis. He was a zealous reformer, and sought justice and excluded nepotism, even refusing his relatives permission to move to Rome. After 22 days of zeal, he died of a stroke. He was the first real reform pope.

Pope Paul IV (1555-1559) combined personal asceticism and humanist intellectualism, as a personal correspondent with Erasmus. As a priest he had founded the order of Theatines, dedicated to strict poverty and to restoring the apostolic way of life. He sought to reform abuses in the church.

---

[277] Kelly (1986), p. 262.

He headed the Inquisition, and, at 79 was elected Pope on Emperor Charles V's wishes. He denounced the Peace of Augsburg which provided for peaceful co-existence of German Lutherans and Catholics. He was a violent anti-Protestant, who refused to reestablish the suspended Council of Trent. Working with the Inquisition, he oversaw the creation of the Index of Forbidden Books.[278] This Index continued in existence until 1966. Paul IV was apparently something of a paranoid fanatic, and persecuted the Jews of Rome whom he suspected of abetting Protestants. He died a very unpopular man.

Pope Pius IV (1559-1565) had been an accomplished lawyer. He had three natural children, and became a rising star when his brother married into the family of Pope Paul III. As Pope his great accomplishment was to reconvene, and bring to a successful conclusion, the Council of Trent. The Council was dissolved in its 25th session on December 4, 1563. Pius confirmed its decree orally on January 26, 1564, and published a formal bull, *Benedictus Deus*, on June 30, 1564. He spent his remaining time seeking to have the council's decrees obeyed throughout Catholic dominions. Pius IV altered eucharistic practice by allowing the chalice to be served to the faithful in Germany, Austria, Hungary, and other regions to quell Protestant growth.[279] The question of the marriage of priests was deferred. Bishops and theo-

---

[278] Duffy (1997), p. 215.

[279] One of the valid Protestant criticisms of the papacy was that it did not permit lay Christians to receive the chalice, but were only given the host.

logians were required to subscribe formally to the council's decrees and profession of faith. Bishops were required to return to and take up residence in their own dioceses. Pius IV initiated but did not complete the compilation of the new catechism and recension of the missal and breviary before his death. These were published by his successor, Pius V, who was to place the Tridentine stamp on the Catholic Church for ages to come and eventually be canonized as a Catholic saint.

## The Jesuits

Several new religious orders were founded in the 1520s, including the Capuchins. These orders are considered to be the first organic signs of the internal Catholic Reformation. In 1540, the Catholic saint, Ignatius of Loyola, founded the Jesuit Order, known formally as the Society of Jesus, and this order became the beacon of the Counter Reformation.[280] The influence of the Jesuits was most poignantly felt through their universities – both the Roman College (Gregorianum) and the German and English Colleges in Rome. More than 500 colleges were established and staffed by the Jesuits in the first century of the order's existence.[281] The educated Jesuits sought to revive the Roman Catholic Church and thoroughly catechize its flock against the Protestant movement. Ignatius wrote a manual, *The Spir-*

---

[280] For more on the Jesuits see O'Malley (1993).
[281] This averages to five per year for 100 years.

*itual Exercises*, which was to provide guidance in the spiritual life
for the Jesuits, as well as a tract
entitled *Rules for Thinking With
the Church*, designed to counter
anti-ecclesiastical and individualistic Protestantism. Early figures
in the Jesuit Order included, besides Ignatius Loyola, the Catholic saints Francis Xavier and
Robert Bellarmine. The Jesuits
were intense missionaries, and

Ignatius of Loyola

many of them, after being educated in Rome, returned to
Protestant lands to preach Catholicism, a fair number of
them suffering martyrdom. If one visits the Tower of London on a tour, it is possible still to see the wall etchings of
imprisoned Jesuit priests from the 16th and 17th centuries. Besides the 16th century monastic orders, there were
also esteemed Roman Catholic churchmen like Charles
Borromeo (1538-1584), Archbishop of Milan, and Francis
de Sales (1567-1622), Bishop of Geneva, who himself won
many Calvinists back to Catholicism. Both of these were
later canonized.

### *The Council of Trent 1545-1563*

There were many components of the reaction by the
papacy and Roman Catholic Church to the tragic split in

Western Christendom. Besides the founding of the Jesuits and the radical educational and missionary endeavors, there was convened the special Council of Trent which met from 1545-1563, and is deemed an ecumenical council by the Roman Catholic Church.[282] Though the Council first convened in 1545 it was originally called by Paul III in 1537. The 18 years during which the Council was in and out of session were punctuated by serious political problems as successive popes negotiated alignments with the prevalent Catholic powers, notably between between France, the Holy Roman

Council of Trent

[282] In fact, most of the bishops who attended the Council were Italians. Its opening session had less than forty in attendance, and that number did double for some later sessions. It is estimated that some six hundred bishops in Europe remained more or less loyal to the papacy, but only 226 bishops signed the Council's documents. MacCulloch (2003), pp. 234, 305.

Empire and Habsburg Spain. When political matters got hot, the council sessions had to be suspended, sometimes for years. Some Protestant theologians attended the second major period of the Council, but were disheartened that so much had already been decided definitively in the first period in their absence and was not going to be renegotiated.

According to the Council itself, as articulated in its third session, its purpose was "the rooting out of heresy and the reform of conduct."[283] This Council was summoned in response to the repeated requests of theologians, churchmen and even the emperor himself for a general church council to address the areas of disputed theology and to stem corruption amongst the clergy. By the time the Council finally convened, the schism between the Protestants and the papacy was firmly fixed, and no plan for reunification was ever under serious consideration. Sporadic meetings took place over almost 20 years, in three distinct periods. The first period covered sessions 1-8, under Pope Paul III, and met during the years 1545-1547. This period addressed decrees on faith (session 3), Scripture and tradition (session 4), original sin (session 5), justification and good works (session 6), and the theology of the sacraments (session 7). The second period covered sessions 9-16, met under Pope Julius III from 1551-1552, and issued decrees on the Eucharist, penance, and last rites. The third period, sessions 17-25,

---

[283] Pelikan (2003), *Creeds and Confessions*, Vol. 2, p. 817.

met from 1561-1563 under Pope Pius IV, and focused more intimately on the nature of the Mass and holy orders.

### The Dogmatic Decrees of the Council of Trent

The dogmatic decrees begin, as do our Orthodox Ecumenical Councils, with an affirmation of the Nicene Creed as the true and authentic confession of Christian faith. Unfortunately, the Council of Trent proclaimed the Nicene Creed with the *filioque* heresy in it, and affirmed that these were the exact words in which the creed is read in "all the churches." The Council affirmed the Roman canon of Scripture which, contrary to the Protestant canon, contains the books of the Longer Canon of the Old Testament (what the Protestants call "Apocryphal books"), and affirmed the old Latin Vulgate edition as the standard edition of the Scriptures. Those who deny this are anathematized.

The Council used the anathema quite extensively, and in so doing effectively anathematized the entire Protestant West. In yet another Roman paradigm shift, this attitude, which was normative for the coming centuries right up until the 20th, became passé and is no longer the Roman Catholic position on Protestantism. Since Vatican II, a Latin ecclesiology of Protestants as "separated brethren" and not as "anathematized heretics" has come to be the official Catholic teaching.[284]

---

[284] The *Decree on Ecumenism* of Vatican II uses this terminology to establish the new papal doctrine. By virtue of this new doctrine, many non-Roman

The second decree of the council insists on interpreting the Holy Scriptures in accord with patristic teachings, and in continuity with the Holy Fathers. The council placed strict censures upon book printers who would print works that advanced hermeneutical novelties, or works published without authorial attribution. All religious books and copies of the Scriptures must be first examined and approved by the local bishop on pain of anathema.[285] The decree on original sin affirms the passing on of the guilt of that sin, and exempts the Virgin Mary from such an inheritance.

### The Decree on Justification

The decree on justification is the longest decree of all the decrees of the council, and constitutes 16 chapters followed by 33 canons. The length and detail of this decree bears

Christians are explicitly affirmed, by the Latin teaching, to be children of the Roman Church without even knowing it by virtue of their baptism. This change in ecclesiology is in harmony with the new Latin "common baptism" theory. Vatican II, *Decree on Ecumenism: Unitatis Redintegratio*, Ch. 1, Sect. 3, 19-23. An excellent and scholarly evaluation of the re-configuration of Roman Catholic theology in the areas of baptism and ecumenism, with special reference to Protestantism, is the soon to be published dissertation (Aristotle University, Thessaloniki, Greece) by Rev. Peter Heers (2014) entitled: *The Ecclesiological Renovation of Vatican II: An Orthodox Examination of Rome's Ecumenical Theology Regarding Baptism and the Church*, Greek edition by Apostoliki Diakonia; English edition TBD.

[285] Between 1576 and 1773 not a single edition of an Italian-language Bible was printed anywhere in the Italian peninsula. Bibles were ceremonially burned, like heretics. Pope Paul V in 1606 castigated the Venetian ambassador saying, "Do you not know that so much reading of Scripture ruins the Catholic religion?" MacCulloch (2003), p. 406.

witness to the centrality of the issue of justification in the whole Reformation conflict. I will now summarize the logic of this decree on justification. Chapter 1 begins with an affirmation that all humans are by nature children of wrath, under the power of the devil and death, and are slaves of sin. In this condition, neither nature nor the law of God given to Moses are able to justify man before God. It is this reality that is the backdrop for the mystery of the Gospel, for the Father of mercies sent His Only-Begotten Son Jesus Christ in order to redeem *both* the Jews, who could not be redeemed by the Law, *and* the Gentiles, who were not even pursuing righteousness. Chapter Three affirms that though Christ died for all, yet not all benefit from his death, but only those to whom the salvation of His Cross is imparted. This transition from being an unregenerate and unjustified person in Adam to being a justified person in Christ cannot take place without the waters of rebirth or a desire for them, as it is written: "Unless a person is born again of water and the Holy Spirit, he cannot enter the kingdom of God." Chapter Five explains that actual justification in adults has its origin in a predisposing grace of God in Jesus Christ, which is God's calling and invitation given to those who have no good deeds at all. God's grace and calling incite and help sinners "to turn towards their own justification by giving free assent to and cooperating with" God's grace. Human beings touched by God's invitation and inviting grace are able to reject it or assent to it and cooperate with it. In preparation for Baptism people are roused and helped by divine grace and "freely move towards God and believe to be true what has been divinely revealed and promised, and in particular that the wicked are justified by God by his grace through the redemption which is in Christ Jesus." At the same time, acknowledging that they are sinners, they turn from fear of divine justice, which profitably strikes them, to thoughts of God's mercy; they rise to hope, with confidence that God will be favorable to them for Christ's sake...They are thereby turned against sin by a feeling of hatred and detestation, namely by that repentance which must occur before Baptism. Finally, when they are proposing to receive Baptism, they are moved to begin a new life and to keep God's commandments. These preparations, actualized by God's grace and the assent of human free will, precede actual justification, "which consists not only in the forgiveness of sins but also in the sanctification and renewal of the inward being by a willing acceptance of the grace and gifts whereby someone from being unjust becomes just, from being an enemy becomes a friend, so that he is an heir in hope of eternal life."

The decree on justification goes on to enumerate the "causes" of justification as the following: the final cause is the glory of God and of Christ, and eternal life; the efficient cause the God of mercy who, of his own free will, washes and sanctifies, placing his seal and anointing with the promised Holy Spirit, who is the guarantee of our inheritance; the meritorious cause, the Lord Jesus Christ who merited justification by his holy passion on the wood of the Cross; the instrumental cause, the sacrament of baptism; and the one formal cause is the justness of God, by which he makes us just, each one of us receiving individually his own justness according to the measure which the Holy Spirit apportions to each one as he wills.

When a person is justified in Baptism the love of God is poured out by the agency of the Holy Spirit in the hearts of those who are being justified, and abides in them. Consequently, in the process of justification, together with the forgiveness of sins a person receives, through Jesus Christ into whom he is grafted, all these infused at the same time: faith, hope, and charity. For faith, unless hope is added to it and charity too, neither unites him perfectly with Christ nor makes him a living member of his body. Hence, it is very truly said that faith without works is dead and barren, and in Christ Jesus neither circumcision is of any avail nor uncircumcision, but faith working through love.

Chapter 9 is entitled *Against the Vain Confidence of the Heretics.* It is necessary to believe that sins have only been forgiven freely by the divine mercy on account of Christ, yet no one should have a proud assurance and certainty that they have been forgiven, or rely solely on that. This assurance as it is preached by the heretics is "empty" and an "ungodly assurance." "No devout person ought doubt the mercy of God, the merit of Christ or the power and efficacy of the sacraments...but it is certainly possible for anyone to be anxious and fearful about his own state of grace, since no one can know, by that assurance of faith which excludes all falsehood, that he has obtained the grace of God." Chapter 10 affirms that justification can be increased as faith, hope, and love grow in the Christian. Chapter 11 insists on the necessity of keeping the commandments of God and of suffering with Christ in order to be glorified with Him. In this section the decree rejects the Protestant teaching that in every good work the just person sins at least venially. Chapter 12 posits that no believer should presume to know about the hidden mystery of predestination and affirm that he is unquestionably among the number of the predestined, as if one justified is no longer capable of sin. Chapter 14 affirms that those who fall away by sin from the grace of justification can be recovered and again justified by the sacrament of repentance. The conciliar decree on justification was followed by 33 canons which define and express the decree, and target specific teachings of Protestant faith.

*Decrees and Canons on the Sacraments.*

The Council issued other decrees and canons on the sacraments in general, and on each sacrament in particular as well as on purgatory, and the invocation and veneration of saints, relics, and sacred images. Canon 6 of the general canons on the sacraments is representative of the explicit effort to counter Protestant assertions: "If anyone says that the sacraments of the new law do not contain the grace which they signify, or that they do not confer that grace on those who place no obstacles in its way, as though they are only outward signs of grace or justice received through faith and certain marks of Christian profession, whereby among men believers are distinguished from unbelievers, let him be anathema." Sacraments are affirmed as working *ex opere operato.*[286]

### Canons on the Eucharist

Canon 1 reads, "If anyone denies that in the sacrament of the most holy Eucharist are contained truly, really and substantially the body and blood together with the soul and divinity of our Lord Jesus Christ, but says that he is in it only as in a sign, or figure or force, let him be anathema." Canons continue which specifically address and reject various Lutheran, Calvinist, and Zwinglian interpretations of the Eucharist. Of interest for us Orthodox Christians is Canon 6,

> If anyone says that in the holy sacrament of
> the Eucharist, Christ, the only begotten Son of

---

[286] From the Latin meaning "from the work done." This sacramental teaching affirms that the unworthiness of a priest administering the sacraments does not nullify the sacraments.

God, is not to be adored with the worship of
latria, also outwardly manifested, and is consequently neither to be venerated with a special
festive solemnity, nor to be solemnly borne
about in procession according to the laudable
and universal rite and custom of holy church,
or is not to be set publicly before the people
to be adored and that the adorers thereof are
idolaters, let him be anathema.

Here Orthodox Christians, who have kept the faith
unaltered of the ancient church, find themselves anathematized. While confessing with all certitude that the Holy
Mystery of the Eucharist is truly the Body and Blood of Jesus Christ, we additionally confess that the Eucharist was
given to us by Jesus Christ to be consumed, not to be pa-
raded with outside of the divine service as in Latin Corpus Christi processions nor to be placed in a monstrance
and adored by the faithful in "holy hours." This is, in fact,
a Latin abuse of the Eucharist itself. Our Lord's words are,
"Take, eat," not "Take, parade" or "Take, adore."

The Council of Trent also published canons on penance
and other sacraments, as well as numerous reform decrees
on important subjects such as establishing church schools
and the importance of preaching, so important to coun-
tering Protestantism. The Council published its rules on
the new Papal Index of prohibited books in which Luther,

Zwingli, Calvin, Balthasar, etc. are named. Taken together these decrees and canons sum up the formal position of the Catholic or Counter Reformation. In 1564, a *Tridentine Profession of Faith* was published, and all bishops, professors at Catholic Universities, and holders of papal benefices were required to openly and formally accept each and all of the decisions of the Council of Trent by making the Tridentine profession.

### When Did the Counter Reformation End?

This is a question not easily answered. At the time of the Reformation, the continued existence of Protestantism was not at all certain. In 1590, about half of Europe was under the control of Protestant government or culture. By 1690 only a fifth was. The Counter Reformation appeared massively victorious.[287] The religious conflict between Catholicism and Protestantism flared up in the Thirty Years War (1618-1648) and left Christian Europe blood-soaked and exhausted by religious conflicts. It gave way to centuries of Catholic-Protestant cold war in which each of these Western communions has failed to maintain the theological discipline of their own confessions, and have fallen prey to many heresies–from theological liberalism/secularism to liberation theology. Catholic-Protestant relations have morphed yet again since Vatican II (1962-1965) when the

---

[287] MacCulloch (2003), p. 669.

Catholic Church refashioned its ecclesiology to find a place for Protestantism, and adopted, at least in practice, many things that the Protestants of the 16th century were calling for. Today, especially in the West, the divide between Catholicism and Protestantism is thinner than ever, the traditional Tridentine Mass is virtually non-existent, and the Catholic services have been radically Protestantized, degraded, and denuded of their traditional liturgical, aesthetic, and linguistic grandeur. Centuries of traditional Gregorian chant and ecclesiastical architecture have often given way to banjos and guitars and architectural monstrosities, all of which bear witness to a radical break from tradition. The teaching on penance, so emphasized at the Council of Trent, has vanished together with long confessional lines and numerous priests. Now, in the local Catholic diocese here in the Inland Empire (Riverside-San Bernardino-Ontario, CA), there are 5000 parishioners for every priest, and so few Catholics confessing their sins and living a normal sacramental life that there is often but one published confessional hour per week. Monasteries have closed throughout the West, and there has been a reduction in the number of Roman Catholic monks, nuns, and members of religious orders in our land by some 95%. Parochial schools which were educating some 6 million children before Vatican II are now educating about 25% that number.

New alignments have come into existence in recent decades, in which the Catholic Church has engaged in extensive dialogue with Judaism and Islam, and set its polemic
sights upon the rising secularism permeating the West and
leaving traditional Christian Europe faithless. The recent
popes have called for a re-evangelization of Europe, and
have emphasized a new *rapprochement* with the Orthodox
East with whom they claim to share so much affinity in a
common battle against the tenets of post-modernity and
secularist mores.

## The Contemporary Counter Reformation

One might be led to believe that the Counter Reformation has ceased to exist, but the Vatican has recently announced a major new initiative designed to reconcile Protestants to its fold. In the previous chapter on the Church
of England it was noted that the Anglican communion has
been fracturing between its extreme secularism in England
and America and its more evangelical churches in Africa
and elsewhere, who aggressively protest the ordination of
women and the legitimization of homosexuality. Recently,
Cardinal William Levada, the former Archbishop of San
Francisco,[288] and the current head of the Congregation for
the Doctrine of the Faith in Rome, announced in a press

---

[288] While in this position Cardinal Levada fought valiantly against the
legalization of same-sex marriage, and endured the persecution of the San
Francisco Supervisors.

conference in London (where he was meeting with Rowan Williams, then Archbishop of Canterbury for the Anglican communion) that a special canonical structure has been established by Pope Benedict XVI that would assist the members of the Anglican communion in becoming Roman Catholics, while maintaining "the distinctive Anglican spiritual and liturgical patrimony." Not only will elements of Anglican liturgical practice be preserved, but married priests retained, and special unmarried bishops commissioned as archpastors. This is a bold move which expresses a certain abandonment of confidence on the part of the papacy in traditional ecumenical dialogue with the Anglican churches. Cardinal Levada in his announcement articulated that the creation of a permanent Anglican structure within the Roman Catholic Church was established in response to the "many requests" directed to the pope by disaffected Anglicans which he said was a "worldwide phenomenon."[289] Perhaps the Counter Reformation continues in some fashion yet today.

---

[289] http://212.77.1.245/news_services/bulletin/news/24513.php?index=24513&lang=en

A page from the illuminated *Lindisfarne Gosepl*, c. 696 AD

# 9

# *America's Folk Religion: Evangelicalism and the Rise of Non-Denominationalism*

O ur survey in the preceding chapters of the history and theology of various Protestant denominations is not complete without a chapter on the subject of evangelicalism. The traditional forms of Protestantism are no longer the self-identification of choice for most Protestants. Many modern Protestants do not even recognize themselves as the heirs of the Protestant Reformation. The most vibrant and demographically explosive forms of Protestantism are so a-historical, so radically detached from the historic Christian ethos that an organic association even with their own Protestant lineage is too much of a chronological and dogmatic commitment. For many of these Protestant Christians the only relevant history of Christianity began with the history of their own particular congregation, or even the history of their particular preacher, and no tangible connection to the Christian past is considered essential. What matters to them is that their spiritual experience is real, not that their spiritual experience is in harmony with that of their forebears.

223

## *Evangelicalism*

This relatively new expression of Protestant Christianity is called evangelicalism, and its growth over the last century has been astronomical. By some estimates, there are approximately 800 million evangelicals in the world, or about 1 in every 8 persons on the earth. Competently affirming evangelical demographics, however, is not easily done because evangelicalism is a movement, not a denomination. There is no evangelical consensus on what it means to be an evangelical, nor is there any official or authoritative definition of the word "evangelical." Evangelicals come from all the branches of traditional Protestantism, and from many traditions that have only the faintest association with traditional Protestantism. The evangelical movement has grown out of Protestant soil, and was fashioned out of the great American revivals of the 18th and 19th centuries. As such, the movement is defined more by a form of spiritual experience than by a confessional commitment or a sacramental participation.

Many evangelicals are fervently attached to denominational particularities, but the majority of evangelicals today have found the historical Protestant denominational structures wanting, and, in a vain effort, have sought to identify themselves as post-denominational. These "non-denominational" congregations, or independent "fellowships" as they are often called, are, in fact, the very worst form of denominationalism itself, being in essence *denominations of one congregation*. It is precisely these non-denominational evangelicals who are most active in missionary labors today.[290] Many of these missionary labors are directed explicitly at traditionally Orthodox lands, and these evangelicals are zealously committed to "saving the Orthodox."[291]

Who are these evangelicals? How has this metamorphosis of the Protestant movement come about? How is it that denominations have multiplied out of all relevance? What is this new identity that so many Protestants have affirmed based on spiritual experience instead of dogmatic confession?

*The Great Awakenings as the Cradle of Evangelicalism.*

During the American colonial period, prior to the formation of the United States of America, various colonies

---

[290]  That missionary zeal is no guarantee of an authentic Christian nature, even from an evangelical point of view, is demonstrated by the extreme missionary zeal of such heretical sects as the Church of Jesus Christ of Latter Day Saints (Mormons) and the Jehovah Witnesses. These sects are zealous for the propagation of their religion, and members often make tremendous personal sacrifices in their sincerity, but they remain *sincerely* outside the acceptable dogmatic norm of traditional Christian faith. Though Mormons and Jehovah Witnesses have jettisoned a far greater amount of the Orthodox Christian faith than have evangelicals, nevertheless the Orthodox view evangelicals on the same continuum of heresy, and evangelical missions as no proof that evangelicalism is the true faith. It takes only one heresy to be a heretic.

[291]  I have in my personal library a copy of a doctoral dissertation from the Southern Baptist Seminary in Louisville, Kentucky, entitled, "How to Win the Orthodox to Christ."

aligned themselves with distinct expressions of the Protestant Christian faith. The New England colonies were associated with Reformed confessions. The middle colonies were more closely tied to the Church of England. Rhode Island was the site of the founding of the first Baptist congregation in America. As the colonies amalgamated into a new nation, one of the fundamental religious principles that the new republic articulated was to establish a boundary between church and state that would forbid any official form of Protestantism from being the new country's official religion.[292]

Over the last two and a half centuries of American Protestant religious history numerous religious movements have deeply affected the American psyche. Chief among these movements are the First and Second Great Awakenings. This First Great Awakening began in Great Britain and the American colonies in the 18th century with the public preaching of such figures as Revs. John Wesley, George Whitefield, and Jonathan Edwards. Each of these exceed-

---

[292] This original notion of the separation of church and state has morphed over time and under secularist influence into the notion that Christianity should have no influence on the government whatsoever. This notion of the "separation of church and state" that banishes religious conviction from the public square has nothing to do with the authentic and original notion articulated in the 1st Amendment of the United States Constitution. Some religious historians believe that religion has flourished in America as it has precisely because of its formal disassociation from the state. Proponents of this theory point to the radical decline in state churches like the Church of England, and the successful request of the state Lutheran Church of Sweden to disestablish.

Jonathan Edwards

ingly gifted preachers claimed to have been converted in heart *after* some time already as clergymen.[293] Defining this conversion of heart as essential Christian repentance and then calling upon others to pursue it at all costs became the focus of the preaching of the Great Awakenings. During the First Great Awakening thousands of late colonial persons were moved to religious conversion.[294] The preachers of this awakening were predominantly Reformed in their theology, and associated with classical Protestant denominations: Anglican, Presbyterian, and Congregational.

The Second Great Awakening took place under the preaching of the Presbyterian-turned-Congregationalist, Rev. Charles Finney,[295] and on principle rejected the strict Calvinism of the leaders of the first revival, often embracing instead a radical Arminianism.[296] Finney's approach to

---

[293] Wesley and Whitefield were Anglican clergymen, and Edwards originally served a Presbyterian church and then a Congregational.

[294] Two classic accounts of this revival were written by Jonathan Edwards and are entitled: *A Faithful Narrative of a Surprising Work of God and Thoughts on the Revival of Religion in New England. The Works of Jonathan Edwards*, 2 Vols., (1834, 1987), Ed. Edward Hickman, Carlisle, PA: Banner of Truth Trust, Vol. 1, pp. 344-430.

[295] Finney was earlier in his life a Master Mason. He left freemasonry and wrote against it. He was also thrice-married and twice widowed.

[296] Finney articulated his theology of revival, so distinct from that of the 1st Great Awakening, in his *Lectures on Revivals of Religion* (1860), Cambridge,

revivalist preaching established a paradigm that has been replicated by evangelical preachers for the last two hundred years. This paradigm includes lengthy religious gatherings often in tents out-of-doors (tent meetings), aggressive advertising to raise awareness and expectation, personal testimonies from men and women, the oratorical climax of the altar call, and an emphasis on making a "decision for Jesus Christ." This religious paradigm of conversion which is so well known to American evangelicals has the additional unique quality of being detached from the sacrament of Holy Baptism. Thus, entire generations of evangelicals have been formed to define and articulate their conversion experiences without reference to Baptism at all.

Finney and other leaders of the Second Great Awakening downplayed denominational association, and carried the rejection of traditional religious forms for preaching and religious gatherings–inherent in the First Great Awakening–to even greater extents. The emphasis in the Second Great Awakening on the potentiality of the human will to do good for one's own salvation and for the greater society led to the unleashing of a reforming zeal unmatched in

Charles Finney

the annals of American history.[297] Protestants were at the forefront in the efforts for civil rights, women's suffrage, the abolition of slavery, and labor reform to protect children and the Lord's Day.

## The "Born-Again" Experience

America's theologian, Jonathan Edwards,[298] articulated for future generations the contours of the "born-again" experience in a number of theological texts in which he sought to articulate the nature of true conversion and revival. These texts included his own story in *A Personal Narrative*, as well as his *Distinguishing Marks of a Work of the Spirit of God, Some Thoughts Concerning Revival*, and *Religious Affections*. In these texts he described how by a mysterious work of God within him he became completely enamored with the beauty of the Lord God and aflame with desire to read the Holy Scriptures and live according to the Gospel commandments. In addition to these new loves, came the unquenchable thirst for the conversion of all the nations to Christianity. These twin emphases on a personal desire for God and a deep impulse to proselytize defined the evangelical notions of being "born-again."

---

[297] Balmer, p. 30.

[298] The description of Edwards as "America's Theologian" comes from the title of the excellent book on Edwards by Robert W. Jensen (1992). Edwards, 1703-1758, besides his pastoral and theological fame, was the President of Princeton University and the grandfather of Aaron Burr.

We Orthodox Christians find these religious affections familiar from the lives of our saints, such as St. Seraphim of Sarov. St. Seraphim lived with an unquenchable thirst for God and for the Scriptures. He read the entire New Testament every week: St. Matthew on Sunday, St. Mark on Monday, St. Luke on Tuesday, St. John on Wednesday, the Acts of the Apostles on Thursday, the Epistles on Friday, and the Revelation on Saturday. He burned for the salvation of others. He sought personal communion with the living God with such intensity that he spent one thousand nights and days on a rock in unceasing prayer.[299]

What then is the Orthodox Christian perspective of this evangelical notion of the "born again" experience? We recognize the outlines of the work of God in the spiritual experience described by Jonathan Edwards. The quest for God, His word, and the evangelization of the world are the fruits of the Spirit of God within the human mind and heart. However, we must point out that the evangelical use of the term "born-again" is a misinterpretation of St. John 3:3 and 3:5 and a tragic misuse of Scripture. In his conversation with Nicodemos our Lord Jesus Christ affirmed that unless a man is born again he cannot see the Kingdom of God (v. 3), and then again (v. 5) that unless a man is born of water and the Spirit he cannot enter into the Kingdom of God. To be born again is to be born of water and the Spirit in Holy Baptism. The evangelical notion of being "born-

---

[299] Rose (2008), p. 67.

again" places that experience definitively outside of the realm of true Christian baptism, and substitutes a tent-revival, altar-call, or some such intangible, pseudo-sacrament for the mystery of Holy Baptism. There is no place for "water" in the evangelical definition of being born-again. As a result, evangelicals have very little respect for Holy Baptism. Most do not know or celebrate the day of their baptisms. They recount and celebrate not the day of their baptism, but the day of their "praying the sinner's prayer" or "receiving Jesus."[300] Most have been baptized more than once, and some even many times. This last notion is especially scandalous to all historic Christians.

Orthodox Christians ought to share with evangelicals an appreciation for a living faith and tangible repentance, for personal prayer in the confines of one's own secret room, and a deep concern for the evangelization of the world, for this is the inheritance we have received from our Holy Fathers. This is the patristic tradition. But we cannot abide by definitions of spiritual experience which negate the sacraments and establish revivalist paradigms[301] unknown in the history of the Church. These revivalistic paradigms produced a great storm of personal judgment between Protes-

---

[300] The language of "receiving Jesus" is scriptural, being taken from John 1:12. However, the method of receiving Jesus in typical revivalist practice is truncated and reductionistic, not involving significant catechesis or the sacrament of baptism.

[301] The evangelical rhetoric of revival has its roots in 17th century Scotland and Ulster. MacCulloch (2003), p. 604.

tant believers, each one evaluating whether or not the other had truly been converted, had gone through the appropriate steps, etc., and the result was an exponential increase in denominational splits in the aftermath of the Great Awakenings. Wesley and Whitefield could no longer work together, and established two competing Methodist traditions. Jonathan Edwards was ejected from his parish. The Congregationalist churches separated into several "Old Light" and "New Light" divisions. More than 100 congregations were gripped by contentiousness and divided into two. The Presbyterian Church divided into rival "Old Side" and "New Side" groups. Numerous Protestant clergymen embraced new heresies. Preachers made public pronouncements about the "lack of grace" of other ministers.[302] A tree can be judged by its fruits. True conversion, authentic spiritual experience, leads not to judgment but to humility and zeal to maintain the unity of the bond of peace.

Evangelicals might argue that the Great Awakenings helped to establish a new form of unity amongst themselves in which denominational distinctives were no longer central but rather were replaced by the common quest to preach the Gospel to the world and secure the conversion of the nations. At the time of the American Revolution

---

[302] David Brainerd, made famous by the publication of his autobiography by Jonathan Edwards which portrayed him as a model of youthful dedication to God and the evangelization of the natives, was himself expelled from Yale because he insulted one of his teachers asserting that the teacher "had no more grace than a chair." Sweeney, p. 56.

more than half of America's church-goers went to Congregational, Presbyterian, and Anglican churches. By 1850, after the Second Great Awakening, less than 20 percent of church-goers went to these established Protestant denominations, but new and growing Baptist and Methodist denominations[303] had gathered over half of America's attendees. New denominations multiplied with ever greater haste, and the movement has not ceased.

Orthodox Christians might suggest that the Great Awakening, rather than serving to unify evangelicals and re-align them along more simplistic evangelical tenets, added complexity and new fissures to an already divided Protestant Christendom, and in so doing established a new form of Protestantism whose litmus test was revivalism and a conversion experience. The resultant de-emphasis on dogma and church polity, even as it was found in thin expression in the traditional Protestant denominations, caused an outbreak of denominations with little theological weight.

## *Pentecostalism and the Charismatic Movement*

In the Protestant world today the majority of evangelicals are from Holiness, Pentecostal, or Charismatic congregations, and they are the fastest growing segment of evangelicalism. The most influential Pentecostal denomination is the Assemblies of God, with a membership in the millions. The Great Awakenings defined the evangelicalism of

---

[303] Methodism was America's largest denomination in 1844.

the 18th and 19th centuries, but the 20th century has been the century of the Holiness, Pentecostal, and Charismatic movements.

On the first day of the new century in Topeka, Kansas, Agnes Ozman, a student at Charles Fox Parham's Bethel Bible College, began "speaking in tongues." News spread and an African-American hotel waiter, William J. Seymour, carried this Pentecostal gospel with him to Los Angeles in early 1906, and speaking in tongues erupted on April 9th at a house on Bonnie Brae Street, where Parham was staying in Azusa, CA. The Bible College moved to a warehouse at 312 Azusa St. where for the next several years the Azusa Street Mission promoted "divine healings," Pentecostal enthusiasm, and missionaries to promote the Pentecostal

Azusa Street Mission

movement throughout the world. This Pentecostal movement not only replicated Pentecostal churches throughout
the world but deeply influenced both established Protestant denominations and even the Roman Catholic Church.

These movements share in common a quest for a higher
spiritual life, sometimes called a "second blessing." Leaders of this movement have placed tremendous emphasis
on moral purity, and have given the Protestant churches a
moral uplift. At the same time, many of these movements
have established an externalized ethos in which dancing,
drinking, and smoking rather than pride, vainglory, and
self-love, are the great taboos to be avoided, and abstinence
from these external "vices" is seen as the defining characteristics of holiness. Such erroneous visions of holiness have
led evangelicals into the promotion of such things as teetotalism,[304] which is seen as the demonization of creation.

Pentecostals emphasize "the work of the Holy Spirit"
in the life of the believer. The movement has normalized
certain charismatic expressions of spiritual life, most no-
toriously the gift of "speaking in tongues." For many Pen-

---

[304] Teetotalism is the practice of abstaining on moral principle from all al-
coholic beverages. Moderation in the use of God's gifts has been rejected
and replaced with the complete rejection of the gift itself. This heretical
ethic finds its parallel in those who today, in reaction to America's obesity,
argue for the complete rejection of meat-eating and the embrace of a vegan
diet on principle. Of course, both of these ethics stigmatize our Lord Jesus
Christ as a sinner (for he ate fish and meat–at least the Passover lamb–and
drank wine), and are inadvertently blasphemous.

tecostals this is the experience *sine qua non*. Speaking in tongues authenticates one's spiritual life, and according to this teaching should be sought daily from God until it is given. In contrast to the *glossolalia* of the Apostles as recorded in Acts 2, most Pentecostals do not believe that they are speaking recognizable human languages designed to enable speakers of those languages to hear and understand the Gospel proclamation in their own tongues. Rather, most Pentecostals affirm that they are speaking a special 'angelic' or 'divine' language which enables them to commune with God at a deeper level than the human mind.

Aside from an emphasis on speaking in tongues, Pentecostals seek to manifest the 'charismatic' gifts of healing, the expulsion of demons, etc. Evangelicals of these persuasions often are "slain in the Spirit" during worship, or are found to have jerking movements, or even to bark as dogs on the ground. The legitimacy of this or that spiritual manifestation has often been a source of profound controversy in Pentecostal circles.

Orthodox Christians appraise such spiritual experiences with reservation. Some of these experiences and practices reek as the work of charlatans. The demonic provenance of other manifestations, such as barking like a dog or spasmodic movements, is obvious to anyone familiar with traditional Christian teaching. An Orthodox opinion of the Pentecostal practice of "speaking in tongues" is not as easy to establish. The Scriptures deal with tongues primarily as the miraculous ability to speak another language previously unknown for the purpose of evangelization. That this reality is almost completely absent from Pentecostal experience should raise caution flags. The Scriptures also speak of tongues being a means of "praying with the spirit" instead of "praying with the mind." If, indeed, some Pentecostals are participating in this gift of prayer by a work of the Holy Spirit, then it would benefit them greatly to listen to the voice of the Holy Spirit and embrace the fullness of the Christian faith which is Holy Orthodoxy. It would also benefit the Pentecostal to de-emphasize the importance of speaking in tongues in order to remember that the Apostle Paul explicitly affirms that, even in the Apostolic age, not all Christians spoke in tongues.[305] Speaking in tongues is therefore not capable of being a litmus test for spiritual life. The Great Apostle also affirmed that he would rather speak five words with his mind, in order that he might instruct others also, rather than 10,000 words in a tongue.[306] Charismatic gifts are no certainty of salvation, nor of virtue.[307]

The esteemed spiritual elder, Father Zacharias (Zacharou), writes of the gift of speaking in tongues,

> The best explanation for God's gifts of tongues to the early Church lies in the necessity of teaching newly converted Christians to

---

[305] 1 Cor. 12:30.
[306] 1 Cor. 14:19.
[307] Matt. 7:21ff.

pray with their heart rather than just externally, as they were likely to have been used to doing. But the Church soon discovered a deeper way to educate the heart, for She was concerned to cultivate the inner man. She discovered the invocation of the Name of our Lord Jesus Christ. And little by little, the Prayer of the Heart replaced the gift of speaking in tongues. The Jesus Prayer is the way of praying in the spirit without losing any control of the spirit, and therefore, without running the risk of usurping the space of the other members of the Body of Christ....If this gift has indeed been given temporarily to some people, perhaps it will enable them to discover the true unbroken Tradition of the Church, the Tradition of the Prayer of the Heart....Through this prayer we receive the greatest of all the gifts of the Holy Spirit, the gift which will heal our nature and strengthen it 'guiding us into all truth' (John 16:3). It will enable us to bear the fullness of divine love. And this gift will never outlive its purpose–indeed it will accompany us beyond the grave. It is important that we understand this phenomenon of glossolalia–we must not be seduced by it. But let us above all be gracious to those who believe they have experienced this gift and gen-

tly point out to them that it is the beginning of
something far greater that will lead them to the
heart of the tradition.[308]

## *Missions to the Ends of the Earth*

The heart of evangelicalism is missionary work. Pentecostals share with all evangelicals a profound commitment
to preaching the Gospel to the entire world. In fact, Pentecostalism has grown more in the undeveloped world than
it has in the West. Following the Great Awakenings, Protestant missions exploded. Leading the way for innumerable
Protestant missionary boards was the Baptist Missionary
Society established by William Carey. The 19th century
witnessed the conversion of
more persons to Catholic and
Protestant Christianity than
at any other time in history.
The 19th century was the century of Protestant missions,
and many hoped that the 20th
century would be the preeminent Christian century. These
hopes were short-lived and
their bearers extremely disillu-

William Carey

---

[308] Zacharou (2007), pp. 240ff. Fr. Zacharias' comments on speaking in
tongues are derived from the teaching of Elder Sophrony (Sakharov) and
St. Philaret of Moscow in the latter's sermon on 1 Cor. 14:15.

sioned as the 20th century was unveiled as the barbarian century, a century during which more blood was shed in war and political repression than in any other century in human history. By the turn of the 20th century, millions of Protestant men and women were either financially supporting missionaries or in the mission field themselves.

Participation in missions is the cornerstone of evangelical spirituality. It was a fervor for missionary co-operation that lay behind the establishment of the modern Ecumenical movement.[309] In 1952, America provided more than 52% of the world's missionaries. By the turn of the 21st century, Korea had surpassed America in the number of missionaries sent to evangelize.[310] Mission work and Bible-reading are the twin evangelical drives and the measuring rod of evangelical spirituality. However, these two disciplines have not been placed within the bouquet of spiritual disciplines that traditionally have ensured a proper Christian formation. As a result, evangelicalism has been racked with: serious and systemic moral failures; its lack of humility and divisiveness; to its complicity in slavery and sustained commitment to racism well into the mid-20th century;[311]

---

[309] Heers (2007).

[310] Sweeney (2005), p. 102.

[311] This sad reality must be counter-balanced by the evangelical leadership in the abolition movement, and the good success that the evangelicals had at evangelization of the African-American community. To this day our land has a great number of black Christians, the majority of whom are Baptists. Having said this, we must also remember that still the most segregated hour

its current divorce epidemic—the divorce rate of active evangelicals is higher than the average divorce rate for all Americans.

## Mainline Protestant Decline

In the 19th and early 20th centuries, as Protestants came into their own in the great missionary movements, Protestantism also was unable to dissociate itself from its factious nature. A fundamental division took place between "mainline" Protestant denominations and the formation of a denominationally unaffiliated "evangelicalism." This fissure erupted over the course of the 19th century as some Protestants, following the tragedy of the Civil War and the embrace of a new form of eschatology called "premillennialism", distanced themselves from involvement with society and wrote off the quest for the moral improvement of society as a vain ambition. Revivalist preacher, Dwight L. Moody, represented this new mood amongst some of America's Protestants when he queried, "Why polish the brass on a sinking ship?" If, as the new eschatology suggested, Jesus was to come back very soon and until then the world was only going to get worse and worse, why invest in the betterment of society?

At the same time as this cultural retrenchment was taking place amongst some Protestants, others were being

in the week in America is Sunday morning—only some 5% of American congregations are inter-racial.

deeply influenced by secularizing trends of theological thought. These Protestants also took up a new focus on engaging society with the message of Jesus for the betterment of the poor and disadvantaged. The message of these Christians began to be dubbed the "social gospel," and as some of these Protestants became influenced by German higher criticism of the Bible, a strong opposition developed within Protestant circles between "liberals" (those of the social gospel) and "conservatives" (those who resisted theological change and had a firm belief in the inerrancy of the scriptural text). These divisions led to the modernist-fundamentalist controversy of the early 20th century over the authority of Scripture and the validity of the scientific theory of evolution.[312]

During the 20th century virtually every traditional Protestant denomination was to split over these issues. The original denominations bodies were hobbled with the label mainline and numerous new denominations were founded. The second quarter of the 20th century witnessed a remarkable flurry of conservative Protestant building projects as those Protestants who had separated themselves from the mainline bodies set about forming their own congrega-

---

[312] Controversy has also erupted over the abiding authority of traditional denominational creeds. Both the mainline denominations and the more recently formed conservative denominations have distanced themselves from classical Protestant confessions of faith. This distance is expressed by the numerous confessional revisions which have taken place at regular intervals, and manifest no evidence of slowing their pace.

tions, denominations, missionary societies, publishing houses, Bible institutes and colleges, Bible camps, and seminaries. This was an attempt to build a whole new conservative Protestant ecclesiastical apparatus, and to some degree insulate themselves from the outside world. The result was the creation of an evangelical subculture.

Some of the major leaders of this movement are well-known names in all American households, like Billy Graham, whose Billy Graham Evangelistic Association has been a tool Graham used to preach to more persons on the face of the earth than any other evangelist. He was instrumental in the founding of the flagship evangelical magazine, *Christianity Today*. Other leaders followed like Chuck Smith, who founded the *Calvary Chapel* movement in southern California, combining the hippie-beach culture of southern California with its casual and slang norms and its rock music with evangelical Bible teaching; Pat Robertson with his *Christian Broadcasting Network* and the *700 Club*, Jim Bakker with his *PTL Network*, and Paul and Jan Crouch with *Trinity Broadcasting Network*.[313] None of these lead-

---

[313] The Crouches, together with a host of other evangelical personalities have taken the identification of religion with American cultural mores to new heights by preaching a "prosperity Gospel" which posits that it is God's will for His people to be rich. It is the religious version of the so-called "American Dream." That such a paradigm, the exact opposite of the life of Jesus Christ and his most-eminent servants, could become religiously normative for so many American evangelicals bears witness to just how far from traditional Christianity those under the evangelical umbrella can stray.

ers were much rooted in traditional Christian theology, but they had hearts full of enthusiasm that united with their savvy grasp of marketing and tele-communications. Pastors of this ilk became fundamentally Bible-teachers detached from any essential interaction with their flocks. They have built mega-churches around their charisma, and multiplied their pastoral ministries on the business franchise model. They have connected intimately to the penchant of modern suburbanites for fast-food religion—quick, casual, often anonymous, unfettered by traditional customs, personal obligations of sacred community, denominational associations, and often even parish membership.

### Evangelical

Over the course of this same century, the religious designation 'evangelical' has become more fundamental to these Protestants than denominational affiliation. This word, evangelical, has a long history and a broad semantic range. The word *evangelion* (εὐαγγέλιον) is a Greek word which means "good news" and refers to the Gospel of Jesus Christ as good news for sinners. Throughout church history, the word evangelical has been an adjective used to describe many things, and Orthodox Christians would understand our monks and nuns, those who have dispossessed themselves of all things for the sake of the Gospel of Christ, as the world's true "evangelicals." True Christians seek to heed our Lord Jesus' call to do all "for the sake of the Gospel."

In early Protestant history the term "evangelical" became associated with Martin Luther and the early history of the Reformation, so much so that the Lutheran Church in Germany is called the "evangelical church."[314] The term "evangelical" has a rich semantic history in America, and America has its own definitions of "evangelical" which are peculiar to America. It is estimated that there are perhaps 70 million evangelicals in America today. No individual evangelical has a corner on the definition of the term, and many evangelical theologians have made their own attempts to define the term. The rise in popularity of self-identification by the term "evangelical" has paralleled the decline in fervent association with a particular Protestant denomination.

Evangelicals in the 21st century, having tasted the bitter and embarrassing fruits of a divisive ecclesiology that has produced thousands of Protestant denominations in America, are thoroughly disenchanted with the concept and reality of denominations. Many have simply jumped into the naïve ocean of "non-denominationalism" and made the divisions all the worse, but some, a wise few, are calling for *evangelical reunion*.[315]

---

[314] Protestant churches in Germany are called *Evangelische*.

[315] Frame (1991). This pioneering text, from perhaps evangelicalism's most brilliant theologian, makes many excellent appraisals about the tragedy of denominationalism together with courageous proposals for reunion, including the embrace of the theology of the 1st four Ecumenical Councils For another evangelical theologian who argues in this vein see the work of Peter Leithart.

Evangelicals hold certain basic tenets in common, including the embrace of the Bible as the inspired word of God,[316] an emphasis on personal conversion to Jesus Christ often called being "born again," and the central commitment to missionary work and evangelism.[317] Beyond these basic contours which form a "lowest common denominator" creed, there exists tremendous latitude. Influential Oxford evangelical theologian, Alister McGrath, posits a definition with more theological content under six headings.[318] Popular evangelical church historian David Bebbington offers a definition with four tenets.[319] The challenge for evangelical scholars in defining their movement is that the more content they give the definition the larger portion of their constituency they remove from the label. The reality is that evangelicalism lacks serious definition, and is a term with an exceedingly broad semantic range that threatens to render it meaningless. The term's popularity exists uniquely because of the failure of Protestantism itself, and its divisive character. Evangelicals gather around the term because it enables them to assimilate some common identity with other Christians from whom their denominations have for-

---

[316] The nature of this inspiration, however, is hotly debated in evangelical circles and has been the subject of many controversies and evangelical divisions.

[317] These three characteristics are posited by Randall Balmer (2010).

[318] McGrath (1995).

[319] Bebbington (1989), pp. 2-3.

mally separated them. The term 'evangelical' is the offspring of Protestant divisiveness.[320]

The broad umbrella term 'evangelical' shadows innumerable varieties of the many-faces of evangelicalism, including modern Pentecostalism and "holiness" churches, charismatics, baptistic fundamentalists, portions of all traditionally main-line denominations, ethnic churches, and the popular mega-churches. Besides these identifiable groups, American Protestantism has provided fertile soil for the creation of innumerable religious cults, and expressions of religious deviance inspired by the ideas of this or that spiritual guru. No culture in the history of mankind has produced more religious quacks, peddling their eccentric brands of religious expression, than the free market of American religion.

Evangelicals can perhaps be understood by Orthodox Christians as having been formed by two primary sources. Evangelicals are the distant offspring of the Protestant Reformation, which explains the general adherence to Protestant theological tenets though with much less zeal and commitment to these tenets than Protestants have traditionally had. Evangelicals are also the children of the American revivals known as the First and Second Great Awakenings, which explains the fundamental emphasis within evangelicalism upon the "born again" spiritual ex-

---

[320] Some of evangelicalism's most accomplished scholars have come to the conclusion that the very term evangelical has become meaningless. Dayton and Johnston (1991).

perience of conversion. Both of these "mothers of evangelicalism" are only nebulous associations since the exact nature of the Protestant dogma and the spiritual experience is not prescribed for evangelicals. More than a positive affirmation, evangelicalism functions as a rejection of certain traditional Christian beliefs in the two areas of dogma and spiritual life. In the area of dogma, evangelicals radically reject traditional Christian reliance on the modes of Holy Tradition including patristic teachings, canon law, the lives of the saints, liturgics, iconography and the sacred arts, and the Creed in order to adhere exclusively to the authority of Scripture. In the area of spiritual life, evangelicals radically reject traditional Christian emphasis on the holy mysteries, ascetical practices, and liturgical centricity in order to embrace and reproduce an individualistic and revivalist understanding of conversion (the "born-again" experience) detached with a Gnostic[321] zeal from any sacrament.

Beyond sharing these common renunciations, evangelicals express the thin lineaments of their common faith with a dizzying array of worship styles, Bible translations, governance structures, and ever-revised statements of faith. In general, they also share an aversion to anything traditional, have no culture of the sacred arts, and share an a-historical

---

[321] Gnostic forms of religion have as one of their primary characteristics a disdain for the spiritual potentiality of physical things. Gnosticism is expressed in many forms of Evangelical Christianity by the latter's rejection of the normative bestowal of grace through sacraments. For more on the appearance of gnosticism in modern Protestantism see Philip Lee (1993) *Against the Protestant Gnostics.*

approach to Christian history in which anything that is not recent is unimportant. Evangelicalism is a populist religion, and as such, being disconnected from tradition, casts itself in whatever forms are acceptable to the populace. To justify the cult of novelty as it is expressed in evangelical worship, many evangelicals simply believe that God has given no clear direction about worship form to His people and thus has left them free to innovate.[322] Evangelicals ought to be praised for avoiding in general the mainline Protestant collapse into secular theological liberalism, and for their fervent attachment to many teachings of the One, Holy, Catholic, and Apostolic Church, including such dogmatic pillars as the deity of Jesus Christ and the infallibility of Scripture. However, evangelicalism is no stronghold itself of traditional Christian theology. It floats naively in an ocean of theological relativity with no secure anchor, having cut its connection to Holy Tradition. As a result, many of its leaders fall in and out of heresies, and during their ministries alter theological course. Examples of such well-respected and powerhouse evangelical leaders who have at one time or another advocated very serious Trinitarian heresies are Pastors John McArthur,[323] T. D.

---

[322] Orthodox Christians point out that the Lord God appears to be especially interested in clearly guiding His people as regards His own worship. Significant portions of the Scriptures are entirely dedicated to the subject of worship form and content. See Ex. 25-40, Lev. 1-7, 1 Cor. 14, Rev., etc.

[323] John MacArthur is the pastor of the Grace Community Church (Sun Valley, CA) and one of the most respected pastor-teachers in American evangelicalism. He has started and presides over the Master's College and Seminary, and disciples thousands of pastors globally. His theology has changed over the years of his ministry, which is a characteristic of many in

Jakes,[324] Chuck Smith,[325] and Benny Hinn.[326] They themselves represent a wide-array of white and fundamentalist,
black and evangelical, and Pentecostal evangelicals. The
truth is, evangelicalism is permeated by theological chaos.

the evangelical movement since the movement is not anchored to sacred
tradition. MacArthur at one time formally taught Trinitarian heresy in the
first edition of his *Commentary on Galatians* in which he affirmed that Jesus
is not the "co-eternal" Son of God, but became the Son of God in time (a
form of adoptionism).

[324] T. D. Jakes is an African-American Pentecostal, and pastor of The Potter's House of Dallas. He does not subscribe to the traditional doctrine of
the Holy Trinity, but is a modalist.

[325] Chuck Smith is the founder of the Calvary Chapel movement, and pastor of the flagship church of the movement in Costa Mesa, CA. The Calvary
churches have as large a backdoor as they do a front door, and many of their
one-time parishioners have become ardent critics. The internet is replete
with documentation from former Calvary members who are exposing the
various heresies articulated by a wide array of Calvary pastors. Chuck Smith
himself has preached many heresies, involving such matters as the nature of
the Incarnation and the resurrection body.

[326] Pastor Benny Hinn is a very popular television evangelist and Pentecostal preacher. Hinn was born and raised in Jaffa, Israel, as an Orthodox
Christian. He immigrated with his parents to Toronto, Canada, where he
left the Orthodox faith and became a Pentecostal. Hinn moved to the USA,
and founded the Orlando Christian Center in Orlando, Florida, where he
began his "miracle crusades." In 1999, Hinn left Florida, and moved his
family to Orange County, CA. Sadly, after relocating to southern California Hinn's wife filed for divorce. While in Orlando he published a book
in which he argued that there was a Trinity of persons within each of the
persons of the Trinity. I was a seminarian at that time in Orlando, Florida,
and my systematic theology professor, Dr. R. C. Sproul, sent Pastor Hinn a
letter to inform him that he was preaching Trinitarian heresy. According to
Sproul, Pastor Hinn was apologetic and promised to make the change in the
next edition of his book. Besides his theological heresy, Hinn has, like many
in the "word of faith" movement, made many unfulfilled prophecies.

# 10

# *An Orthodox Appreciation of Protestant Virtues*

In previous chapters we have surveyed the major personalities and teachings of the principal branches of Protestantism: Lutheran, Reformed, Anglican, and Anabaptist. In these chapters we have sought to establish the historical context in which the Reformation took place, because the Reformation was not simply a theological revolution, but also a movement inextricably tied to politics, power, and technology such as the printing press,[327] without which it would never have flowered into an abiding 500-year Western schism and a distinct group of churches. We have also attempted to survey the essential Roman Catholic response to the Protestant Reformation as the Latin Church sought to offer articulate refutations of the major Protestant assertions. Lastly, we have also made an effort to note the interaction of the Orthodox East with the major Protestant Reformers and their theological heirs, from the 100-year correspondence between the Lutheran theologians of Tübingen and the Ecumenical Patriarch, to the intrigues

---

[327] The oldest surviving datable printed book is from 1457 and is a Latin edition of the Book of Psalms. MacCulloch (2003), p. 73.

surrounding Patriarch Cyril Lucaris and the Calvinists, to the 17th century unified Orthodox refutation of Protestantism in general, and Calvinism in particular, known as the Council of Jerusalem (1672) and its *Confession of Dositheos.*

In these concluding chapters a more elaborate and indepth Orthodox critique of the major tenets of the Protestant faith will be proffered. Before launching this exercise in Orthodox apologetics, however, which must by necessity be highly critical, I would like to share with you an exercise that I require my catechumens to perform in the catechetical program that seekers are asked to engage in. I pass out to our catechumens a form entitled *Affirmations and Renunciations.* What follows is a description of that exercise.

> **Exercise:** Divide a piece of paper into two columns. Title the left-hand column *Orthodox Beliefs* and the right-hand column *Heresies / Errors.* In the column on the left write down the doctrines of your former confession which are Orthodox. In the column on the right write down the doctrines of your former confession which are heretical. Be thorough. Part of the formal process of conversion is clearly identifying the heresies of one's previous confession and renouncing them. Heresy is from the devil, and all Christians are called upon by God to hate with righteous hatred all heresy. Having identified your heresies you will be asked by the

priest who is catechizing and receiving you into the Orthodox Church to renounce these heresies and to affirm Orthodox teachings. In some traditions this formal renunciation takes place at the beginning of the service of the reception of converts.

At the same time it is of the utmost importance for converts to realize that wherever truth is found, its author is God Himself. In virtually all religious traditions there are true beliefs and practices, and in some there are many. In the process of conversion the catechumen should also be able to identify and appreciate the Orthodox elements of his previous confession and be genuinely thankful for them. It is very important to avoid a critical and negative spirit.

The intention of this catechetical exercise is two-fold. First it raises the issue of heresy to the proper intensity. Heresy is not to be played with, and it certainly does not save. Christ, Incarnate Truth, saves. The theological divisions that afflict Christendom are extremely serious, and are not to be swept under the rug by naïve theological peaceniks who assume that, just because they do not understand theology, it therefore must be unimportant. Some catechumens are tempted to interpret their conversion to Holy Orthodoxy as a mere denominational switch, and not what it is: a conversion from heresy to orthodoxy.

On the other hand, this catechetical exercise guides the person in process of conversion to a deep appreciation of the good of their previous confession. Whether the convert approaches the Orthodox Church from Roman Catholicism, Protestantism, Judaism, Islam, or Buddhism, there are precious truths which have been bequeathed to the convert from his previous tradition. These truths should be loved, and those who communicated these truths to the catechumen should be sincerely thanked and appreciated. Many converts to Holy Orthodoxy come to the Church with a sincere and deep belief in the Holy Trinity, with the knowledge that all creation is the magnificent work of the Almighty, the Creator of heaven and earth, with belief in the divinity of Jesus Christ and indeed with a confidence in most of the teaching of the Nicene Creed, having read and studied the 27 books of the New Testament and with an unshakeable conviction in the truth of Holy Scripture, with an appreciation and practice of repentance and faith, with a confidence in the promise of the Second Coming of Jesus Christ to the earth and the Great Judgment, with a love for the church of Jesus Christ as they understand it, and in conviction of many more eternal truths. Besides these convictions that so many converts bring with them as they approach the One, Holy, Catholic and Apostolic Church, the Orthodox Church, they also often bring a life of cultivated virtues: notable among these virtues is a commitment to worship and church attendance. In fact, many of our converts have decades of spiritual life in which they attended church Sunday morning, often Sunday evening, and on Wednesday evenings. Besides church attendance, many converts bring with them a generosity that leads them to tithe religiously to their new parish, to pray daily and seek to deepen their personal devotion and relationship to God, a willingness to obey and listen to their pastor, a desire to promote the Christian faith and support the missionary enterprises of their community, and a hearty American optimism about what a single parish can do for God on its own by pulling up its own bootstraps and rolling up its own sleeves.

When we prepare catechumens to make public renunciation of their heresies, we most certainly do not mean them to renounce these beautiful things. Most converts in our current milieu are not converting from heathen darkness and the darkness of idols. This is why our catechism is typically one year, rather than the three years on average that most Greeks and pagans converting to Christianity in the early centuries of the Church's missionary outreach endured in formal ecclesiastical instruction. Hence, we teach our catechumens to love and adore the truth and piety found in their previous confession, and not only not to renounce these things but to embrace them ever more fully and with more love and zeal than ever before as they embrace the fullness of the faith which is Orthodoxy.

We also teach them to recognize that this truth and piety existed in their previous confession as *borrowed capital*.

The truth which upholds the universe and cannot be conquered is the truth of the Holy Apostolic Orthodox Christian Church. The Protestant Reformers were not those who sacrificed all in order to defend the deity of Jesus Christ against the Arian heretics at the First Ecumenical Council and establish Christianity in the world. Rather, it was the Orthodox bishops, and indeed the entire flock of the Orthodox, who articulated the Christian faith, established the canon of Holy Scripture, evangelized the known world, and taught us by word and deed how to love God, pray, repent, and worship. These are simple historical facts. Take any Protestant Reformer you like Calvin, Luther, Zwingli, it matters not—pluck him up from his 16th century milieu, transport him back several centuries, place him in any locale in which the Church existed, and what would he be? He would be an Orthodox Christian or a heretic. Nothing else. Calvinism, Lutheranism, and the Anabaptism simply did not exist.

As a matter of fact, here is a fine question to put to any Protestant who insists on the necessity and virtue of his Protestantism: What kind of Christian would you have been if you had lived in 4th century Egypt, or 8th century Gaul, or 12th century Greece? Certainly not a Protestant since there were no Protestants. There were only Orthodox and heretics. Whether or not a Protestant has a priest, an altar,[328] or the holy mysteries now, he would most cer-

---

[328] Many Protestants have "altar calls" but, strangely, no altars.

tainly have had such if he was a Christian prior to the 16th century.

Hence, our *Affirmations and Renunciations* exercise is designed to create *balance* in a catechumen. Balance is not always in large supply in the often tumultuous lives of persons in the process of conversion, who have not just the devil but often family members and mentors in opposition to their catechism. We seek to nurture a deep appreciation for all those Orthodox teachings and tenets the catechumen was given in his previous confession, though given under another name and without due credit acknowledged, and at the same time to nurture a piercing aversion to all heresy.

### *The Virtues of Protestantism*

Besides the remnants of Orthodoxy that exist, often abundantly, in Protestantism itself that we Orthodox ought to love and cherish, I also suggest that we American Orthodox have benefited from and ought to appreciate the virtues and accomplishments of Protestantism that exist in our land. Inasmuch as America can still be understood as a Christian nation, we owe much of this Christian identity to the seventy million Protestants of our land, and to their forefathers in the faith.

The Protestant faith has historically placed an exceedingly *high value upon the text of Holy Scripture*, and we are all the better for it. Of course, there are negatives we could follow up with immediately as we articulate each of these

Protestant virtues, such as the fact that Protestants have also led the way in so-called higher-critical studies of the Scripture which have decimated its authority in the West. But rather than elaborating the existent negatives associated with each of the virtues I now articulate, I am choosing simply to make a positive list, and first on my list is the Protestant commitment to the value and importance of Holy Scripture in the life of the individual, church, and nation. Protestants in America have, until quite recently when Chinese publishers became predominant,[329] consistently published more Bibles for sale than anyone else. The Anglican Reformer, Thomas Cranmer, was right to quote extensively from the great Orthodox saint and hierarch John Chrysostom, while he was writing his introduction to the Great Bible of 1540, in which he argued so vociferously for the importance of daily Bible reading in the Christian's life. This is Orthodox teaching, though often ignored by Orthodox believers. I am certain that I would be no Christian at all were it not for having a copy of the Holy Scriptures in my possession. I read the Scriptures in three English versions: the King James Version (KJV), the Revised Standard Version (RSV), and the New American Standard (NASB) version. All three versions are Protestant accomplishments. I read the original Greek New Testament in a United Bible Society version, edited by esteemed Protestant scholars in-

---

[329] Out-sourcing to Chinese publishers is being done, however, mostly by Protestant businesses.

cluding the late Bruce Metzger. I read the original Greek Old Testament, the Septuagint, in a German edition edited by a famous German Protestant scholar. Even the English Altar Gospel used in many Orthodox dioceses in America is a slightly amended RSV. Besides providing us with the best English and critical edition texts of the original languages, Protestant scholars also teach the exegesis of the Bible at Protestant institutes of higher learning throughout our land. I remain deeply indebted to my Protestant professors of Old and New Testament in both college and seminary. Even the recent scholarly effort to gather together in English an anthology of patristic commentary on the entire Bible in the *Ancient Christian Commentary* series has been spearheaded by and has as its general editor a Protestant theologian.

Another virtue of Protestants is *zeal for missionary work*, and the commitment to preach the Gospel to all human beings, and especially to those who have never had the opportunity to become Christians. This has not always been a strength of Protestants. In the first two hundred years of Protestantism, Protestants themselves were too busy fighting for their very existence against Roman Catholicism and seeking to establish their self-identity to invest significantly in missions.[330] Today it is common for Protestant young people to engage in summer and short-term mission trips

---

[330] During the early Reformation centuries it was the Roman Church that was zealously promoting Christian missions in America and Asia using the

that expose them to the needs of the world and foster a larger Christian vision than that of the local parish alone. Many Protestants choose missionary work as an honorable calling, and are sent by and supported by mission boards and local churches. It is common for Protestant churches to support many missionaries financially every year. This engagement of the non-Christian with the Gospel is not just a commitment to overseas missions but to domestic missions as well. Efforts at neighborhood evangelism, vacation Bible schools, and evangelistic crusades all bear witness to the Protestant thirst for evangelizing the man on the street, and furthering the influence of Christian truth in American life. This missionary emphasis also nurtures the ability of Protestant Christians to articulate concisely to others what Jesus Christ has done for them, what they call "giving a testimony."

Another virtue found among Protestants is a *deep and costly commitment to Christian education*. America is now scattered with Protestant day schools that are educating millions of America's youth as an alternative to the secularized state school system. Protestant schools are doing on a comparable scale today, what Catholic schools were doing in the first half of the 20th century: reaching the youth with an education that includes faith. This commitment reaches past secondary education into university life. Private, lib-

Spanish and Portuguese empires and their tools. MacCulloch (2003), p. 427.

eral arts universities and colleges associated with Protestantism have never been so influential in our land as they are today. In our city of Riverside, two of the three major universities are private and Protestant. In the United States alone there are several hundred colleges and universities affiliated with the Protestant Churches. For example, the Presbyterian Church USA has 2.2 million members, and has 63 colleges and universities, including large universities like the University of Tulsa and prestigious small colleges like Davidson and Macalester, both included by *Newsweek* in their list of 25 "New Ivies."[331] This commitment to higher learning is a traditional Protestant characteristic, which was transplanted to America in the early colonial period and led to the creation of the great Ivy League schools like Harvard and Yale, originally established as seminaries to train Protestant clergy.

Another virtue of Protestants is an *aggressive commitment to cultural engagement with Christian values*. This has not always been a steady commitment on the part of American Protestants, but it certainly characterizes the most dynamic and growing portions of Protestantism now. This engagement includes political lobbying and influence up to

---

[331] August 21, 2006. See the unpublished paper, "Higher Education and the Orthodox Tradition in America: A Prescriptive Consideration" presented June 3, 2009 at the conference, "Orthodox Christianity and the University," organized by the Orthodox Scholars Initiative (OSI) and sponsored by the Office of Vocation and Ministry (OVM) at Hellenic College in Brookline, MA.

the highest levels of the administration. Gone is the rhetoric of an eschatology that led to cultural abandonment, and powerfully present is an attitude of engagement and combat with secularism. Protestant organizations like *Focus on the Family,* the *Family Research Council,* and the *American Family Association* are locked in a cultural wrestling match with the secular elite and their activist foot soldiers. We Orthodox are most thankful for the manifold labors by Protestant Christians to influence our cultural mores with the teaching of Jesus Christ.

Besides the cultural witness for Christian values that many Protestants provide today, there is also the personal witness of many Protestant believers. Many Orthodox Christians have been deeply blessed and edified by the personal devotion to Jesus Christ of particular Evangelical Christians who have labored to love God and to acquire the Christian virtues. Many Evangelical believers have modeled a spirit of sacrifice, generosity, chastity and devotion to Jesus Christ, and this witness is deeply appreciated and revered by Orthodox Christians.

## *The False Teachings of Protestantism*

I could go on, but I think this is enough to understand that the Orthodox theological critique of Protestantism here found does not derive from blind prejudice, or a lack of appreciation of the virtues of Protestantism. I admire the virtues of Protestantism most sincerely and make myself its student in those areas where it is exceptional. However, these virtues do not validate the Protestant faith or justify heretical Protestant teachings. And Protestantism is certainly riddled with heresy. In what follows I will focus upon those tenets of Protestant faith common to virtually all Protestants, and not erroneous teachings that are particular to certain branches of Protestantism.

For pedagogical purposes, I will categorize the major Protestant heresies under the following four thematic heads: authority, theology proper (doctrine of God), soteriology (doctrine of salvation), and ecclesiology (doctrine of the Church).

### The Heresy of 'Sola scriptura'

The first principle of Protestantism, universally embraced by the main branches of Protestantism, is the principle of *sola scriptura. Sola scriptura,* "by scripture alone," is the doctrine that the Bible alone is the only infallible rule for faith and practice, and that the Bible alone contains all the knowledge that is necessary for salvation. From this fountain do the other major Protestant mistakes, errors, and heresies flow. The Protestant Reformers were convinced that their teaching and church practice were simply an expression of fidelity to the Word of God. They articulated in their confessions, as we have seen, the foundational tenet that all dogma must rest upon clear and explicit teaching of Scripture, and that anything not found in Scripture cannot itself be a matter of required belief for Christians. Orthodox Christians respond to this Protestant affirmation with a firm and steady anathema, and we do this for many reasons.

First and foremost is the fact that the Lord Jesus Christ and His Holy Apostles did not teach such a thing but explicitly rejected it in teaching and practice.

The *scriptura* itself does not teach that it is *sola*. Scripture is the foundational authority in the Church, being itself the very words of the living God, the inspired and infallible truth, quoted supremely by Councils and Holy Fathers to establish doctrine, and read in depth and explained in every Orthodox liturgy, and in every Orthodox home by prescription of the Fathers. It is just this traditional biblicism that has always led the Orthodox Church to reject the heresy of *sola scriptura*, for the Bible itself clearly teaches that it is not a stand-alone authority. Our problem with the Protestants is that on this point they are not biblical enough.

The New Testament itself affirms that the foundational authority for the Christian and the Church is the Apostles' teaching. "And they were continually devoting themselves to the apostles' teaching and to fellowship, and to the breaking of bread and to prayer."[332] The teaching of the Apostles is the teaching of Jesus Christ. It is impossible to receive Christ, to hear Christ, to obey Christ, or to follow Christ, if

---

[332] Acts 2:42.

The Synaxis of the Holy Apostles
*Image Courtesy of Uncut Mountain Icons*

one does not receive, hear, obey, and follow the Holy Apostles. They are literally Christ's ambassadors, beseeching the world, on behalf of Christ, to be reconciled to the Father.[333] The teaching of the Apostles is itself called 'tradition' in the New Testament. A word commonly used for this is the Greek word *paradosis* (παράδοσις) meaning teachings or commandments that are handed over or down. "Now we command you, brethren, in the name of our Lord Jesus Christ, that you keep aloof from every brother who leads an unruly life and not according to the tradition which you received from us" (2 Thess. 3:6). Tradition is the Christian way of life, or life in the Holy Spirit. Tradition is the Bible rightly interpreted. St. Paul praised the Corinthians for adhering to the Church's tradition, "Now I praise you because you remember me in everything, and hold firmly to the traditions, just as I delivered them to you."[334] Again St. Paul wrote to the Corinthians using the verbal form of the word 'tradition': "Now I traditioned/handed on to you as of first importance what I also received..."[335] Here is the heart of the Holy Tradition according to the Scriptures. The Christian faith was "once for all" delivered to the saints according to the Apostle Jude.[336] Christ delivered the faith to the Apostles, and the Apostles delivered the faith to the

---

[333] 2 Cor. 5:20.
[334] 1 Cor. 11:2.
[335] 1 Cor. 15:3.
[336] Jude 3.

Church. It is a passing of the baton of truth, each generation receiving the unchanging Christian faith from the previous generation as we all run the race set before us. This is why the Orthodox Church refers to the "teaching of the Holy Fathers" so often. This canon of faith, this touchstone of theological certainty we have called the consensus of the Fathers,[337] was common parlance in the Church from the 2nd century, expressing the universal Christian sense of being heirs of the pristine faith of our fathers. This is why theological innovation is so despised by the Church. Innovation is a break, an alteration, of this sacred passing on of truth. Truth does not need to be improved but preserved. Hence, we Orthodox conclude our services each day with these words, "Preserve, O God, the Holy Orthodox Faith and all Orthodox Christians unto ages of ages. Amen." *Preserve* O God—not *improve* O God.

St. Paul did not just teach the preservation of the traditions but he lived it. For instance, we are all no doubt familiar with that beautiful teaching of our Lord Jesus Christ, "It is more blessed to give than to receive," are we not? Where is this found in the Holy Gospels? The answer is that it is not found anywhere in the Holy Gospels. It is recorded in Acts 20:35 where St. Paul says, "In everything I showed you that by working hard in this manner you must help the weak and remember the words of the Lord Jesus, that He

---

[337] Also called the "mind of the Church."

Himself said, 'It is more blessed to give than to receive.'" How did St. Paul know that Jesus said this if it is not written in the Gospels? He knew because there existed more of Jesus' teaching than was recorded in writing in the canon, and that teaching was authoritative and remains so.

Apostolic Tradition, therefore, is the ultimate authority in the Church, the very touchstone of all truth, that by which all is judged. Holy Tradition is the umbrella under which truth is communicated to us by various means, chief of which is *written* Apostolic Tradition or what we call *the Holy Scriptures.* The Holy Scriptures are an expression of Apostolic Tradition, and are therefore not above tradition. The Bible is tradition, Holy Tradition. And this is an exaltation of the Bible, not a degradation. We Orthodox kiss the Bible every Sunday. We form a line in the temple and walk one-by-one up to venerate the sacred words of God. We do not dare move when it is read for we know that God is speaking to us.

Of course, there is such a thing, as our Savior has warned us, of unholy and man-made tradition which nullifies the very Word of God.[338] I would, in fact, argue that one of the clearest examples of *unholy tradition* is Protestantism itself, and especially the heretical teaching that the Bible alone is the authority of the Church. *Sola scriptura* is unholy and man-made tradition. One of the Apostolic traditions

---

[338] Matt. 15.

is that the Scriptures are to be read in and by the Church Herself in hermeneutical continuity with the Holy Fathers, with that which the Church teaches. This mindset would have saved Zwingli, and indeed all the Reformers, from outrageous interpretations.

Unholy tradition is tradition that is not of God, that is not apostolic, and neither Jesus nor His Apostles ever passed on to the Church the teaching that the Bible alone is the authority for Christians. The existence of the unholy tradition does not negate the existence of Apostolic or Holy Tradition. There are, in fact, according to the New Testament, two kinds of Tradition: Apostolic and Unholy or Man-Made. One must be embraced, the other rejected.

The teaching of the Apostles, what we know as Holy Tradition, is expressed in the Church in two forms: in oral form and in written form. There is oral Apostolic teaching and there is written Apostolic teaching, and both are equally authoritative. This is, of course, the express teaching of the Holy Apostles themselves. Listen to St. Paul in his 2nd Letter to the Thessalonians, "So then, brethren, stand firm and hold to the traditions which you were taught, whether by word of mouth or by letter from us."[339] Here you have St. Paul again using the word "tradition." St. Paul's spiritual children, the Christians of Thessalonica (still to this day a great beacon of Orthodox Christianity), were called upon

---

[339] 2 Thess. 2:15.

to stand firm and hold fast to tradition. This is the Christian's duty. We cannot be blown here and there by theological fads and innovations and still be faithful to God and the Apostles. We must stand firmly upon the traditions of the Church, says the Great Apostle. And he continues, "... whether by word of mouth or by letter from us." Here the Apostle teaches us how Apostolic Tradition comes in two forms: in an oral form and in a written form. The Protestant proponents of *sola scriptura* would have us believe that there is only one binding source of Apostolic authority: the written Scriptures. This is a direct contradiction to the Apostle Paul's teaching to the Thessalonians.

Imagine that you lived in Thessalonica in the first century and were converted to Christ under St. Paul's ministry. From the Apostle's own mouth you received hours of instruction, teaching, and moral guidance, and later from St. Timothy whom St. Paul sent back to Thessalonica to continue his Apostolic ministry. This Timothy was charged with the task of "traditioning" others when St. Paul wrote to him, "You therefore, my son, be strong in the grace that is in Christ Jesus. And the things which you have heard from me in the presence of many witnesses, these entrust to faithful men, who will able to teach others also."[340] According to St. Paul, St. Timothy had learned much from Paul's mouth, and was to pass on this oral teaching to other

---

[340] 2 Tim. 2:2.

The Holy Apostle Paul

Christian men who themselves were to pass it on. This is how oral Holy Tradition works. Now remember again that you are a Christian in Thessalonica, and you have received the Apostolic teaching and are living the Holy Tradition of the Church. Are we to suppose, as the *sola scriptura* theory would have it, that you were only to obey the Apostolic teachings and injunctions that St. Paul wrote down and not those that you heard from his own mouth? Are we to imagine that after the Holy Apostle's martyrdom in Rome (some 17 years after his initial evangelization of Thessalonica) the Christians in Thessalonica disregarded the oral Apostolic traditions and only followed what had been written down? Such conclusions are untenable.

Oral Apostolic Tradition is lived in the Church and evidences herself in universal customs such as the making of the Holy Cross, Baptism by triple immersion and emersion, prayer facing the East, and many more things. St. Basil the Great lists some of the content of oral tradition in a famous passage in his text *On the Holy Spirit*. The Church Herself is the guardian of the sacred deposit of all Apostolic Tradition.

In fact, Apostolic or Holy Tradition as expressed and maintained in the Holy Church is the authority of the Christian and of our pristine faith. The innovations of the scholastic papacy and the post-Schism Latin church fallen into heresy make the Protestant embrace of the *sola scrip-*

*tura* doctrine and its concomitant rejection of Holy Tradition more understandable but no more correct. We Orthodox Christians share many of the Protestant criticisms of the inauthentic traditions of the Roman Catholic Church, including such things as indulgences, papal supremacy, the poorly-named petrine theory of universal jurisdiction of the pope, purgatory, supererogation, mandatory priestly celibacy, the withholding of the chalice from the laity, etc. and *we even to the list add many additional charges* and criticisms of the papacy not advocated by Protestants themselves, including the rejection of the traditional form of Baptism, the use of unleavened bread, the *filioque* and the change of the Nicene Creed to posit this heresy, the change of the calendar and paschalion, the change of Apostolic fasting rules, the change in the making of the sign of the Cross, the practice of serving more than one liturgy on an altar on one day and the serving of the liturgy on weekdays in Lent, the practice of multiple ordinations at one time, the doctrine of the indelible mark of ordination,[341] etc.

---

[341] The Latin teaching on the indelible mark of ordination is that once a priest is ordained his priesthood cannot be expunged by an act of church discipline. This teaching is ably refuted by Orthodox saints such as Nicodemos of the Holy Mountain. Scouteris (2006), pp. 81-85. The doctrine of the indelible mark attained at ordination to the priesthood appears to have originated in the scholastic period of the Western church. This teaching divorces the priesthood from its organic context of the ecclesial life, and affirms that the ordained person possesses a self-sufficient power, higher than the Church.

Nevertheless, a rejection of abusive Latin customs formed as the Western church grew further distant from the patristic spirit and merged herself with kingdoms of this world, does not in any way logically lead to the rejection of authentic Holy Tradition and the embrace of *sola scriptura*. The Protestant Reformers threw the proverbial baby out with the bathwater. They rejected the innovations of the papacy by becoming still yet greater innovators. They rejected the pope and each Reformer made himself a pope,[342] and demonstrated great indignation at those Protestants who did not follow in theological lock-step. This is why we Orthodox, when asked if we are closer to Protestantism or to Roman Catholicism, have at times answered: Neither. One might consider the post-Schism popes to be the first Protestants. They set themselves up as infallible interpreters of the Bible, and Protestants ran with a version of the papal theory and applied it to every reader of the Bible. In many ways both Roman Catholicism and Protestantism are closer to each other than either is to Holy Orthodoxy. They often give diametrically opposite answers, but they are asking the same questions. Orthodox Christianity maintains the patristic mind, and asks different questions.

We also believe that the history of Protestantism, from its very root, bears witness to the lack of Apostolic authenticity of the *sola scriptura* doctrine. Why do Lutheran,

---

[342] The Swiss Reformed accused Luther of acting like a pope. Brecht (1987), p. 330.

Calvinistic, Zwinglian, and Anabaptist creeds all differ on fundamental points if the Bible alone is the only authority of the Reformers? Why could not Luther and Zwingli and the other Reformers agree on the nature of the very central act of Christian worship, the Holy Eucharist, if they were both simply reading the Bible and following its teachings? By cutting the cords of Holy Tradition, and placing in its stead the doctrine of *sola scriptura,* the Protestants ensured theological divisiveness and fracture between themselves and their descendants, and have only multiplied divisions, theories, and interpretations *ad infinitum,* with no end in view to this day. We may judge a tree by its fruit. The *sola scriptura* tree has borne the fruit of division and every conceivable heresy.

The Lord Cursing the Barren Fig Tree

# 11
## *The Heresies of Protestantism*

This critique of Protestantism is not borne from a disregard of Protestant virtues, or a negative or reactionary spirit. I deeply appreciate the Protestant roots of the American nation, and though no longer a Protestant, have lived most of my life in a Protestant milieu. I have been educated in Protestant schools of higher learning, and have worked with Protestants extensively in the pro-life, traditional marriage, and homeschooling movements. Protestant Christians exercise a tremendous positive influence in these places and through these movements. Most forms of Protestant faith have maintained a great amount of Orthodox dogma, though this is often maintained as borrowed capital, and its Orthodox provenance more often than not unacknowledged. Despite the many virtues of Protestants, the Protestant faith has at its core many tragic heresies which serve to demonstrate that Protestantism is not the "faith once delivered to the saints" but is a man-made tradition, despite all claims to being biblical.

As previously stated, for pedagogical purposes I have categorized the major Protestant heresies under the following four thematic heads: authority, theology proper (doctrine of God), soteriology (doctrine of salvation), and ecclesiology (doctrine of the Church). In the last chapter the Protestant doctrine of *sola scriptura* was examined, and it was demonstrated that this doctrine is in direct contradiction to Scripture itself, and is the source from which all other Protestant heresies flow. This is so because this dogma undermines the authority of Apostolic Tradition, and provides an apparent justification for abrogating universal Christian teaching by the claim of scriptural precedent. By theologically overreacting to papal tradition, the Reformers became authors of conflicting traditions themselves. By refusing the authority of the see of Peter, they established the sees of Geneva, Wittenberg, Strasbourg, and Canterbury as virtual centers of infallibility, and launched a divisive religious hermeneutic that has produced thousands of competing Protestant denominations, all in dogmatic conflict and all certain that their variant is the biblical one.

Here is continued an Orthodox critique of Protestant dogma under the headings of theology, soteriology, and ecclesiology. The categories are distinct, but they are all intimately interconnected.

### Heresies of Protestant Theology Proper

*The Filioque Heresy*

We Orthodox Christians wish most sincerely that the Protestant Reformers had protested against papal abuses in that area in which papal innovation was most grievous and scandalous: the *filioque* heresy. No action of the scholastic papacy was more offensive and a greater attack upon the conscience of the Church than the 11th century decision of the Pope to change the text of the Nicene Creed, to assert his authority over the Ecumenical Councils, and to make the heresy of the procession of the Holy Spirit from the Father *and the Son* (*filioque*) the official faith of the Roman Church.

St. Photios the Great, 9th century Patriarch of Constantinople, is the greatest Orthodox champion of the true faith against the heresy of the *filioque* and the arrogance of papal supremacy. The conflict over the *filioque*, however, preceded the life of St. Photios. *Filioque* is the Latin word meaning "and the Son," which in the West was promulgated by St. Augustine of Hippo. The teaching was meant to affirm that the Holy Spirit proceeded not only "from the Father" as our Lord Jesus Christ explicitly taught, but also "from the Son." In his 5th century work, *On the Trinity*, St. Augustine articulated the double procession of the Holy Spirit without patristic precedent. Though this was Augustine's opinion, it was not expressed in the Creed he confessed. The *filioque* doctrine was formally endorsed less than two decades after St. Augustine's death by a Synod in Toledo in 447. The doctrine was added to the third paragraph of the Nicene Creed at a Spanish council in the same city in 589.[343]

---

[343] Siecienski, p. 69.

Though without patristic support, Augustine's philosophical model of the Trinity passed into the Western Middle Ages as if there were no other theological paradigm.[344] In 633 and 653, two more synods at Toledo approved the recitation of the Creed with the *filioque*. With the help of a Western Creed falsely attributed to St. Athanasius the Great, this Augustinian teaching became firmly entrenched in Gaul. Alcuin of York (735-804) added the *filioque* to the Sacramentary of St. Gregory the Great. In the late 8th and early 9th century Charlemagne and the Franks embraced the *filioque*, and accused the Greeks of heresy for *removing* the *filioque* from the original Creed. This wrong-headed polemic was taken up by Thomas Aquinas in the 13th century, and continued as a standard Latin polemic against the Orthodox until about 100 years ago.[345]

From France the *filioque* heresy pressed into Germany, and German missionaries used the interpolated Creed in their efforts to evangelize the Bulgarians. Consequently, disputes erupted between the German missionaries and the Eastern missionaries, who rejected the interpolation as

---

[344] St. Augustine's works became a second canon in the West. It should be noted that St. Augustine was attempting to explain how the Spirit is the Spirit of the Son, and would be grieved at the thought that he was innovating and not following patristic precedent.

[345] For more on Aquinas' *Contra Errores Graecorum* and his evaluation of the *filioque* debate see Siecieski (2010), pp. 128-131. Aquinas was on his way to the reunion council at Lyons, carrying his *Against the Errors of the Greeks* text with him, when he died on March 7, 1274.

a heresy and as an illicit alteration of the Creed. In 808, the monks of the Monastery of St. Saba in the Holy Land violently protested the recitation of the *filioque* in the Creed at the Western Monastery on the Mount of Olives, where the Frankish monks adhered to the practices they had learned at the Royal Chapel in Aix which had been using the interpolated Creed since 796. Again in 808, Pope Leo III wrote a letter to these Western monks in which he forbade the interpolation, and he also wrote a letter to Charlemagne himself in which he denounced altering the Creed. Pope Leo III wrote in this letter that not even he himself, the Pope, "would presume equality with the authority of the Fathers" as the Frankish synod had presumed to do. Soon, such humility would become non-existent at the Vatican. Leo III also had the original Greek text of the Creed (which did not have the *filioque*) and a Latin translation inscribed on silver plaques and set up in St. Peter's in Rome.[346]

St. Photios, in an encyclical addressed to the other patriarchs in 866,[347] attacked both the doctrine of the double procession and the illegitimacy of the Pope altering the Creed, calling those bishops who taught the *filioque* "bishops of darkness." St. Photios asks,

---

[346] The best history of the filioque controversy is Siecienski's magisterial work (2010). Kolbaba (2008) is less comprehensive, but a significant work as well. Prior to these recent works the last significant treatment of the *filioque* controversy in English was Swete (1876).

[347] Pelikan and Hotchkiss (2003), *Creeds and Confessions*, Vol. 1, pp,. 298ff.

Who will not close his ears to the excess of
their blasphemy? This opposes the Gospels. It
resists the holy councils. It cancels the blessed
and holy fathers: the great Athanasius; Gregory preeminent in theology; the great Basil,
the royal robe of the church; John who is truly
called Chrysostom, the golden mouth of the
inhabited world, the sea of wisdom. But why do
I mention one or another? This blasphemous
and godless expression takes up arms against
all the holy prophets together, the apostles, the
hierarchs, the martyrs, the Lord's own words.[348]

In his retirement in 886, St. Photios wrote a lengthy refutation of the *filioque* heresy entitled *The Mystagogy of the
Holy Spirit*. In this treatise, St. Photios calls the doctrine a
heresy, and a noxious venom of impiety.

In time the papal legates of John VIII accepted the decrees of the Photian council of 879-80 in Constantinople
(attended by some 343 bishops) which stated, in agreement
with the Ecumenical Councils, that the Creed cannot be
altered in any way. All agreed to anathematize anyone tampering with the Creed. This Council of Constantinople of
879-880[349] formally anathematized the *filioque* doctrine as
heresy, and a new *Synodikon* for use on the Sunday of Or-

---

[348] *Ibid.*, p. 302.

[349] Many Orthodox teach that this council is to be numbered as the Eighth
Ecumenical Council.

St. Photios the Great

thodoxy was written to memorialize the condemnation of the *filioque* doctrine as heresy and so to protect future generations of Orthodox from this poison.[350]

Sadly, this papal reasonableness did not last. In 1009, the newly-elected Pope Sergius IV sent a letter to Constantinople which may have contained an affirmation of the *filioque* heresy. It is certain that at this time the Patriarch of Constantinople removed the Pope's name from the diptychs, a liturgical expression of a break in communion. Sometime in or around 1014 it is thought that the *filioque* was first used in Rome by directive of Pope Benedict VIII. When Pope Leo IX officially promoted the *filioque* in the Nicene Creed through his legate Cardinal Humbert of Silva in 1053, the East viewed this action as blasphemy.[351] This papal abuse was reaffirmed by the 13th century Council of Lyons and the 15th century Council of Ferrara-Florence. The *filioque* doctrine remains the faith of the Roman Catholic Church, and was codified with

---

[350] "Synodicon on the Holy Spirit," Archives De L'Orient Chretien, no. 16, ed. V. Laurent et J. Darrouzes, "Dossier Grec, De L'Union de Lyons (1273-74)," Institut Francais d'Etudes Byzantines (Paris, 1976).

[351] Siecienski, p. 113.

only one exception into all Protestant confessions of faith. Though very few Catholics and Protestants today have any idea what the *filioque* is or means, due to the extreme decrease of ecclesiastical knowledge in general, and to the replacement of a God-centered Trinitarian worship form with a man-centered entertainment service, still the *filioque* remains official Catholic and Protestant teaching and the greatest obstacle to union with the Orthodox Church and the traditional Christian faith.

Why is the *filioque* such a travesty? Why is it a diabolical and heretical attack upon the Lord God Himself? For many reasons. Chief among these reasons is that it nullifies the unique and personal characteristics of the Persons of the Holy Trinity. The unique hypostases of the Father, and of the Son, and of the Holy Spirit are expressed in Scripture and in the Creed by an affirmation that God is the Father, that Jesus is the Only-Begotten Son of the Father, and that the Holy Spirit proceeds from the Father. These personal characteristics are the sum of what we know about the Persons of the Holy Trinity, and define each Person's uniqueness. The Father is not the Son, but the Begetter of the Son. The Father is not the Spirit, but the origin from whom the Spirit proceeds. What the *filioque* heresy does is to make what is unique to the Father, His being the origin and sender of the Holy Spirit, common also with the Son, Jesus Christ. By affirming that the Holy Spirit proceeds from the Father and the Son, the advocates of the *filioque* denude the Father of His own unique personal characteristic. This heresy either divides the *hypostasis*[352] of the Father into two parts, or else the hypostasis of the Son becomes a part of the hypostasis of the Father.

Additionally, we Christians worship One God. We worship One God because there is One Father of us all, and the Father is the origin, source, and monarch of the Holy Trinity. In St. Paul's language, the Father is the *head* of Christ.[353] By affirming that the Holy Spirit proceeds from the Father and the Son, the promoters of the filioque make the Son a co-origin, a co-head of the Holy Spirit, and as such they strip the Father of His sole monarchy in the Trinity. This heresy also makes Jesus something that He is not: it makes Him both the Only-Begotten *and* the origin of the Holy Spirit. Not only does it attack the Person of the Father and the Son, but it subordinates the Holy Spirit to the Father and the Son by affirming that the Father and Son share in something together (i.e. being the co-origins of the Holy Spirit) from which the Spirit is excluded. The Father and the Son have a communion therefore, according to this heinous teaching, that the Holy Spirit does not share. What is

---

[352] The Greek term *hypostasis* (ὑπόστασις) was used in the mid-4th century as a synonym for *physis* (φύσις) or "nature." The Cappadocian Fathers, in their articulation of Trinitarian theology forged a redefinition of hypostasis to mean "person" as opposed to "nature." Hence, there is but one divine "nature" shared by each of the three "hypostases/persons" of the divinity.

[353] 1 Cor. 11:3.

The Hospitality of Abraham
*A Traditional Orthodox Icon of the Holy Trinity*

different about the Holy Spirit from the Father and the Son that something does not proceed from Him?[354] This again violates the unity of the Godhead, for it posits that the Persons of the Father and Son do not only share a common essence as they do with the Holy Spirit, but also something unique to their Persons that is not shared by the Holy Spirit (i.e. being co-origins of the Holy Spirit). As such the Holy Spirit is demoted to a lower rank than the Son, since the Son possesses not only the Father's nature/essence but also the property of His Person, which the Holy Spirit does not possess. The double procession cannot be reconciled with the patristic principle that that which is not common to all three Persons belongs exclusively to only one of the three Persons. The *filioque* attacks the very unity of the Godhead, and so Latins argue for the unity of the divine nature, or essence, as the basis of the unity of the Godhead.

The *filioque* doctrine also imposes St. Augustine's philosophical categories onto the Holy Trinity,[355] emasculates the Father's hypostasis, unbalances the Trinity, and depersonalizes the peculiar characteristics of the divine Persons.

The Orthodox Church considers the actions of the papacy concerning the *filioque* to be the greatest scandal of the Latins, involving both a damnable heresy and moral

---

[354] St. Photios the Great, Encyclical, p. 302.

[355] St. Augustine's theological ethos in this treatise is far more philosophical and speculative than comparable works on the Trinity in the Greek tradition of the time.

fratricide. It was the embrace of theological error, and by presumptuously altering the Creed, it was a sin against the unity of the Church itself. If there was something to be protested by Protestant Christians, it was certainly the embrace of the unscriptural and untraditional *filioque* doctrine and the papal arrogance of altering the Creed of the Church. Yet this greatest papal abuse was accepted by the Protestant Reformers, who reiterated and continue to reiterate the *filioque*.

### Heresies of Protestant Soteriology

Moving on from the Protestant doctrine of God, about which more could be said, let us turn our attention to the teaching of Protestantism on the subject of salvation. The great problem with Protestant teaching on salvation is its thorough-going reductionism. In the Holy Scripture and in the writings of the Holy Fathers salvation is a grand accomplishment with innumerable facets, a great and expansive deliverance of humanity from all its enemies: sin, condemnation, the wrath of God, the devil and his demons, the world, and ultimately death. In Protestant teaching and practice, salvation is essentially a deliverance from the wrath of God. This reductionism can be helpfully evaluated by two means.

First is the use of the word "saved." This word is found many times in the New Testament. It translates the Greek word *sozo* (σώζω), which is used in all three tenses in the

New Testament: past, present and future. Protestant soteriology is focused on salvation as a past act, accomplished
in response to the act of faith. Here the words of St. Paul
to the Ephesians are often quoted: "For by grace you have
been saved through faith." The definitive focus in Protestant soteriology is the calling upon the name of the Lord
by faith, which leads to the glorious exchange, in which the
sins of the sinner are imputed to Jesus Christ the Savior and
the righteousness of Jesus Christ is imputed to the believing
sinner. From this moment on the sinner has been radically
transferred from being under the wrath of God to being
under grace. Not all Protestant confessions agree on whether or not this salvation can be lost, but all these confessions,
sharing a perspective on salvation as winning a court room
declaration of pardon, produce a spiritual life that focuses
on the concept of salvation as past act. The great quest for
the Protestant is to make sure that one has been saved, and
then to help others "get saved."

Orthodox Christians acknowledge the immense importance of the act of faith, and of the need to be saved. We categorically deny, however, that one is saved by faith *alone*.[356]

---

[356] The 2nd chapter of the Epistle of St. James explicitly affirms that we are
not saved by faith alone. Luther's importation of the word "alone" into his
German translation of Romans 3:28 where the word does not exist in the
Greek original is yet another Protestant abuse of New Testament translation. Brecht (1987), p. 108. Luther affirmed that his doctrine of justification
by faith alone is the article "on which the church stands or falls." *Ibid.*, p.
180.

We also share the earnest desire that others "get saved" as well. However, we understand this differently. We associate the definitive moment of salvation with holy Baptism. There, in the Baptism, is one forgiven, washed, cleansed, incorporated into the Church, united to Christ, and made a Holy Temple indwelt by the Holy Spirit. As emphasized as this past event is, Orthodox Christians are very much aware that salvation is a process as much as it is a definitive act. We are saved by faith when we are baptized, for sure. However, the New Testament uses the word *sozo* also in the present and future tenses. In fact, the most common use of the word *sozo* in the New Testament is the future, not the past. Hence, to be "biblical" we must consider salvation to be primarily, not exclusively, a future reality.

As a result, the Orthodox teaching is that we are saved by faith when we are baptized, and we are being saved as we draw near to God and walk in the commandments of Christ, and we will be saved when Jesus Christ returns in glory to judge the world. Hence, an Orthodox Christian might confidently affirm that he has been saved, and at the same time labors to be saved. In the language of the New Testament, the Christian is in the process of being saved: "For the word of the Cross is folly to those who are perishing, but to us who are being saved it is the power of God."[357] St. Paul writes, "Work out your salvation with fear

---

[357] 1 Cor. 1:18.

and trembling."[358] In most Protestant theology, to fear and tremble about salvation is a sign of a lack of faith, but for Orthodox to fear and tremble about salvation is a sign of great faith and apostolic obedience, for we are commanded to fear and tremble. Why? Because we know that salvation is a present work, and a dynamic and synergistic work that involves not just God's power and grace but also our own human wills holding fast to the word of truth so that we do not become Judases. Until our Lord Jesus returns in glory with all His holy angels in flaming fire and rendering recompense, we are fighting a great war against mortal enemies that are trying to kill us and ruin our salvation. We have many enemies to be saved from in the present: the Evil One and his demons, our passions, and death itself which wants to swallow us. Certainly our Savior has triumphed over all of our enemies definitively in His Cross and Passion. He has bound the Evil One. He has atoned for our sins, and given us the Mysteries and His Spirit to mortify our passions and desires. He has crushed death. However, our participation in His victory is not complete or final in Baptism. Jesus has saved us, is saving us, and will save and deliver us from the wrath to come,[359] unless we ruin ourselves.

Salvation is not just a matter of the past or a courtroom declaration of forgiveness. Salvation is much more than forgiveness. Forgiveness is at its heart, but salvation

---

[358] Phil. 2:12.
[359] 1 Thess. 1:10.

involves much more than forgiveness. We have real and tangible present enemies from which we need to be saved. In Protestant theology the focus is reduced to being saved from God Himself by taking refuge in God. Once a Protestant has believed and been justified there is not much left to fear, especially if one attains to the inner witness of the Holy Spirit through which one gains assurance that he is of the elect, and that he will be saved in the future. We believe this teaching leads to great overconfidence, a lack of ascetic discipline, and sinful presumption about intimacy with God and future salvation. In contrast to these Protestant presumptions, hear the words of the Apostle Paul as he describes his thoughts about his own salvation: "Do you not know that in a race all the runners compete, but only one receives the prize? So run that you may obtain it...I do not run aimlessly, I do not box as one beating the air; but I pommel my body and make it my slave, lest after preaching to others I myself should be disqualified."[360] Disqualification was considered a possibility by the Apostle. He knew, even though he had been so dramatically saved by Christ, that he still had enemies including his own fallen body and its lusts. So he sought to make his body his slave, rather than having his body make him its slave. He ran, he boxed, he engaged in the spiritual disciplines so that he might be saved.

With the New Testament, our focus is on our *hope to be saved* in the future. Listen to the words of the Holy Apostle

---

[360]  1 Cor. 9:24, 26-27.

Paul, "Since we are now justified by His blood, much more shall we be saved by Him from the wrath of God. For if while we were enemies we were reconciled to God by the death of His Son, much more, now that we are reconciled, shall we be saved by His life" (Romans 5:9-10). Here we see that our hope is to be saved at the Second Coming of our Lord. Toward this day we strive each day to grow, to repent, to seek God's face, to reduce the chasm between us and Him, and to eliminate prayerlessness and all manner of life without communion with Him. This understanding of salvation as a present work is why the Orthodox tradition has such an emphasis upon spiritual life, asceticism, and prayer. It is why we have a *Philokalia*[361] and Protestantism does not. It is why most of the writings of the Holy Fathers are devoted to the subject of holiness and the acquisition of the Holy Spirit. It is why we have a 2000-year history of

---

[361] Philokalia is a Greek word meaning "love of the beautiful." As early as the 4th century it was used to describe a type of literary genre in which precious passages of a particular writer were excerpted and published in a devotional collection. Ss. Gregory the Theologian and Basil the Great had a philokalia of Origen's writings *sans* heresies. The Philokalia, as is known today in the Orthodox Church, is a dearly-loved and much read collection of patristic texts on the spiritual life written by various masters of the spiritual life between the 4th and 15th centuries. These texts were published together in Venice in the 18th century by Ss. Nicodemos the Hagiorite and Makarios of Corinth, and since have been published in Russian (by St. Theophan the Recluse), modern Greek, Romanian, Finnish, French and English editions. Apart from the Holy Scriptures themselves no book has had the influence upon the Orthodox Church in the last several centuries that the Philokalia has had.

saints who have arisen above the demands of the earth, and Protestantism does not.

Take, for instance, the Reformed Protestant doctrine of atonement as expressed in the Westminster Confession of Faith: "Christ, by his obedience and death, did fully discharge the debt of all those that are thus justified, and did make a proper, real, and full satisfaction to his Father's justice in their behalf."[362] Here we see the usual Protestant reductionism applied to the Cross of our Savior. The traditional Christian teaching expressed in the New Testament and in the writings of the Fathers on the subject of the atonement of our Savior is that the Cross saved us in three essential ways: on the Cross Jesus conquered death; on the Cross Jesus triumphed over the principalities and powers of this evil age; on the Cross Jesus made atonement for human sins by His blood. Because the Protestants were working out of a soteriological framework of a courtroom and declarative justification, they read the teaching about the Cross through these lenses and as a result articulated a reductionistic theology of the atonement, which ignored the traditional emphases on the conquering of death and the triumph over the demons. Everything for Protestantism becomes satisfaction of God's justice, and by making one image the whole, even that image became distorted in Protestant articulation.

---

[362] Westminster Confession of Faith, VIII.5.

The Crucifixion of our Lord

Besides the reductionism found in Protestant notions of salvation as forgiveness and the atonement, the greatest reductionism is found in the immense neglect of emphasis upon the heart of the New Testament teaching on salvation as union with Jesus Christ, or what Orthodox theology calls theosis or deification. The theology of the Church bears witness to the fact that the mystery of salvation is accomplished not just on the Cross, but from the very moment of Incarnation when the Only-Begotten and Co-Eternal Son united Himself forever with humanity in the womb of the Virgin Mary, His Most Pure Mother. Salvation as union and communion between God and Man drips from every page of the New Testament and in the writings of Holy Fathers. This is why the phrase "in Christ" is St. Paul's fundamental image of salvation and Christian life.

Protestants do not understand the patristic emphasis so beautifully expressed by St. Athanasius the Great, "God became man, so that man might become God." Or the patristic dictum: "All that God is by nature, man can become by grace." For the traditional Christian this is no quest to become the fourth person of the Holy Trinity. It is not an expectation to cease being a creature or negate the Creator-creature distinction. This is a quest to be united by grace to the living God in a mystical transformation expressed by the Holy Transfiguration of our Savior on Mt. Tabor where, due to the union of divinity and humanity, hypostatically bound in the One Person of Jesus Christ, the uncreated divine light shone in and through human flesh. In St. John's words, "Beloved, now we are children of God, and it has not appeared as yet what we shall be. We know that, when He appears, we shall be like Him, because we shall see Him as He is."[363] This coming transfiguration of believers, this glorious resurrection and divinization of human nature in the unspeakable bliss of union with God, this shining as the stars in the Kingdom of His Father as our Savior puts it in his parabolic teachings, is the future of believers. It is hardly just forgiveness.

The tragic reductionism of Protestant concepts of salvation has produced a very serious neglect of theosis, and has led to the serious error of objectifying fallen human life and its limitations and projecting it into the future. It has kept Protestants from understanding the potential of human transformation in this life. The Protestant tradition has no saints. This reductionism has kept them from the natural embrace of saints in Paradise and from an active communion with them. In the Protestant conception of salvation, there is no ability for those in Paradise to transcend fallen human norms of communication and existence so as to maintain a personal communion with Christians on earth. The tradition of the Orthodox Church points out that life in the Spirit, deified life, transcends the fallen boundaries

---

[363] I Jn. 3:2.

that define our current existence. Such life was manifested in the Prophets of old who transcended fallen human limitations as types of redeemed men. The Holy Prophet Moses the God-Seer had his countenance transfigured in uncreated light by communion with God.[364] The Prophet

St. John writing the Ladder of Divine Ascent

---

[364] Ex. 34:29.

Elisha was able to hear and see what the King of Aram in Syria was strategizing in his war rooms, which were many miles away.[365] The saints of God, who dwell in union with Him in heaven, are not bound by fallen human limitations. They are, according to the Scriptures, able to know and are deeply concerned about what concerns the Church militant.[366]

### Protestant Heresies of Ecclesiology

Having examined the heresies of Protestantism regarding authority, the doctrine of God, and the subject of salvation, let us finish our critique with a summary of Protestant errors concerning the doctrine of the Church and her sacraments. At the heart of the Protestant errors on this subject is a deficient definition of the Church itself. This novel understanding, in which the Church is defined as that body of Christians where the Word of God is rightly preached and the sacraments are rightly administered, was a major break with both the New Testament and traditional Christian teaching on the Church.

The Nicene Creed[367] is the statement of the Christian faith. It expresses what must be believed by someone to claim to be a Christian. Its tenets are those that have been

---

[365] 2 Kings 6:12.

[366] Rev. 6:9-11.

[367] The Nicene Creed is called by the Church the "Symbol of Faith of Nicea."

universally embraced by Christians. Having said this, it is important to remember that the Creed has four paragraphs: the first devoted to the Father, the second to the Son, the third to the Holy Spirit, and the fourth to the Church. Ecclesiology therefore is not a matter of personal opinions, or an area where Christians can think and conceive of the Church however they wish. The Creed reads, "I believe in one, holy, catholic and apostolic church. I believe in one baptism for the remission of sins. I look for the Resurrection of the dead and the life of the world to come. Amen." Protestants may formally affirm belief in the Nicene Creed, but no Protestant maintains a belief in the fourth paragraph of the Nicene Creed in a traditional way, or in a way intended by the Holy Fathers who wrote the Creed.

This is so in two fundamental areas. First is the fact that the Protestant Reformers denied the four characteristics or marks of the Church articulated in the Creed and substituted their own marks. The true Church is One, Holy, Catholic, and Apostolic. Protestantism is anything but one. It began as a fractured and splintered protest movement, and over time has only grown in its divisive nature. Protestantism has denied the God-given means of maintaining unity and oneness. Formally denying the four marks of the Church, and bearing no evidence of having these marks itself, Protestantism has been judged by Holy Orthodoxy to be a religious movement *outside of the Church.*

This Orthodox affirmation that Protestant churches are not authentic churches but man-made religious bodies is often very difficult for Protestant Christians to hear because it sounds to them as though we Orthodox Christians are being triumphalistic or arrogant, and perhaps that we are condemning them as being non-Christians or living in total darkness. Such is not the case. We have previously affirmed that Protestantism maintains many Orthodox teachings. We are simply making an ecclesiological affirmation. We know where the Church is and is not. The Church is a historical body and has been on the earth for thousands of years. One need simply ask this question of one's Christian community: "Who founded my church?" If the answer is someone whose name is not Peter, Paul, Andrew, James, John, Philip, Bartholomew, Thomas, Matthew, James, Thaddaeus, Simon the Zealot, or Matthias, then be assured you are not in the One, Holy, Catholic, and Apostolic Church.

Ecclesiological exclusivity is not just an Orthodox reality but a Protestant one, and has always been so. The Protestant Reformers almost universally rejected the Roman Church as being the authentic Church, calling its churches synagogues of Satan and often calling the pope the Antichrist. Even Protestant Churches today practice such ecclesiological exclusivity. Protestants do not allow just any group to claim that it is the Church of Jesus Christ. For a group to do that it must bear the marks of the Church as defined by Protestantism. Protestant exclusivity is demonstrated in a particularly grievous way by the Evangelical Protestant missionizing of Orthodox lands. Ignoring, in many cases, the fact that Orthodox Christianity has existed in the East for thousands of years, many Protestant sects have poured into Eastern Europe after the fall of communism, seeking to convert not just atheists but Orthodox Christians to their forms of Protestantism. This includes often re-baptizing Orthodox Christians.

Protestants manifest their exclusivity by also judging many Protestant sects outside acceptability. The Mormon Church is typically judged to be an inauthentic church by Protestants in general. Protestants point out that Mormons do not maintain fundamental Christian teachings about God and Christ that are essential to a true Christian confession. We Orthodox Christians agree with Protestants on this evaluation of Mormonism, and would simply point out that on the same basis we judge Protestantism itself to be inauthentic. Why must Mormons maintain a belief in the first three paragraphs of the Creed to be Christian, but the Protestants can reject the fourth paragraph of the Creed with impunity? Essential Christian teaching, required to be a member of the Church, involves not just an affirmation of the teaching on the Father, Son and Holy Spirit, but also on the Church as expressed in the fourth paragraph of the Creed.

Protestantism is neither one, nor holy (for it is without saints), nor catholic, nor apostolic. Many Protestants today hold to the "invisible church" theory, which we believe to be aptly named since it does not exist. This theory affirms that individuals become members of the Body of Christ simply by "receiving Jesus into their hearts" or "praying the sinner's prayer" as an act of faith, without any association whatsoever with a concrete church community, a clergyman, or sacraments. Common Protestant teaching on the sacraments is gnostic at its core, denying that the grace of God is communicated in and through the mysteries. This is why most Protestants are unable to affirm the words of the Creed "I confess one baptism for the remission of sins." The affirmation that remission of sins comes through the grace of God *in the water of baptism* is too much for them. Protestantism has rejected most of the traditional mysteries, and formally rejected the sacrament of priesthood itself upon which lies the power and authority to effect all the sacraments. Protestantism is not apostolic in that it has *on principle* rejected apostolic succession, refusing to be governed by bishops and synods, and refusing to maintain the apostolic faith. Protestantism has rejected the canons of the Church and its conciliar definitions. It has rejected iconography in practice, and some denominations are explicitly iconoclastic. It has abandoned sacred architecture and traditional ecclesiastical music. It has rejected monasticism, and offers no sanctified path for any but the married. It has rejected the traditional fasts of the Church. We could continue at great length.

Our examination of the heresies of Protestantism is in no way exhaustive, but is meant to be a general examination of the major errors of the Protestant faith. The critique is offered in love, and with high esteem for many Protestant Christians. The anathema of the Orthodox Church is not offered casually or from rancor or contempt. It is a *charitable anathema.* The apostolic anathema against heresy is an act of love promulgated to guard and protect human beings from soul-destroying heresies. Heresy does not save. Jesus Christ, the Truth Incarnate, saves. To live in the truth is to live in Christ Himself, and every heresy works to separate the believer in the heresy from Jesus Christ. St. Paul calls heresy the "doctrine of demons."[368] May the Almighty God keep us all from such demonic doctrines, and guard us all in the unity of the faith which was once for all delivered to the saints.

## Conclusion

In the preceding chapters an account has been provided of the history of the Protestant Reformation and the theological tenets of its major proponents. We have examined the lives and theological legacies of Martin Luther, Ulrich Zwingli, John Calvin, and Thomas Cranmer, amongst oth-

---

[368] 1 Tim. 4:1.

ers. These weighty historical figures established abiding templates of Protestant religious conviction that were adhered to for centuries.

I seriously doubt that any of these towering figures would be comfortable in any of the religious options available today on the Protestant smorgasbord. Nor is it certain that these "Reformers" would recognize contemporary Protestants or evangelicals as their legitimate spiritual offspring. Protestantism exploded onto history like a theological volcanic eruption, and has been unable to control, in any cohesive way, the new hermeneutic of individualistic authority it established in its efforts to shake off papal dominance. Protestantism has been a runaway theological train from the beginning.

Nevertheless, it has demonstrated immense elasticity and stamina. It has morphed and reinvented itself time and time again over the last five hundred years, more or less while appealing to scriptural authority and the individual's spiritual experience unfettered by sacred Tradition. Some of these metamorphoses have been closer to Holy Orthodoxy than others, but none of them are any substitute for a confession of the faith "once delivered to the saints."[369] It is hoped by a study of the preceding pages that the reader has come to see that the Latin-Protestant conflict was not a conflict involving the entire Christian world, but rath-

---

[369] Jude 3.

er a Western conflict precipitated by papal deviance from traditional Orthodox Christian norms. Regardless of the heat of Western devotion and missionary enterprise, Orthodox Christians are wise to guard their spiritual patrimony against the proselytizing efforts of Western Christians, and, in fact, to hold out to them with humble confidence the glory of the unchanged and unadulterated Orthodox Christian faith.

It is also hoped that the non-Orthodox reader would conclude that there is *another way of faith* that does not mandate either the embrace of the innovations of the medieval papacy nor the overreactions of the Protestant denominations. This other way of faith is the *Orthodox Way*.

Glory to the Holy, Consubstantial, Life-Giving, and Undivided Trinity, always, now and ever, and unto the ages of ages. Amen.

# *Appendix 1*

*On the Use of the Word "Heresy/Heretic"
in the Scriptures and in the Holy Orthodox Church*

The word heresy (αἵρεσις) has a broad semantic range, and a colorful history. In the Old Testament the word is often translated 'choice,' such as in a reference to free-will offerings which are described in Lev. 22:18,21 (LXX) as "gifts according to their choice."[370] Hellenism used the word αἵρεσις to describe various teaching and philosophical schools. Judaism used it in the same neutral, merely descriptive, way until the 2nd century when it began to be used by rabbis (with its Hebrew equivalent) in an evaluative way for Christians and Gnostics with negative connotations.

In the New Testament the word heresy/αἵρεσις is quite common. In Acts 24:14 St. Paul before Felix says that the Jews malign the Way of Christ by calling it a "sect" and the word is αἵρεσις in the accusative (αἵρεσιν). In some cases the word is employed with the same neutral meaning as 1st century Judaism and Hellenism, but in the Christian Church it developed a pejorative meaning from the start.

Besides the meaning "choice," heresy/αἵρεσις sometimes means a chosen opinion, as in 2 Pet. 2:1 where it is rendered

---

[370] *cf.* Gen. 49:15.

"destructive opinions."[371] The word can also be employed to mean "sect" or "school"—in the sense of rooted in the teaching of the person who has fashioned these opinions.

These three definitions are united in the Church's theological understanding of what a heresy is. The true faith is revealed to us by the Lord Jesus Christ through His holy body, the Church. The only "choice" a faithful Orthodox Christian ought to exercise is the choice to be a Christian by embracing the true faith. As such we accept the faith once delivered to the saints, and we seek to preserve it whole and unharmed, and to live it faithfully. We are *not* free to improve it according to our judgments, nor to discard parts of the faith we are not happy with. The exercise of such pernicious choice with regards to the faith is the heart of heresy. According to Tertullian, this is why we call heretics "self-condemned" for the heretic himself is the one who chose that for which he is condemned.[372]

Such choices produce chosen opinions that are different from the rule of faith, the apostolic standard, and this—if joined with a charismatic or highly intelligent personality, or both—creates a sect or school. Hence, one of the characteristics of heresies is that they are often named after a

---

[371] This Petrine understanding of heresy as false opinions and a conscious rejection of revealed truth came to be the essential definition of heresy in the history of the Church.

[372] *On Prescription of Heretics*, Ch. 6, p. 245. Tit. 3:9-11 describes the heretic as "self-condemned."

particular person: Arianism, Nestorianism, Eutychianism, Papalism, Lutheranism, Calvinism, etc. Clement of Alexandria says that heretics receive their appellations from four basic sources: the name of the founder, from a geographical place, from a nation (Egyptians, Armenians), from an action (Encratites), and some from peculiar dogmas, or individuals they have honored.[373]

The appellation "heretic" and the word "heresy" are used by the Holy Fathers *both* to describe heresies that have arisen within the Church itself (which is the normative usage) *and* to describe erroneous teaching of false Christain teachers who are outside the church, pagan teaching like Manichaeanism, as well as Jewish errors.[374] It is not true that the word "heresy" is used in the Orthodox tradition only to describe errors that have arisen within the Church Herself as though it were inappropriate to term Protestantism, for instance, as heresy.

In fact, our Holy Fathers have always described Protestantism as a collection of heresies even though Protestantism never had an organic connection to the Apostolic Church. An example of this traditional Orthodox practice is found in the 1672 *Confession of Dositheos,* the 17th century Orthodox confession that Fr. John Meyendorff dubbed the most important dogmatic statement of the Orthodox

---

[373] *Stromata*, Bk. 7, p. 555.
[374] St. John of Damascus in his famous work *On Heresies* lists Muhammadism/Islam as a heresy.

Church of that time. In the 2nd decree of that confession, the 16th century Protestant Reformer John Calvin is specifically called a "heretic." Many Orthodox saints have written specifically against Protestantism in general, and forms of Protestantism in particular, such as evangelicalism, describing these faith groups as heretical.[375]

The renowned 19th century Russian saint, Theophan the Recluse, had the following to say regarding where one finds the truth of God:

> The truth of God, the whole, pure and saving truth, is to be found neither in the Roman Catholics, nor in the Protestants, nor in the Anglicans, nor in this preacher of yours. It is to be found only in the One True Church, the Orthodox Church. The others may well believe that they possess the truth. In reality, however, they are far from it. The Roman Catholics, who were the first to split from the Church, consider the truth to be with their side. The Protestants, who protested against the Roman Catholics' failure on a score of points, failed themselves to return to the truth and, in fact, strayed from it even further than the former. They did not establish their new faith upon

---

[375] For example, St. Theophan the Recluse's *Preaching Another Christ: Against Evangelicalism*, and St Hilarion Troitsky's *Thou Shalt Have No Other Gods*. We have almost 500 years of patristic testimony against the Protestant movement.

God's truth, but upon heretical sophistries of their own invention. No matter how much they claim to be right, they are very far from the truth...Countless heresies appeared in the West but they were all rejected by Orthodoxy despite the fact that they preached Christ the Savior! Therefore, we must not rush to the conclusion that just because someone preaches Christ, he must necessarily be trustworthy, but we need to ascertain whether or not he preaches the truth about Christ.[376]

Though the word αἵρεσις has a semantic range in the New Testament that covers both what we know as heresy and what we know as schism,[377] over time heresy came to be differentiated from schism in the language of the church. Schism is a split caused by disagreement on church policy and over questions that are usually more easily resolved than issues of heresy. Schismatics can be, and historically have often been, heretics also, but there is no necessity for such. Schism is often caused not by false teaching, but by a lack of virtue, particularly love and patience.

St. Basil the Great in his Epistle 188 makes the following distinctions: heresy, schism, and illegal assemblies. Her-

---

[376] From St. Theophan the Recluse's *Preaching Another Christ: Against Evangelicalism* (p. 20, 22).

[377] 1 Cor. 11:19 and 11:18 schismata, Gal. 5:20. It should also be noted that in the early centuries of the Church there was also a positive use of the term heresy. For instance, in Eusebius' *Ecclesiastical History* he calls the Church "our most sacred heresy" (x.v.21-22).

etics are completely severed from the faith, and examples of these according to St. Basil are Manichaeans, Gnostics (Valentinians and Marcionites), and Montanists; schismatics are those who are separated due to a failure to solve ecclesiastical problems, and include according to Basil the ancient Katharoi, Enkratitai, and Hydroparastatai; and illegal assemblies are assemblies of rebellious bishops and/or priests in disobedience.

*Some New Testament References to Heresy*

**Matt. 7:15** "Beware of false prophets...inwardly ravenous wolves...you will know them by their fruits"

**Matt. 24: 4-5, 11, 13, 24** "See to it that no one misleads you. For many will come in My name saying, 'I am the Christ' and will mislead many...and many false prophets will arise, and will mislead many'...the one who endures to the end will be saved' [endure in the faith]...false Christs and false prophets will arise and will show great signs and wonders so as to mislead, if possible, even the elect..."

**Acts 20:28-30** "Be on guard for yourselves and for all the flock, among which the Holy Spirit made you overseers, to shepherd the Church of God which He purchased with His own blood. I know that after my departure, savage wolves will come in among you, not sparing the flock; and from among your own selves men will arise, speaking perverse things, to draw away the disciples after them."

1 Cor. 11:19 "There must also be heresies/schisms among you, that those who are approved may become recognized among you."

Gal. 5:19-21 "Now the works of the flesh are evident, which are...selfish ambitions, dissensions, heresies/schisms, envy, murders, drunkenness...those who practice such things will not inherit the Kingdom of God."

1 Tim. 4:1 "The Spirit explicitly says that in later times some will fall away from the faith, paying attention to deceitful spirits and doctrines of demons."

2 Tim. 4:3-4 "The time will come when they will not endure sound doctrine, but according to their own desires, because they have itching ears, they will heap up for themselves teachers; and they will turn their ears away from the truth, and be turned aside to fables."

2 Pet. 2:1 "There will be false teachers among you, who will secretly introduce destructive heresies, even denying the Master Who bought them, and bring on themselves swift destruction, because of whom the way of truth will be blasphemed."

2 Pet. 3:16 "Paul, according to the wisdom given to him, has written to you, as also in all his epistles, speaking in them of these things, in which are some things hard to understand, which those who are untaught and unstable twist to their own destruction, as they do also the rest of the Scriptures."

St. Irenaeus of Lyons writes in *Against Heresies* "It is incumbent to obey the priests who are in the church...those who, as I have shown, possess the succession from the apostles. These men, together with the succession of the bishops, have received the certain gift of truth, according to the good pleasure of the Father. But we should hold in suspicion others who depart from the primitive succession, and assemble themselves together in any place whatsoever—either as heretics of perverse minds, or as schismatics puffed up and self-pleasing. Or they may be hypocrites, acting this way for the sake of money and vainglory. For all of those persons have fallen from the truth. The heretics bring strange fire to the altar of God – namely, strange doctrines. So they shall be burned up by the fire from heaven, as were Nadab and Abihu."

## *The Synodikon of Orthodoxy*

The first Sunday of Great Lent, which is called the Triumph of Orthodoxy, climaxes liturgically with the public proclamation of the Synodikon of the Seventh Ecumenical Council which proclaims the true Orthodox faith and anathematizes many heretics and their heresies. This annual liturgical condemnation of heresies keeps alive in the experience of the Orthodox faithful the importance of guarding the true faith from heresy.

*Summing Up the Origins and Characteristics of Heresy*

1. The Orthodox Catholic faith of the Christians was once for all delivered to the saints: revealed and pure.

2. Heresy is a parasitical innovation; an alteration of the true faith, and is always incoherent and deficient. It is reductionistic, which is expressed in its being named often after its founder.

3. Heresy is almost always a deliberate deviation from the apostolic norm due to sin. Common motivations are a love of the new, discontent, pride, indiscreet curiosity, love of power, and greed for ecclesiastical office.

4. Heresy develops under the providence of God and is the fulfillment of New Testament prophecies. Christians should not be surprised nor scandalized by the appearance of heresies, and should accomplish God's work in opposing them. This work includes the love of the heretic and efforts at his recovery, as well as the acknowledgement of and affixation to those leaders of the church who are approved (1 Cor. 11: 18-19).

Patriarch Dositheos II Notarius of Jerusalem (1641 - 1707)

# *Appendix II*

### *The Confession of Patriarch Dositheos (1672)*

Dositheos, by the mercy of God, Patriarch of Jerusalem, to those that ask and inquire concerning the faith and worship of the Greeks, that is of the Eastern Church, how forsooth it thinketh concerning the Orthodox faith, in the common name of all Christians subject to our Apostolic Throne, and of the Orthodox worshippers that are sojourning in this holy and great city of Jerusalem (with whom the whole Catholic Church agreeth in all that concerneth the faith) publisheth this concise Confession, for a testimony both before God and before man, with a sincere conscience, and devoid of all dissimulation.

#### *Decree I*

We believe in one God, true, almighty, and infinite, the Father, the Son, and the Holy Spirit; the Father unbegotten; the Son begotten of the Father before the ages, and consubstantial with Him; and the Holy Spirit proceeding from the Father, and consubstantial with the Father and the Son. These three Persons in one essence we call the All-holy Trinity, — by all creation to be ever blessed, glorified, and adored.

## Decree II

We believe the Divine and Sacred Scriptures to be God-taught; and, therefore, we ought to believe the same without doubting; yet not otherwise than as the Catholic Church[378] hath interpreted and delivered the same. For every foul heresy receiveth, indeed, the Divine Scriptures, but perversely interpreteth the same, using metaphors, and homonymies, and sophistries of man's wisdom, confounding what ought to be distinguished, and trifling with what ought not to be trifled with. For if [we were to receive the same] otherwise, each man holding every day a different sense concerning the same, the Catholic Church would not [as she doth] by the grace of Christ continue to be the Church until this day, holding the same doctrine of faith, and always identically and steadfastly believing, but would be rent into innumerable parties, and subject to heresies; neither would the Church be holy, the pillar and ground of the truth,[379] without spot or wrinkle;[380] but would be the Church of the malignant[381] as it is manifest that of the heretics undoubtedly is, and especially that of Calvin, who are not ashamed to learn from the Church, and then to wickedly repudiate her. Wherefore, the witness also of the Cath-

---

[378] In this context, "Catholic Church" is used to indicate the Holy Orthodox Church; not the church in Rome.

[379] 1 Tim. 3:15.

[380] Eph. 5:27.

[381] Ps. 25:5.

olic Church is, we believe, not of inferior authority to that of the Divine Scriptures. For one and the same Holy Spirit being the author of both, it is quite the same to be taught by the Scriptures and by the Catholic Church. Moreover, when any man speaketh from himself he is liable to err, and to deceive, and be deceived; but the Catholic Church, as never having spoken, or speaking from herself, but from the Spirit of God — who being her teacher, she is ever unfailingly rich — it is impossible for her to in any wise err, or to at all deceive, or be deceived; but like the Divine Scriptures, is infallible, and hath perpetual authority.

### Decree III

We believe the most good God to have from eternity predestinated unto glory those whom He hath chosen, and to have consigned unto condemnation those whom He hath rejected; but not so that He would justify the one, and consign and condemn the other without cause. For that were contrary to the nature of God, who is the common Father of all, and no respecter of persons, and would have all men to be saved, and to come to the knowledge of the truth;[382] but since He foreknew the one would make a right use of their free-will, and the other a wrong, He predestinated the one, or condemned the other. And we understand the use of free-will thus, that the Divine and illuminating

---

[382] 1 Tim. 2:4.

grace, and which we call preventing grace, being, as a light to those in darkness, by the Divine goodness imparted to all, to those that are willing to obey this — for it is of use only to the willing, not to the unwilling — and co-operate with it, in what it requireth as necessary to salvation, there is consequently granted particular grace; which, co-operating with us, and enabling us, and making us perseverant in the love of God, that is to say, in performing those good things that God would have us to do, and which His preventing grace admonisheth us that we should do, justifieth us, and maketh us predestinated. But those who will not obey, and co-operate with grace; and, therefore, will not observe those things that God would have us perform, and that abuse in the service of Satan the free-will, which they have received of God to perform voluntarily what is good, are consigned to eternal condemnation.

But to say, as the most wicked heretics do and as is contained in the Chapter answering hereto — that God, in predestinating, or condemning, had in no wise regard to the works of those predestinated, or condemned, we know to be profane and impious. For thus Scripture would be opposed to itself, since it promiseth the believer salvation through works, yet supposeth God to be its sole author, by His sole illuminating grace, which He bestoweth without preceding works, to shew to man the truth of divine things, and to teach him how he may co-operate therewith, if he will, and do what is good and acceptable, and so obtain salvation. He taketh not away the power to will — to will to obey, or not obey him.

But than to affirm that the Divine Will is thus solely and without cause the author of their condemnation, what greater calumny can be fixed upon God? and what greater injury and blasphemy can be offered to the Most High? For that the Deity is not tempted with evils,[383] and that He equally willeth the salvation of all, since there is no respect of persons with Him, we do know; and that for those who through their own wicked choice, and their impenitent heart, have become vessels of dishonour, there is, as is just, decreed condemnation, we do confess. But of eternal punishment, of cruelty, of pitilessness, and of inhumanity, we never, never say God is the author, who telleth us that there is joy in heaven over one sinner that repenteth.[384]Far be it from us, while we have our senses, thus to believe, or to think; and we do subject to an eternal anathema those who say and think such things, and esteem them to be worse than any infidels.

*Decree IV*

We believe the tri-personal God, the Father, the Son, and the Holy Spirit to be the maker of all things visible and invisible; and the invisible are the angelic Powers, rational

---

[383] *cf.* Jas.1:13.
[384] Lk. 15:7.

souls, and demons, — though God made not the demons
what they afterwards became by their own choice, — but
the visible are heaven and what is under heaven. And because the Maker is good by nature, He made all things very
good[385] whatsoever He hath made, nor can He ever be the
maker of evil. But if there be aught evil, that is to say, sin,
come about contrarily to the Divine Will, in man or in
demon, — for that evil is simply in nature, we do not acknowledge, — it is either of man, or of the devil. For it is a
true and infallible rule, that God is in no wise the author of
evil, nor can it at all by just reasoning be attributed to God.

*Decree V*

We believe all things that are, whether visible or invisible, to be governed by the providence of God; but although
God foreknoweth evils, and permitteth them, yet in that
they are evils, He is neither their contriver nor their author.
But when such are come about, they may be over-ruled by
the Supreme Goodness for something beneficial, not indeed as being their author, but as engrafting thereon something for the better. And we ought to adore, but not curi-
ously pry into, Divine Providence in its ineffable and only
partially revealed judgments.[386] Albeit what is revealed to
us in Divine Scripture concerning it as being conducive
to eternal life, we ought honestly to search out, and then

---

[385] *cf.* Gen. 1:31.
[386] *cf.* Gen. 1:31.

unhesitatingly to interpret the same agreeably to primary notions of God.

## Decree VI

We believe the first man created by God to have fallen in Paradise, when, disregarding the Divine commandment, he yielded to the deceitful counsel of the serpent. And hence hereditary sin flowed to his posterity; so that none is born after the flesh who beareth not this burden, and experienceth not the fruits thereof in this present world. But by these fruits and this burden we do not understand [actual] sin, such as impiety, blasphemy, murder, sodomy, adultery, fornication, enmity, and whatsoever else is by our depraved choice committed contrarily to the Divine Will, not from nature; for many both of the Forefathers and of the Prophets, and vast numbers of others, as well of those under the shadow [of the Law], as under the truth [of the Gospel], such as the divine Precursor, and especially the Mother of God the Word, the ever-virgin Mary, experienced not these, or such like faults; but only what the Divine Justice inflicted upon man as a punishment for the [original] transgression, such as sweats in labour, afflictions, bodily sicknesses, pains in child-bearing, and, in fine, while on our pilgrimage, to live a laborious life, and lastly, bodily death.

## Decree VII

We believe the Son of God, Jesus Christ, to have emp-tied Himself,[387] that is, to have taken into His own Person human flesh, being conceived of the Holy Spirit, in the womb of the ever-virgin Mary; and, becoming man, to have been born, without causing any pain or labour to His own Mother after the flesh, or injury to her virginity, to have suf-fered, to have been buried, to have risen again in glory on the third day, according to the Scriptures,[388] to have ascend-ed into the heavens, and to be seated at the right hand of God the Father. Whom also we look for to judge the living and the dead.

## Decree VIII

We believe our Lord Jesus Christ to be the only medi-ator, and that in giving Himself a ransom for all He hath through His own Blood made a reconciliation between God and man, and that Himself having a care for His own is advocate and propitiation for our sins. Albeit, in prayers and supplications unto Him, we say the Saints are interces-sors, and, above all, the undefiled Mother of the very God the Word; the holy Angels too — whom we know to be set over us — the Apostles, Prophets, Martyrs, Pure Ones, and all whom He hath glorified as having served Him faith-

---

[387] *cf.* Phil. 2:7.
[388] *cf.* 1 Cor. 15:3,4.

fully. With whom we reckon also the Bishops and Priests, as standing about the Altar of God, and righteous men eminent for virtue. For that we should pray one for another, and that the prayer of the righteous availeth much,[389] and that God heareth the Saints rather than those who are steeped in sins, we learn from the Sacred Oracles. And not only are the Saints while on their pilgrimage regarded as mediators and intercessors for us with God, but especially after their death, when all reflective vision being done away, they behold clearly the Holy Trinity; in whose infinite light they know what concerneth us. For as we doubt not but that the Prophets while they were in a body with the perceptions of the senses knew what was done in heaven, and thereby foretold what was future; so also that the Angels, and the Saints become as Angels, know in the infinite light of God what concerneth us, we doubt not, but rather unhesitatingly believe and confess.

### Decree IX

We believe no one to be saved without faith. And by faith we mean the right notion that is in us concerning God and divine things, which, working by love, that is to say, by [observing] the Divine commandments, justifieth us with Christ; and without this [faith] it is impossible to please God.

---

[389] Jas. 5:16.

## Decree X

We believe that what is called, or rather is, the Holy Catholic and Apostolic Church, and in which we have been taught to believe, containeth generally all the Faithful in Christ, who, that is to say, being still on their pilgrimage, have not yet reached their home in the Fatherland. But we do not in any wise confound this Church which is on its pilgrimage with that which is in the Fatherland, because it may be, as some of the heretics say, that the members of the two are sheep of God, the Chief Shepherd,[390] and hallowed by the same Holy Spirit; for that is absurd and impossible, since the one is yet militant, and on its journey; and the other is triumphant, and settled in the Fatherland, and hath received the prize. Of which Catholic Church, since a mortal man cannot universally and perpetually be head, our Lord Jesus Christ Himself is head, and Himself holding the rudder is at the helm in the governing of the Church, through the Holy Fathers. And, therefore, over particular Churches, that are real Churches, and consist of real members [of the Catholic Church], the Holy Spirit hath appointed Bishops as leaders and shepherds, who being not at all by abuse, but properly, authorities and heads, look unto the Author and Finisher of our Salvation,[391] and refer to Him what they do in their capacity of heads forsooth.

---

[390]  cf. Ps. 94:7.
[391]  cf. Heb. 2:10; 12:2.

But forasmuch as among their other impieties, the Calvinists have fancied this also, that the simple Priest and the
High Priest are perhaps the same; and that there is no necessity for High Priests, and that the Church may be governed by some Priests; and that not a High Priest [only],
but a Priest also is able to ordain a Priest, and a number of
Priests to ordain a High Priest; and affirm in lofty language
that the Eastern Church assenteth to this wicked notion —
for which purpose the Tenth Chapter was written by Cyril
— we explicitly declare according to the mind which hath
obtained from the beginning in the Eastern Church.

That the dignity of the Bishop is so necessary in the
Church, that without him, neither Church nor Christian
could either be or be spoken of. For he, as a successor of
the Apostles, having received in continued succession by
the imposition of hands and the invocation of the All-holy
Spirit the grace that is given him of the Lord of binding
and loosing, is a living image of God upon the earth, and
by a most ample participation of the operation of the Holy
Spirit, who is the chief functionary, is a fountain of all the
Mysteries [Sacraments] of the Catholic Church, through
which we obtain salvation.

And he is, we suppose, as necessary to the Church as
breath is to man, or the sun to the world. Whence it hath
also been elegantly said by some in commendation of the
dignity of the High Priesthood, "What God is in the heav-

enly Church of the first-born,[392] and the sun in the world, that every High Priest is in his own particular Church, as through him the flock is enlightened, and nourished, and becometh the temple of God."[393]

And that this great mystery and dignity of the Episcopate hath descended unto us by a continued succession is manifest. For since the Lord hath promised to be with us always, although He be with us by other means of grace and Divine operations, yet in a more eminent manner doth He, through the Bishop as chief functionary make us His own and dwell with us, and through the divine Mysteries is united with us; of which the Bishop is the first minister, and chief functionary, through the Holy Spirit, and suffereth us not to fall into heresy. And, therefore [John] the Damascene, in his Fourth Epistle to the Africans, hath said, the Catholic Church is everywhere committed to the care of the Bishops; and that Clement, the first Bishop of the Romans, and Evodius at Antioch, and Mark at Alexandria, were successors of Peter is acknowledged. Also that the divine Andrew seated Stachys on the Throne of Constantinople, in his own stead; and that in this great holy city of Jerusalem our Lord Himself appointed James, and that after James another succeeded, and then another, until our own times. And, therefore, Tertullian in his Epistle to Papianus called all Bishops the Apostles' successors. To their

392   cf. Heb. 12:23.
393   cf. Eph. 2:21.

succession to the Apostles' dignity and authority Eusebius, the [friend] of Pamphilus, testifieth, and all the Fathers testify, of whom it is needless to give a list; and this the common and most ancient custom of the Catholic Church confirmeth.

And that the dignity of the Episcopate differeth from that of the simple Priest, is manifest. For the Priest is ordained by the Bishop, but a Bishop is not ordained by a Priest, but by two or three High Priests, as the Apostolic Canon directeth. And the Priest is chosen by the Bishop, but the High Priest is not chosen by the Priests or Presbyters, nor is he chosen by secular Princes, but by the Synod of the Primatial Church of that country, in which is situated the city that is to receive the ordinand, or at least by the Synod of the Province in which he is to become a Bishop. Or, if ever the city choose him, it doth not this absolutely; but the election is referred to the Synod; and if it appear that he hath obtained this agreeably to the Canons, the Elect is advanced by ordination by the Bishops, with the invocation of the All-holy Spirit; but if not, he is advanced whom the Synod chooseth. And the Priest, indeed, retaineth to himself the authority and grace of the Priesthood, which he hath received; but the Bishop imparteth it to others also. And the one having received the dignity of the Priesthood from the Bishop, can only perform Holy Baptism, and Prayer-oil, minister sacrificially the unbloody

Sacrifice, and impart to the people the All-holy Body and Blood of our Lord Jesus Christ, anoint the baptised with the Holy Myron [Chrism], crown the Faithful legally marrying, pray for the sick, and that all men may be saved and come to the knowledge of the truth,[394] and especially for the remission and forgiveness of the sins of the Faithful, living and dead. And if he be eminent for experience and virtue, receiving his authority from the Bishop, he directeth those Faithful that come unto him, and guideth them into the way of possessing the heavenly kingdom, and is appointed a preacher of the sacred Gospel. But the High Priest is also the minister of all these, since he is in fact, as hath been said before, the fountain of the Divine Mysteries and graces, through the Holy Spirit, and he alone consecrateth the Holy Myron. And the ordinations of all orders and degrees in the Church are proper to him; and in a primary and highest sense he bindeth and looseth, and his sentence is approved by God, as the Lord hath promised.[395] And he preacheth the Sacred Gospel, and contendeth for the Orthodox faith, and those that refuse to hear he casteth out of the Church as heathens and publicans,[396] and he putteth heretics under excommunication and anathema, and layeth down his own life for the sheep.[397] From which it is mani-

---

[394] cf. 1 Tim. 2:4.
[395] Matt. 16:19.
[396] cf. Matt. 18:17.
[397] cf. Jn. 10:11.

fest, that without contradiction the Bishop differeth from the simple Priest, and that without him all the Priests in the world could not exercise the pastorate in the Church of God, or govern it at all.

But it is well said by one of the Fathers, that it is not easy to find a heretic that hath understanding. For when these forsake the Church, they are forsaken by the Holy Spirit, and there remaineth in them neither understanding nor light, but only darkness and blindness. For if such had not happened to them, they would not have opposed things that are most plain; among which is the truly great mystery of Episcopacy, which is taught by Scripture, written of, and witnessed to, both by all Ecclesiastical history and the writings of holy men, and always held and acknowledged by the Catholic Church.

## Decree XI

We believe to be members of the Catholic Church all the Faithful, and only the Faithful; who, forsooth, having received the blameless Faith of the Saviour Christ, from Christ Himself, and the Apostles, and the Holy Œcumenical Synods, adhere to the same without wavering; although some of them may be guilty of all manner of sins. For unless the Faithful, even when living in sin, were members of the Church, they could not be judged by the Church. But now being judged by her, and called to repentance, and guided into the way of her salutary precepts, though they may be still defiled with sins, for this only, that they have not fallen into despair, and that they cleave to the Catholic and Orthodox faith, they are, and are regarded as, members of the Catholic Church.

## Decree XII

We believe the Catholic Church to be taught by the Holy Spirit. For he is the true Paraclete; whom Christ sendeth from the Father,[398] to teach the truth,[399] and to drive away darkness from the minds of the Faithful. The teaching of the Holy Spirit, however, doth not immediately, but through the holy Fathers and Leaders of the Catholic Church, illuminate the Church. For as all Scripture is, and is called, the word of the Holy Spirit; not that it was spoken immediately by Him, but that it was spoken by Him through the Apostles and Prophets; so also the Church is taught indeed by the Life-giving Spirit, but through the medium of the holy Fathers and Doctors (whose rule is acknowledged to be the Holy and Œcumenical Synods; for we shall not cease to say this ten thousand times); and, therefore, not only are we persuaded, but do profess as true and undoubtedly certain, that it is impossible for the Catholic Church to err, or at all be deceived, or ever to choose falsehood instead of truth. For the All-holy Spirit continually operating through the holy Fathers and Leaders faithfully ministering, delivereth the Church from error of every kind.

---

[398] cf. Jn. 25:26.
[399] cf. Jn. 26:13.

## Decree XIII

We believe a man to be not simply justified through faith alone, but through faith which worketh through love, that is to say, through faith and works. But [the notion] that faith fulfilling the function of a hand layeth hold on the righteousness which is in Christ, and applieth it unto us for salvation, we know to be far from all Orthodoxy. For faith so understood would be possible in all, and so none could miss salvation, which is obviously false. But on the contrary, we rather believe that it is not the correlative of faith, but the faith which is in us, justifieth through works, with Christ. But we regard works not as witnesses certifying our calling, but as being fruits in themselves, through which faith becometh efficacious, and as in themselves meriting, through the Divine promises[400] that each of the Faithful may receive what is done through his own body, whether it be good or bad, forsooth.

## Decree XIV

We believe man in falling by the [original] transgression to have become comparable and like unto the beasts, that is, to have been utterly undone, and to have fallen from his perfection and impassibility, yet not to have lost the nature and power which he had received from the supremely good God. For otherwise he would not be rational, and consequently not man; but to have the same nature, in which

---

[400] cf. 2 Cor. 5:10.

he was created, and the same power of his nature, that is free-will, living and operating. So as to be by nature able to choose and do what is good, and to avoid and hate what is evil. For it is absurd to say that the nature which was created good by Him who is supremely good lacketh the power of doing good. For this would be to make that nature evil — than which what could be more impious? For the power of working dependeth upon nature, and nature upon its author, although in a different manner. And that a man is able by nature to do what is good, even our Lord Himself intimateth, saying, even the Gentiles love those that love them.[401] But this is taught most plainly by Paul also, in Romans chap. i. [ver.] 19, and elsewhere expressly, saying in so many words, "The Gentiles which have no law do by nature the things of the law." From which it is also manifest that the good which a man may do cannot forsooth be sin. For it is impossible that what is good can be evil. Albeit, being done by nature only, and tending to form the natural character of the doer, but not the spiritual, it contributeth not unto salvation thus alone without faith, nor yet indeed unto condemnation, for it is not possible that good, as such, can be the cause of evil. But in the regenerated, what is wrought by grace, and with grace, maketh the doer perfect, and rendereth him worthy of salvation.

A man, therefore, before he is regenerated, is able by nature to incline to what is good, and to choose and work moral good. But for the regenerated to do spiritual good

---

[401] Matt. 5:46; Lk. 6:32.

— for the works of the believer being contributory to salvation and wrought by supernatural grace are properly called spiritual — it is necessary that he be guided and prevented by grace, as hath been said in treating of predestination; so that he is not able of himself to do any work worthy of a Christian life, although he hath it in his own power to will, or not to will, to co-operate with grace.

### Decree XV

We believe that there are in the Church Evangelical Mysteries [i.e., Sacraments of the Gospel Dispensation], and that they are seven. For a less or a greater number of the Mysteries we have not in the Church; since any number of the Mysteries other than seven is the product of heretical madness. And the seven of them were instituted in the Sacred Gospel, and are gathered from the same, like the other dogmas of the Catholic Faith. For in the first place our Lord instituted Holy Baptism by the words, "Go ye and make disciples of all the nations, baptising them in the name of the Father, and of the Son, and of the Holy Spirit;"[402] and by the words, "He that believeth and is baptised shall be saved, but he that disbelieveth shall be condemned."[403]

And that of Confirmation, that is to say, of the Holy Myron or Holy Chrism, by the words, "But ye — tarry ye in the city of Jerusalem, until ye be endued with power from on high."[404] With which they were endued by the coming

---

[402] Matt. 28:19.
[403] Mk. 16:16.
[404] Lk. 24:49.

of the Holy Spirit, and this the Mystery of Confirmation signifieth; concerning which Paul also discourseth in the Second Epistle to the Corinthians, chap. i., and Dionysius the Areopagite more explicitly.

And the Priesthood by the words, "This do ye for My Memorial;"[405] and by the words, "Whatsoever ye shall bind and loose upon the earth shall be bound and loosed in the heavens."[406]

And the unbloody Sacrifice by the words, "Take, eat ye; This is My Body;"[407] and, "Drink ye all of It; This is My Blood of the New Testament;"[408] and by the words, "Except ye eat the Flesh of the Son of Man, ye have not life in yourselves."[409]

And Marriage, when, having recited the things which had been spoken thereof in the Old [Testament], He, as it were, set His seal thereto by the words, "Those whom God hath joined together, let not man put asunder,"[410] and this the divine Apostle also calleth a great Mystery.[411]

And Penance, with which is joined sacramental confession, by the words, "Whose soever sins ye remit, they are remitted unto them; and whose soever sins ye retain, they are

---

[405] Lk. 22:19.

[406] Matt. 18:18.

[407] Matt. 26:26; Mk. 14:22; and *cf.* Lk. 22:19; 1 Cor. 2:24.

[408] Matt. 26:27; and cf. Mk. 14:24; Lk. 22:20; 1 Cor. 2:25.

[409] Jn. 6:53.

[410] Matt. 19:6.

[411] Eph. 5:32.

retained";[412] and by the words, "Except ye repent, ye shall [all] likewise perish."[413] And lastly, the Holy Oil or Prayer-Oil is spoken of in Mark,[414] and is expressly witnessed to by the Lord's brother.[415]

And the Mysteries consist of something natural, and of something supernatural; and are not bare signs of the promises of God. For then they would not differ from circumcision — than which [notion] what could be worse? And we acknowledge them to be, of necessity, efficient means of grace to the receivers. But we reject, as alien to Christian doctrine, the notion that the integrity of the Mystery requireth the use of the earthly thing [i.e., dependeth upon its reception]; for this is contrary to the Mystery of the Offering [i.e., the Sacrament of the Eucharist], which being instituted by the Substantial Word, and hallowed by the invocation of the Holy Spirit, is perfected by the presence of the thing signified, to wit, of the Body and Blood of Christ. And the perfecting thereof necessarily precedeth its use. For if it were not perfect before its use, he that useth it not aright could not eat and drink judgment unto himself;[416] since he would be partaking of mere bread and wine. But now, he that partaketh unworthily eateth and drinketh

---

[412] Jn. 22:23.
[413] Lk. 13:3,5.
[414] Mk. 6:13.
[415] Jas. 5:14.
[416] 1 Cor. 11:26, 28, 29.

judgment unto himself; so that not in its use, but even before its use, the Mystery of the Eucharist hath its perfection. Moreover, we reject as something abominable and pernicious the notion that when faith is weak the integrity of the Mystery is impaired. For heretics who abjure their heresy and join the Catholic Church are received by the Church; although they received their valid Baptism with weakness of faith. Wherefore, when they afterwards become possessed of the perfect faith, they are not again baptised.

## Decree XVI

We believe Holy Baptism, which was instituted by the Lord, and is conferred in the name of the Holy Trinity, to be of the highest necessity. For without it none is able to be saved, as the Lord saith, "Whosoever is not born of water and of the Spirit, shall in no wise enter into the Kingdom of the Heavens."[417] And, therefore, it is necessary even for infants, since they also are subject to original sin, and without Baptism are not able to obtain its remission. Which the Lord shewed when he said, not of some only, but simply and absolutely, "Whosoever is not born [again]," which is the same as saying, "All that after the coming of Christ the Saviour would enter into the Kingdom of the Heavens must be regenerated." And forasmuch as infants are men, and as such need salvation; needing salvation, they need also Baptism. And those that are not regenerated, since they

---

[417] Jn. 3:5.

have not received the remission of hereditary sin, are, of necessity, subject to eternal punishment, and consequently cannot without Baptism be saved; so that even infants ought, of necessity, to be baptised. Moreover, infants are saved, as is said in Matthew;[418] but he that is not baptised is not saved. And consequently even infants must of necessity be baptised. And in the Acts[419] it is said that the whole houses were baptised, and consequently the infants. To this the ancient Fathers also witness explicitly, and among them Dionysius in his Treatise concerning the Ecclesiastical Hierarchy; and Justin in his fifty-sixth Question, who saith expressly, "And they are vouchsafed the benefits of Baptism by the faith of those that bring them to Baptism." And Augustine saith that it is an Apostolical tradition, that children are saved through Baptism; and in another place, "The Church giveth to babes the feet of others, that they may come; and the hearts of others, that they may believe; and the tongues of others, that they may promise;" and in another place, "Our mother, the Church, furnisheth them with a particular heart."

Now the matter of Baptism is pure water, and no other liquid. And it is performed by the Priest only, or in a case of unavoidable necessity, by another man, provided he be Orthodox, and have the intention proper to Divine Baptism. And the effects of Baptism are, to speak concisely,

---

[418] Matt. 19:12.
[419] Acts 8:12; 16:33.

firstly, the remission of the hereditary transgression, and of any sins whatsoever which the baptised may have committed. Secondly, it delivereth him from the eternal punishment, to which he was liable, as well for original sin, as for mortal sins he may have individually committed. Thirdly, it giveth to such immortality; for in justifying them from past sins, it maketh them temples of God. And it may not be said, that any sin is not washed away through Baptism, which may have been previously committed; but to remain, though not imputed. For that were indeed the height of impiety, and a denial, rather than a confession of piety. Yea, forsooth, all sin existing, or committed before Baptism, is blotted out, and is to be regarded as never existing or committed. For the forms of Baptism, and on either hand all the words that precede and that perfect Baptism, do indicate a perfect cleansing. And the same thing even the very names of Baptism do signify. For if Baptism be by the Spirit and by fire,[420] it is manifest that it is in all a perfect cleansing; for the Spirit cleanseth perfectly. If it be light,[421] it dispelleth the darkness. If it be regeneration,[422] old things are passed away. And what are these except sins? If the baptised putteth off the old man,[423] then sin also. If he putteth on Christ,[424] then in effect he becometh free from

---

[420] Matt. 3:11.
[421] Heb. 6:4.
[422] Tit. 3:5.
[423] Col. 3:9.
[424] Gal. 3:27.

sin through Baptism. For God is far from sinners. This Paul also teacheth more plainly, saying: "As through one [man] we, being many, were made sinners, so through one [are we made] righteous."[425] And if righteous, then free from sin. For it is not possible for life and death to be in the same [person]. If Christ truly died, then remission of sin through the Spirit is true also. Hence it is evident that all who are baptised and fall asleep while babes are undoubtedly saved, being predestinated through the death of Christ. Forasmuch as they are without any sin; — without that common [to all], because delivered therefrom by the Divine laver, and without any of their own, because as babes they are incapable of committing sin; — and consequently are saved. Moreover, Baptism imparteth an indelible character, as doth also the Priesthood. For as it is impossible for any one to receive twice the same order of the Priesthood, so it is impossible for any once rightly baptised, to be again baptised, although he should fall even into myriads of sins, or even into actual apostacy from the Faith. For when he is willing to return unto the Lord, he receiveth again through the Mystery of Penance the adoption of a son, which he had lost.

### Decree XVII

We believe the All-holy Mystery of the Sacred Eucharist, which we have enumerated above, fourth in order, to

---

[425] Rom. 5:19.

be that which our Lord delivered in the night wherein He gave Himself up for the life of the world. For taking bread, and blessing, He gave to His Holy Disciples and Apostles, saying: "Take, eat ye; This is My Body."[426] And taking the chalice, and giving thanks, He said: "Drink ye all of It; This is My Blood, which for you is being poured out, for the remission of sins."[427] In the celebration whereof we believe the Lord Jesus Christ to be present, not typically, nor figuratively, nor by superabundant grace, as in the other Mysteries, nor by a bare presence, as some of the Fathers have said concerning Baptism, or by impanation, so that the Divinity of the Word is united to the set forth bread of the Eucharist hypostatically, as the followers of Luther most ignorantly and wretchedly suppose, but truly and really, so that after the consecration of the bread and of the wine, the bread is transmuted, transubstantiated, converted and transformed into the true Body Itself of the Lord, Which was born in Bethlehem of the ever-Virgin, was baptised in the Jordan, suffered, was buried, rose again, was received up, sitteth at the right hand of the God and Father, and is to come again in the clouds of Heaven; and the wine is converted and transubstantiated into the true Blood Itself of the Lord, Which as He hung upon the Cross, was poured out for the life of the world.[428]

---

[426] Matt. 26:26.

[427] Matt. 26:28.

[428] Jn. 6:51.

Further [we believe] that after the consecration of the bread and of the wine, there no longer remaineth the substance of the bread and of the wine, but the Body Itself and the Blood of the Lord, under the species and form of bread and wine; that is to say, under the accidents of the bread.

Further, that the all-pure Body Itself, and Blood of the Lord is imparted, and entereth into the mouths and stomachs of the communicants, whether pious or impious. Nevertheless, they convey to the pious and worthy remission of sins and life eternal; but to the impious and unworthy involve condemnation and eternal punishment.

Further, that the Body and Blood of the Lord are severed and divided by the hands and teeth, though in accident only, that is, in the accidents of the bread and of the wine, under which they are visible and tangible, we do acknowledge; but in themselves to remain entirely unsevered and undivided. Wherefore the Catholic Church also saith: "Broken and distributed is He That is broken, yet not severed; Which is ever eaten, yet never consumed, but sanctifying those that partake," that is worthily.

Further, that in every part, or the smallest division of the transmuted bread and wine there is not a part of the Body and Blood of the Lord — for to say so were blasphemous and wicked — but the entire whole Lord Christ substantially, that is, with His Soul and Divinity, or perfect God and perfect man. So that though there may be many celebrations in the world at one and the same hour, there are not many Christs, or Bodies of Christ, but it is one and the same Christ that is truly and really present; and His one Body and His Blood is in all the several Churches of the Faithful; and this not because the Body of the Lord that is in the Heavens descendeth upon the Altars; but because the bread of the Prothesis set forth in all the several Churches, being changed and transubstantiated, becometh, and is, after consecration, one and the same with That in the Heavens. For it is one Body of the Lord in many places, and not many; and therefore this Mystery is the greatest, and is spoken of as wonderful, and comprehensible by faith only, and not by the sophistries of man's wisdom; whose vain and foolish curiosity in divine things our pious and God-delivered religion rejecteth.

Further, that the Body Itself of the Lord and the Blood That are in the Mystery of the Eucharist ought to be honoured in the highest manner, and adored with latria. For one is the adoration of the Holy Trinity, and of the Body and Blood of the Lord. Further, that it is a true and propitiatory Sacrifice offered for all Orthodox, living and dead; and for the benefit of all, as is set forth expressly in the prayers of the Mystery delivered to the Church by the Apostles, in accordance with the command they received of the Lord.

Further, that before Its use, immediately after the consecration, and after Its use, What is reserved in the Sacred

Pixes for the communion of those that are about to depart [i.e. the dying] is the true Body of the Lord, and not in the least different therefrom; so that before Its use after the consecration, in Its use, and after Its use, It is in all respects the true Body of the Lord.

Further, we believe that by the word "transubstantiation" the manner is not explained, by which the bread and wine are changed into the Body and Blood of the Lord, — for that is altogether incomprehensible and impossible, except by God Himself, and those who imagine to do so are involved in ignorance and impiety, — but that the bread and the wine are after the consecration, not typically, nor figuratively, nor by superabundant grace, nor by the communication or the presence of the Divinity alone of the Only-begotten, transmuted into the Body and Blood of the Lord; neither is any accident of the bread, or of the wine, by any conversion or alteration, changed into any accident of the Body and Blood of Christ, but truly, and really, and substantially, doth the bread become the true Body Itself of the Lord, and the wine the Blood Itself of the Lord, as is said above. Further, that this Mystery of the Sacred Eucharist can be performed by none other, except only by an Orthodox Priest, who hath received his priesthood from an Orthodox and Canonical Bishop, in accordance with the teaching of the Eastern Church. This is compendiously the doctrine, and true confession, and most ancient tradition of the Catholic Church concerning this Mystery; which must not be departed from in any way by such as would be Orthodox, and who reject the novelties and profane vanities of heretics; but necessarily the tradition of the institution must be kept whole and unimpaired. For those that transgress the Catholic Church of Christ rejecteth and anathematiseth.

## Decree XVIII

We believe that the souls of those that have fallen asleep are either at rest or in torment, according to what each hath wrought; — for when they are separated from their bodies, they depart immediately either to joy, or to sorrow and lamentation; though confessedly neither their enjoyment, nor condemnation are complete. For after the common resurrection, when the soul shall be united with the body, with which it had behaved itself well or ill, each shall receive the completion of either enjoyment or of condemnation forsooth.

And such as though envolved in mortal sins have not departed in despair, but have, while still living in the body, repented, though without bringing forth any fruits of repentance — by pouring forth tears, forsooth, by kneeling while watching in prayers, by afflicting themselves, by relieving the poor, and in fine by shewing forth by their works their love towards God and their neighbour, and which the Catholic Church hath from the beginning rightly called satisfaction — of these and such like the souls depart into

Hades, and there endure the punishment due to the sins they have committed. But they are aware of their future release from thence, and are delivered by the Supreme Goodness, through the prayers of the Priests, and the good works which the relatives of each do for their Departed; especially the unbloody Sacrifice availing in the highest degree; which each offereth particularly for his relatives that have fallen asleep, and which the Catholic and Apostolic Church offereth daily for all alike; it being, of course, understood that we know not the time of their release. For that there is deliverance for such from their direful condition, and that before the common resurrection and judgment we know and believe; but when we know not.

## Question 1

### Ought the Divine Scriptures to be read in the vulgar tongue by all Christians?

No. For that all Scripture is divinely-inspired and profitable[429] we know, and is of such necessity, that without the same it is impossible to be Orthodox at all. Nevertheless they should not be read by all, but only by those who with fitting research have inquired into the deep things of the Spirit, and who know in what manner the Divine Scriptures ought to be searched, and taught, and in fine read. But to such as are not so exercised, or who cannot distinguish,

---

[429] cf. 2 Tim. 3:16.

or who understand only literally, or in any other way contrary to Orthodoxy what is contained in the Scriptures, the Catholic Church, as knowing by experience the mischief arising therefrom, forbiddeth the reading of the same. So that it is permitted to every Orthodox to hear indeed the Scriptures, that he may believe with the heart unto righteousness, and confess with the mouth unto salvation;[430] but to read some parts of the Scriptures, and especially of the Old [Testament], is forbidden for the aforesaid reasons and others of the like sort. For it is the same thing thus to prohibit persons not exercised thereto reading all the Sacred Scriptures, as to require infants to abstain from strong meats.

## Question 2

### Are the Scriptures plain to all Christians that read them?

If the Divine Scriptures were plain to all Christians that read them, the Lord would not have commanded such as desired to obtain salvation to search the same;[431] and Paul would have said without reason that God had placed the gift of teaching in the Church;[432] and Peter would not have said of the Epistles of Paul that they contained some things hard to be understood.[433] It is evident, therefore, that the

---

[430] Rom. 10:10.

[431] Jn. 5:39.

[432] 1 Cor. 13:28.

[433] 2 Pe. 3:16.

Scriptures are very profound, and their sense lofty; and that they need learned and divine men to search out their true meaning, and a sense that is right, and agreeable to all Scripture, and to its author the Holy Spirit.

So that as to those that are regenerated [in Baptism], although they must know the faith concerning the Trinity, the incarnation of the Son of God, His passion, resurrection, and ascension into the heavens, what concerneth regeneration and judgment — for which many have not hesitated to die — it is not necessary, but rather impossible, that all should know what the Holy Spirit manifesteth to those alone who are exercised in wisdom and holiness.

## Question 3

### What Books do you call Sacred Scripture?

Following the rule of the Catholic Church, we call Sacred Scripture all those which Cyril collected from the Synod of Laodicea, and enumerated, adding thereto those which he foolishly, and ignorantly, or rather maliciously called Apocrypha; to wit, "The Wisdom of Solomon," "Judith," "Tobit," "The History of the Dragon," "The History of Susanna," "The Maccabees," and "The Wisdom of Sirach." For we judge these also to be with the other genuine Books of Divine Scripture genuine parts of Scripture. For ancient custom, or rather the Catholic Church, which hath delivered to us as genuine the Sacred Gospels and the other

Books of Scripture, hath undoubtedly delivered these also as parts of Scripture, and the denial of these is the rejection of those. And if, perhaps, it seemeth that not always have all been by all reckoned with the others, yet nevertheless these also have been counted and reckoned with the rest of Scripture, as well by Synods, as by how many of the most ancient and eminent Theologians of the Catholic Church; all of which we also judge to be Canonical Books, and confess them to be Sacred Scripture.

## Question 4

### How ought we to think of the Holy Eikons, and of the adoration of the Saints?

The Saints being, and acknowledged by the Catholic Church to be, intercessors, as hath been said in Eighth Chapter, it is time to say that we honour them as friends of God, and as praying for us to the God of all. And the honour we pay them is twofold; — according to one manner which we call hyperdulia, we honour the Mother of God the Word. For though indeed the Theotokos be servant of the only God, yet is she also His Mother, as having borne in the flesh one of the Trinity; wherefore also is she hymned, as being beyond compare, above as well all Angels as Saints; wherefore, also, we pay her the adoration of hyperdulia. But according to the other manner, which we call dulia, we adore, or rather honour, the holy Angels, Apostles,

Prophets, Martyrs, and, in fine, all the Saints. Moreover, we adore and honour the wood of the precious and life-giving Cross, whereon our Saviour underwent this world-saving passion, and the sign of the life-giving Cross, the Manger at Bethlehem, through which we have been delivered from irrationality, the place of the Skull [Calvary], the life-giving Sepulchre, and the other holy objects of adoration; as well the holy Gospels, as the sacred vessels, wherewith the unbloody Sacrifice is performed. And by annual commemorations, and popular festivals, and sacred edifices and offerings; we do respect and honour the Saints. And then we adore, and honour, and kiss the Eikons of our Lord Jesus Christ, and of the most holy Theotokos, and of all the Saints, also of the holy Angels, as they appeared to some of the Forefathers and Prophets. We also represent the All-holy Spirit, as He appeared, in the form of a dove.

And if some say we commit idolatry in adoring the Saints, and the Eikons of the Saints, and the other things, we regard it as foolish and frivolous. For we worship with latria the only God in Trinity, and none other; but the Saints we honour upon two accounts: firstly, for their relation to God, since we honour them for His sake; and for themselves, because they are living images of God. But that which is for themselves hath been defined as of dulia. But the holy Eikons [we adore] relatively since the honour paid to them is referred to their prototypes. For he that adoreth the Eikon doth, through the Eikon, adore the prototype; and the honour paid to the Eikon is not at all divided, or at all separated from that of him that is pourtrayed, and is done unto the same, like that done unto a royal embassy.

And what they adduce from Scripture in support of their novelties, doth not help them as they would, but rather appeareth agreeable to us. For we, when reading the Divine Scriptures, examine the occasion and person, the example and cause. Wherefore, when we contemplate God Himself saying at one time, "Thou shalt not make to thyself any idol, or likeness; neither shalt thou adore them, nor serve them;"[434] and at another, commanding that Cherubim should be made;[435] and further, that oxen and lions[436] were placed in the Temple, we do not rashly consider the import of these things. For faith is not in assurance; but, as hath been said, considering the occasion and other circumstances, we arrive at the right interpretation of the same; and we conclude that, "Thou shalt not make to thyself any idol, or likeness," is the same as saying, "Thou shalt not adore strange Gods,"[437] or rather, "Thou shalt not commit idolatry." For so both the custom obtaining in the Church from Apostolic times of adoring the holy Eikons relatively is maintained, and the worship of latria reserved for God alone; and God

---

[434] Ex. 20:4,5; Deut. 5:8,9.
[435] Ex. 25:18.
[436] 1 Kings 7:29.
[437] Ex. 20:4.

doth not appear to speak contrarily to Himself. For if the Scripture saith [absolutely], "Thou shalt not make," "Thou shalt not adore," we fail to see how God afterwards permitted likenesses to be made, even though not for adoration. Wherefore, since the commandment concerneth idolatry only, we find serpents, and lions, and oxen, and Cherubim made, and figures and likenesses; among which Angels appear, as having been adored.

And as to the Saints whom they bring forward as saying, that it is not lawful to adore Eikons; we conclude that they rather help us; since they in their sharp disputations inveighed, as well against those that adore the holy Eikons with latria, as against those that bring the eikons of their deceased relatives into the Church, and subjected to anathema those that so do; but not against the right adoration, either of the Saints, or of the holy Eikons, or of the precious Cross, or of the other things of which mention hath been made; especially since the holy Eikons have been in the Church, and have been adored by the Faithful, even from the times of the Apostles, as is recorded and proclaimed by very many; with whom and after whom the Seventh Holy Œcumenical Synod putteth to shame all heretical impudence.

Since it giveth us most plainly to understand that it behoveth to adore the Holy Eikons, and what have been mentioned above. And it anathematiseth, and subjecteth to excommunication, as well those that adore the Eikons with latria as those that say that the Orthodox commit idolatry in adoring the Eikons. We also, therefore, do anathematise with them such as adore either Saint, or Angel, or Eikon, or Cross, or Relic of Saints, or sacred Vessel, or Gospel, or aught else that is in heaven above, or aught on the earth, or in the sea, with latria; and we ascribe adoration with latria to the only God in Trinity. And we anathematise those that say that the adoration of Eikons is the latria of Eikons, and who adore them not, and honour not the Cross, and the Saints, as the Church hath delivered.

Now we adore the Saints and the Holy Eikons, in the manner declared; and pourtray them in adornment of our temples, and that they may be the books of the unlearned, and for them to imitate the virtues of the Saints; and for them to remember, and have an increase of love, and be vigilant in ever calling upon the Lord, as Sovereign and Father, but upon the Saints, as his servants, and our helpers and mediators.

And so much as to the Chapters and Questions of Cyril. But the heretics do find fault with even the prayers of the pious unto God, for we know not why they should calumniate those of the Monks only. Moreover, that prayer is a conversation with God, and a petitioning for such good things as be meet for us, from Him of whom we hope to receive, an ascent too of the mind unto God, and a pious expression of our purpose towards God, a seeking what is above, the support of a holy soul, a worship most acceptable to God, a token of repentance, and of steadfast hope, we do know; and prayer is made either with the mind alone, or with the mind and voice; thereby engaging in the contemplation of the goodness and mercy of God, of the unworthiness of the petitioner, and in thanksgiving, and in realising the promises attached to obedience to God. And it is accompanied by faith, and hope, and perseverance, and observance of the commandments; and, as already said, is a petitioning for heavenly things; and it hath many fruits, which it is needless to enumerate; and it is made continually, and is accomplished either in an upright posture, or by kneeling. And so great is its efficacy, that it is acknowledged to be both the nourishment and the life of the soul. And all this is gathered from Divine Scripture; so that if any ask for demonstration thereof, he is like a fool, or a blind man, who disputeth about the sun's light at the hour of noon, and when the sky is clear. But the heretics, wishing to leave nothing unassailed that Christ hath enjoined, carp at this also. But being ashamed thus openly to impiously maintain as much concerning prayer, they do not forbid it to be made at all, but are distributed at the prayers of the Monks; and they act thus, that they may raise in the simple-minded a hatred towards the Monks; so that they may not endure even the sight of them, as though they were profane and in-

novators, much less allow the dogmas of the pious and Orthodox faith to be taught by them. For the adversary is wise
as to evil, and ingenious in inventing calumnies. Wherefore
his followers also — such as these heretics especially — are
not so much anxious about piety, as desirous of ever involving men in an abyss of evils, and of estranging them into
places, which the Lord taketh not under his care.[438]

They should be asked therefore, what are the prayers of
the Monks; and if they can shew that the Monks do anything entirely different from themselves, and not in accordance with the Orthodox worship of Christians, we also
will join with them, and say, not only that the Monks are no
Monks, but also no Christians. But if the Monks set forth
particularly the glory and wonders of God, and continually,
and unremittingly, and at all times, as far as is possible for
man, proclaim the Diety, with hymns and doxologies; now
singing, forsooth, parts of Scripture, and now gathering
hymns out of Scripture, or at least giving utterance to what
is agreeable to the same; we must acknowledge that they
perform a work apostolical and prophetical, or rather that
of the Lord.

Wherefore, we also, in singing the Paracletikê, the Tri-
odion, and the Menæon, perform a work in no wise unbe-
coming Christians. For all such Books discourse of the Diety as one, and yet of more than one personality, and that
even in the Hymns; now gathered out of the Divine Scrip-

---

[438] cf. Deut. 11:12.

tures, and now according to the direction of the Spirit; and in order that in the melodies, the words may be paralleled by other words, we sing parts of Scripture; moreover, that it may be quite plain that we always sing parts of Scripture, to every one of our Hymns, called a Troparion, we add a verse of Scripture. And if we sing, or read the Thecara [Threasury], or other prayers composed by the Fathers of old; let them say what there is in these which is blasphemous, or not pious, and we with them will prosecute these [Monks].

But if they say this only, that to pray continually and unremittingly is wrong, what have they to do with us? Let them contend with Christ — as indeed they do contend — who spake the parable of the unjust judge,[439] how that prayer should be made continually; and taught us to watch and pray,[440] in order to escape trials, and to stand before the Son of man.[441] Let them contend with Paul, [who] in the [5th] Chapter of the First [Epistle] to the Thessalonians, and elsewhere in many places [exhorteth to pray unremittingly]. I forbear to mention the divine leaders of the Catholic Church, from Christ until us; for to put these [heretics] to shame sufficeth the accord of the Forefathers, Apostles, and Prophets concerning prayer.

If, therefore, what the Monks do is what the Apostles and Prophets did; and, we may say, what the holy Fathers and Forefathers of Christ Himself did; it is manifest that the

[439] Lk. 28:2.
[440] Mk. 13:33.
[441] Lk. 21:36.

prayers of the Monks are fruits of the Holy Spirit, the giver of graces. But the novelties which the Calvinists have blasphemously introduced concerning God and divine things, perverting, mutilating, and abusing the Divine Scriptures, are sophistries and inventions of the devil.

Unavailing too is the assertion, that the Church cannot, without violence and tyranny, appoint fasts and abstinence from certain meats. For the Church for the mortification of the flesh and all the passions, and acting most rightly, carefully appointeth prayer and fasting, of which all the Saints have been lovers and examples; through which our adversary the devil[442] being overthrown by the grace from on high, together with his armies and his hosts — the race[443] that is set before the pious is the more easily accomplished. In making these provisions the undefiled[444] Church everywhere useth neither violence nor tyranny; but exhorteth, admonisheth, and teacheth, in accordance with Scripture, and persuadeth by the power of the Spirit.

And to what hath been mentioned a certain fellow at Charenton — we mean the beforementioned Claud — addeth certain other ridiculous objections against us, and unworthy of any consideration; but what hath been said by him we regard as idle tales; and the man himself we consider as a trifler and altogether illiterate. For from [the time

---

[442] *cf.* 1 Pe. 5:8.

[443] *cf.* 2 Tim. 4:7.

[444] *cf.* Eph. 5:27.

of ] Photius what vast numbers have there been, and there are now, in the Eastern Church, eminent for wisdom, and theology, and holiness, by the power of the Spirit. And it is most absurd [to argue] that because certain of the Eastern Priests keep the Holy Bread in wooden vessels, within the Church, but without the Bema, hung on one of the columns; that, therefore, they do not acknowledge the real and true transmutation of the bread into the Body of the Lord. For that certain of the poor Priests do keep the Lord's Body in wooden vessels, we do not deny; for truly Christ is not honoured by stones and marbles; but asketh for a sound purpose and a clean heart.

And this is what happened to Paul. "For we have," [445] saith he, "the treasure in earthen vessels." But where particular Churches able, as with us here in Jerusalem, the Lord's Body is honourably kept within the Holy Bema of such Churches, and a seven-light lamp always kept burning before it.

And I am tempted to wonder, if it may be that the heretics have seen the Lord's Body hanging in some Churches without the Bema, because perhaps the walls of the Bema were unsafe on account of age, and so have arrived at these absurd conclusions; but they did not notice Christ pourtrayed on the apse of the Holy Bema as a babe [lying] in the Paten; so that they might have known, how that the East-

---

[445] 2 Cor. 4:7.

erns do not represent that there is in the Paten a type, or grace, or aught else, but the Christ Himself; and so believe that the Bread of the Eucharist is naught else, but becometh substantially the Body Itself of the Lord, and so maintain the truth.

But concerning all these things it hath been treated at large and most lucidly in what is called *The Confession of the Eastern Church*, by George, of Chios, from Coresius in his [Treatises] concerning the Mysteries, and of predestination, and of grace, and of free-will, and of the intercession and adoration of Saints, and of the adoration of Eikons, and in the Refutation composed by him of the illicit Synod of the heretics holden on a certain occasion in Flanders, and in many other [Treatises]; by Gabriel, of Peloponnesus, Metropolitan of Philadelphia; and by Gregory Protosyncellus of Chios in his [Treatises] concerning the Mysteries; by Jeremias, the Most Holy Patriarch of Constantinople, in three dogmatic and Synodical Letters to the Lutherans of Tubingen in Germany; by John, Priest, and Economus of Constantinople, surnamed Nathaniel; by Meletius Syrigus, of Crete, in the Orthodox Refutation composed by him of the Chapters and Questions of the said Cyril; by Theophanes, Patriarch of Jerusalem, in his dogmatic Epistle to the Lithuanians, and in innumerable other [Epistles]. And before these hath it been spoken most excellently of these matters by Symeon, of Thessalonica, and before him by all the Fathers, and by the Œcumenical Synods, by ecclesiastical historians too; and even by writers of secular history under the Christian Autocrats of Rome, have these matters been mentioned incidentally; by all of whom, without any controversy, the aforesaid were received from the Apostles; whose traditions, whether by writing, or by word, have through the Fathers descended until us. Further, the argument derived from the heretics also confirmeth the aforesaid. For the Nestorians after the year of Salvation, 428, the Armenians too, and the Copts, and the Syrians, and further even the Ethiopians, who dwell at the Equator, and beyond this towards the tropics of Capricorn, whom those that are there commonly call Campesii, after the year...of the Incarnation broke away from the Catholic Church; and each of these hath as peculiar only its heresy, as all know from the Acts of the Œcumenical Synods. Albeit, as concerning the purpose and number of the Sacred Mysteries, and all what hath been said above — except their own particular heresy, as hath been said — they entirely believe with the Catholic Church; as we see with our own eyes every hour, and learn by experience and conversation, here in the Holy City of Jerusalem, in which there either dwell, or are continually sojourning, vast numbers of them all, as well learned, such as they have, as illiterate.

Let, therefore, prating and innovating heretics keep silence, and not endeavour by stealing some sentences, [as] against us, from the Scriptures and the Fathers, to cunningly bolster up falsehood, as all apostates and heretics have ever done; and let them say this one thing only, that in contriving excuses[446] for sins they have chosen to speak wickedness against God,[447] and blasphemies against the Saints.

## *Epilogue*

Let us briefly suffice for the reputation of the falsehoods of the adversaries, which they have devised against the Eastern Church, alleging in support of their falsehoods the incoherent and impious Chapters of the said Cyril. And let it not be for a sign to be contradicted[448] of those heretics that unjustly calumniate us, as though they spake truly; but for a sign to be believed, that is for reformation of their innovations, and for their return to the Catholic and Apostolic Church; in which their forefathers also were of old, and assisted at those Synods and contests against heretics, which these now reject and revile. For it was unreasonable on their part, especially as they considered themselves to be wise, to have listened to men that were lovers of self; and profane, and that spake not from the Holy Spirit, but from the prince of lies, and to have forsaken the Holy, Catholic, and Apostolic Church, which God hath purchased with the Blood of His own Son;[449] and to have abandoned her.

---

[446] *cf.* Ps. 140:4.

[447] *cf.* Ps. 74:6.

[448] *cf.* Lk. 2:34.

[449] *cf.* Acts 20:28.

For otherwise there will overtake those that have separated from the Church the pains that are reserved for heathens and publicans; but the Lord who hath ever protected her against all enemies, will not neglect the Catholic Church; to Him be glory and dominion unto the ages of the ages. Amen.

In the year of Salvation 1672, on the 16th [day] of the month of March, in the Holy City of Jerusalem: —

I, DOSITHEOS, by the mercy of God, Patriarch of the Holy City of Jerusalem and of all Palestine, declare and confess this to be the faith of the Eastern Church.

*(Translation omits over five full pages of signatories)*

Translated from the Greek by J.N.W.B. Robertson (London: Thomas Baker, 1899).

St. Raphael of Brooklyn

# *Appendix III*

*Letter of St. Raphael of Brooklyn to the American Branch of the Anglican and Eastern Orthodox Churches' Union (1911)*

320 Pacific Street,
Brooklyn, New York,

September 25, 1911.

*To the American Branch of the Anglican and Eastern Orthodox Churches' Union.*

Right Rev. Brother and Rev., and dear Lay Brothers:

It is with great reluctancy that I must write you this letter. However, it is absolutely necessary for me to do so – my health, duties and convictions all combine as factors, as well as sincerity toward you, my Anglican friends.

**First:** My health and duties prevent me from giving attention to the work of the Union. For instance: - I am at present enlarging my Cathedral, collecting funds for a Parish House and also for the purchase of a farm for an orphanage. If my health sustains me these matters together with the enormous work of such a scattered and still growing Diocese will occupy all of my time, and perhaps, over-power my remaining strength.

**Second:** I have a personal opinion about the usefulness of the Union. Study has taught me that, there is a vast difference between the doctrine, discipline and even worship of the Holy Orthodox Church and those of the Anglican Communion. While on the other hand, experience has forced upon me conviction that, to promote courtesy and friendship, which seem to be the only aims of the Union at present, is not only killing precious time, at best, but also somewhat hurtful to the religious and ecclesiastical welfare of the Holy Orthodox Church in these United States.

There is a great and growing misunderstanding on the part of the Laity *to wit*, that, there is actually a union , or that, there will be, in the very near future, *a corporate Union*, between the Protestant Episcopal Church and the Holy Orthodox in America at least. The result is that the Laity in some sections are being confused in their doctrinal belief as well as growing careless about other requirements of the Holy Orthodox Church. In fact they neither know what to believe nor to reject, - much less which Church it is their duty to sustain.

Very many of the Bishops of the Holy Orthodox Church, – at the present time – especially myself, have observed that, the Anglican Communion is associated with the numerous Protestant Bodies, many of whose doctrines and teachings as well as practices are condemned by the

Holy Orthodox Church. And furthermore Freemasonry is a commonly accepted society of some of the highest and influential Prelates, Clergymen and Laymen of the Anglican Communion. Indeed it would be hard to select any Diocese or parish in the Anglican Communion where Freemasonry had not great influence amongst its Clerical and Lay-members.

You are aware, without my reminding you, that, this fact brings the members of the Anglican Communion into the closest relationship, for purposes other than those of business and religion, with a body of men which includes Atheists, infidels, heretics and unconverted Jews: – men who, to my knowledge, and I am sure to yours also, are opposers of our *common Holy Religion* – deniers of the Divinity of Our one Lord and Saviour Jesus Christ and all that is uplifting in the true spirit of Christianity in its self-sacrificing methods of spreading the Gospel of that *One Who* so loved us that, He gave Himself for us on the Cross of Calvary. For this reason, alone, I view union as only a pleasing dream.

Indeed, as it is impossible for the Holy Orthodox Church to receive, - as she has a thousand times proclaimed, and which even the Papal See of Rome declared for the Holy Orthodox Church's credit, - anyone into her fold or into union with her who does not accept her faith in full without any qualifications, - the Faith which she claims is most surely apostolic, - I cannot see how she can unite with the

Anglican Communion, or the latter expect, in the near future, to unite with her while the Anglican Communion holds so many Protestant tenets and doctrines and also is so closely associated with the non-Catholic religions about her.

**But finally:** I am in perfect accord with the views expressed by His Grace Archbishop Platon in his address, delivered this year before the Philadelphia Protestant Episcopal Brotherhood, as to the impossibility of union under present circumstances.

Indeed, I fell grieved that very tender explanation and permission granted by me as contained in my address before our Union, which address had been widely published and circulated, have proven very harmful and confusing to the Holy Orthodox Laity. Some of the Protestant Episcopal Clergy have taken upon themselves, through misunderstanding, to offer their services to Orthodox people, when even Orthodox Priests were within calling distance to minister to them; thus conveying the idea that, they, the Protestant Episcopal Clergy, were accepted as Holy Orthodox and that, there was no need of the ministrations or pastoral care of their own Orthodox Bishops and Clergy. There has been much injury done to the cause of friendly relation and reunion by such overt, or confusing acts.

I assure you nothing that I have said in this letter indicates, in the slightest way, a lack of personal regard and love for the individual members on the Anglican side of the Union here in America. I shall always cherish the names of my Right Reverend Brother, Dr. Parker, and the Rev. Dr. Perry, with those of the others that I cannot find space to insert in this lengthy letter. And the sincere friendship which I hold for you all, and especially for Bishop Parker, causes grief when I must tenderly, yet firmly and without revocation, offer you my resignation both from the office of Vice-President, on the Holy Orthodox side of the Union and also from membership in the Union.

Commending the future into His care Who has a way mapped out to reunite the torn-apart Church for which He has shed His Sacred Blood,

I remain, in His Love,

Your friend and brother,

†RAPHAEL,
*Bishop of Brooklyn.*

First Ecumenical Council - 16th c. Cretan
*Image Courtesy of Uncut Mountain Icons*

# *Appendix IV*

*Pastoral Letter of St. Raphael of Brooklyn
Concerning Orthodox/Episcopal Relations (1912)*

To My Beloved Clergy and Laity of the Syrian Greek-Orthodox Catholic Church in North America:

Greetings in Christ Jesus, Our Incarnate Lord and God.

My Beloved Brethren:

Two years ago, while I was Vice-President and member of the Anglican and Eastern Orthodox Churches Union, being moved with compassion for my children in the Holy Orthodox Faith once delivered to the saints,[450] scattered throughout the whole of North America and deprived of the ministrations of the Church; and especially in places far removed from Orthodox centers; and being equally moved with a feeling that the Episcopalian (Anglican) Church possessed largely the Orthodox Faith, as many of the prominent clergy professed the same to me before I studied deeply their doctrinal authorities and their liturgy—the Book of Common Prayer—I wrote a letter as Bishop and Head of the Syrian-Orthodox Mission in North

---

[450] Jude 1:3.

America, giving permission, in which I said that in extreme cases, where no Orthodox priest could be called upon at short notice, the ministrations of the Episcopal (Anglican) clergy might be kindly requested. However, I was most explicit in defining when and how the ministrations should be accepted, and also what exceptions should be made. In writing that letter I hoped, on the one hand, to help my people spiritually, and, on the other hand, to open the way toward bringing the Anglicans into the communion of the Holy Orthodox Faith.

On hearing and in reading that my letter, perhaps unintentionally, was misconstrued by some of the Episcopalian (Anglican) clergy, I wrote a second letter in which I pointed out that my instructions and exceptions had been either overlooked or ignored by many, to wit:

They (the Episcopalians) informed the Orthodox people that I recognized the Anglican Communion (Episcopal Church) as being united with the Holy Orthodox Church and their ministry, that is holy orders, as valid.

The Episcopal (Anglican) clergy offered their ministrations even when my Orthodox clergy were residing in the same towns and parishes, as pastors.

Episcopal clergy said that there was no need of the Orthodox people seeking the ministrations of their own Orthodox priests, for their (the Anglican) ministrations were all that were necessary.

I, therefore, felt bound by all the circumstances to make a thorough study of the Anglican Church's faith and orders, as well as of her discipline and ritual. After serious consideration I realized that it was my honest duty, as a member of the College of the Holy Orthodox Greek Apostolic Church, and head of the Syrian Mission in North America, to resign from the vice-presidency of and membership in the Anglican and Eastern Orthodox Churches Union. At the same time, I set forth, in my letter of resignation, my reason for so doing.

I am convinced that the doctrinal teaching and practices, as well as the discipline, of the whole Anglican Church are unacceptable to the Holy Orthodox Church. I make this apology for the Anglicans whom as Christian gentlemen I greatly revere, that the loose teaching of a great many of the prominent Anglican theologians are so hazy in their definitions of truths, and so inclined toward pet heresies that it is hard to tell what they believe. The Anglican Church as a whole has not spoken authoritatively on her doctrine. Her Catholic-minded members can call out her doctrines from many views, but so nebulous is her pathway in the doctrinal world that those who would extend a hand of both Christian and ecclesiastical fellowship dare not, without distrust, grasp the hand of her theologians, for while many are orthodox on some points, they are quite heterodox on others. I speak, of course, from the Holy Orthodox Eastern Catholic point of view. The Holy Orthodox Church has never perceptibly changed from Apostolic times, and, therefore, no one can go astray in finding out what She teaches. Like Her Lord and Master, though at times surrounded with human malaria — which He in His mercy pardons — She is the same yesterday, and today, and forever[451] the mother and safe deposit of the truth as it is in Jesus.[452]

The Orthodox Church differs absolutely with the Anglican Communion in reference to the number of Sacraments and in reference to the doctrinal explanation of the same. The Anglicans say in their Catechism concerning the Sacraments that there are "two only as generally necessary to salvation, that is to say, Baptism and the Supper of the Lord." I am well aware that, in their two books of homilies (which are not of a binding authority, for the books were prepared only in the reign of Edward VI and Queen Elizabeth for priests who were not permitted to preach their own sermons in England during times both politically and ecclesiastically perilous), it says that there are "five others commonly called Sacraments" (see homily in each book on the Sacraments), but long since they have repudiated in different portions of their Communion this very teaching and absolutely disavow such definitions in their "Articles of Religion" which are bound up in their Book of Common Prayer or Liturgy as one of their authorities.

---

[451] Heb. 13:8.
[452] cf. Eph. 4:21.

The Orthodox Church has ever taught that there are seven Sacraments. She plainly points out the fact that each of the seven has an outward and visible sign and an inward and spiritual Grace, and that they are of gospel and apostolic origin.

Again, the Orthodox Church has certain rites and practices associated and necessary in the administration of the Sacraments which neither time nor circumstances must set aside where churches are organized. Yet the Anglicans entirely neglect these, though they once taught and practiced the same in more catholic days.

In the case of the administration of Holy Baptism it is the absolute rule of the Orthodox Church that the candidate must be immersed three times (once in the name of each Person of the Holy Trinity). Immersion is only permissory in the Anglican Communion, and pouring or sprinkling is the general custom. The Anglicans do not use holy oil in the administration, etc., and even in doctrinal teaching in reference to this Sacrament they differ.

As to the doctrine concerning Holy Communion the Anglican Communion has no settled view. The Orthodox Church teaches the doctrine of transubstantiation without going into any scientific or Roman Catholic explanation. The technical word which She uses for the sublime act of the priest by Christ's authority to consecrate is "transmuting."[453] She, as I have said, offers no explanation, but She

---

[453] Liturgy of Saint John Chrysostom.

believes and confesses that Christ, the Son of the living God Who came into the world to save sinners, is of a truth in His "all-pure Body" and "precious Blood"[454] objectively present, and to be worshiped in that Sacrament as He was on earth and is now in risen and glorified majesty in Heaven; and that "the precious and holy and life-giving Body and Blood of Our Lord and God and Saviour Jesus Christ are imparted" (to each soul that comes to that blessed Sacrament) "Unto the remission of sins, and unto life everlasting".[455]

Confirmation or the laying on of hands, which the Orthodox Church calls a Sacrament — "Chrismation" — in the Anglican Church is merely the laying on of hands of the Bishop accompanied by a set form of prayers, without the use of Holy Chrism, which has come down from Apostolic days as necessary.

Holy Matrimony is regarded by the Anglican Communion as only a sacred rite which, even if performed by a Justice of the Peace, is regarded as sufficient in the sight of God and man.

Penance is practiced but rarely in the Anglican Communion, and Confession before the reception of Holy Communion is not compulsory. They have altogether set aside the Sacrament of Holy Unction, that is anointing the sick as commanded by St. James.[456] In their priesthood they do not

---

[454] *Ibid.*

[455] *Ibid.*

[456] *See* Jas. 5:14.

teach the true doctrine of the Grace of the Holy Orders. Indeed they have two forms of words for ordination, namely, one which gives the power of absolution to the priest, and the alternative form without the words of Our Lord, whosoever sins ye remit, etc.[457] Thus they leave every bishop to choose intention or non-intention in the act of ordination as to the power and Grace of their priesthood.[458]

But, besides all of this, the Anglican Communion ignores the Orthodox Church's dogmas and teachings, such as the invocation of saints, prayers for the dead, special honor to the blessed Virgin Mary the Mother of God, and reverence for sacred relics, holy pictures and icons. They say of such teaching that it is "a foul thing, vainly invented, and grounded upon no warranty of Scripture, but rather repugnant to the word of God".[459]

There is a striking variance between their wording of the Nicene Creed and that of the Holy Orthodox Church; but sadder still, it contains the heresy of the "filioque."

I do not deem it necessary to mention all the striking differences between the Holy Orthodox Church and the Anglican Communion in reference to the authority of holy tradition, the number of Ecumenical Councils, etc. Enough has already been said and pointed out to show that the Anglican Communion differs but little from all other Protestant bodies, and therefore, there cannot be any in-

---

[457] Jn. 20: 23.
[458] "Ordination of Priests," *Book of Common Prayer.*
[459] Article of Religion, XXII.

tercommunion until they return to the ancient Holy Orthodox Faith and practices, and reject Protestant omissions
and commissions.

Therefore, as the official head of the Syrian Holy Orthodox Catholic Apostolic Church in North America and as
one who must give account[460] before the judgment seat of
the Shepherd and Bishop of our souls,[461] that I have fed the
flock of God,[462] as I have been commissioned by the Holy
Orthodox Church, and inasmuch as the Anglican Communion[463] does not differ in things vital to the well-being of
the Holy Orthodox Church from some of the most errant
Protestant sects, I direct all Orthodox people residing in
any community not to seek or to accept the ministrations
of the Sacraments and rites from any clergy excepting those
of the Holy Orthodox Catholic and Apostolic Church,
for the Apostolic command that the Orthodox should not
commune in ecclesiastical matters with those who are not
of the same household of faith,[464] is clear: "Any bishop, or
presbyter or deacon who will pray with heretics, let him be
anathematized; and if he allows them as clergymen to perform any service, let him be deposed."[465] "Any bishop, or
presbyter who accepts Baptism or the Holy Sacrifice from

---

[460] Heb. 13:17.

[461] 1 Pet. 2:25.

[462] *Ibid.*

[463] Protestant Episcopal Church in the USA.

[464] Gal. 6:10.

[465] Apostolic Canon 45.

heretics, we order such to be deposed, for what concord hath Christ with Belial, or what part hath he that believeth with an infidel?"[466]

As to members of the Holy Orthodox Church living in areas beyond the reach of Orthodox clergy, I direct that the ancient custom of our Holy Church be observed, namely, in cases of extreme necessity, that is, danger of death, children may be baptized by some pious Orthodox layman, or even by the parent of the child, by immersion three times in the names of the (Persons of the) Holy Trinity, and in case of death such baptism is valid; but, if the child should live, he must be brought to an Orthodox priest for the Sacrament of Chrismation.

In the case of the death of an Orthodox person where no priest of the Holy Orthodox Church can be had, a pious layman may read over the corpse, for the comfort of the relatives and the instruction of the persons present, Psalm 90 and Psalm 118, and add thereto the Trisagion ("Holy God, Holy Mighty," etc.). But let it be noted that as soon as possible the relative must notify some Orthodox bishop or priest and request him to serve the Liturgy and Funeral for the repose of the soul of the departed in his cathedral or parish Church.

As to Holy Matrimony, if there be any parties united in wedlock outside the pale of the holy Orthodox Church

---

[466] *Ibid.*, 46.

because of the remoteness of Orthodox centers from their home, I direct that as soon as possible they either invite an Orthodox priest or go to where he resides and receive from his hands the Holy Sacrament of Matrimony; otherwise they will be considered excommunicated until they submit to the Orthodox Church's rule.

I further direct that Orthodox Christians should not make it a practice to attend the services of other religious bodies, so that there be no confusion concerning the teaching or doctrines. Instead, I order that the head of each household, or a member, may read the special prayers which can be found in the Hours in the Holy Orthodox Service Book, and such other devotional books as have been set forth by the authority of the Holy Orthodox Church.

Commending our clergy and laity unto the safekeeping of Jesus Christ, and praying that the Holy Spirit may keep us all in the truth and extend the borders of the Holy Orthodox Faith, I remain,

Your affectionate Servant in Christ

†RAPHAEL,
Bishop of Brooklyn,
*Head of the Syrian Greek Orthodox Catholic Mission in North America*

# Bibliography

### Reference Works

Cross, F. L. and Elizabeth A. Livingstone. *The Oxford Dictionary of the Christian Church*. Oxford: Oxford University Press, 1997.

Fossier, Robert. *The Cambridge Illustrated History of the Middle Ages*. Cambridge ; New York: Cambridge University Press, 1986.

Pelikan, Jaroslav and Valerie R. Hotchkiss. *Creeds & Confessions of Faith in the Christian Tradition*. New Haven: Yale University Press, 2003.

*The Great Book of Needs : Expanded and Supplemented*. South Canaan: St. Tikhon's Seminary Press, 1998.

### Translations

Baylor, Michael G. *The Radical Reformation*. New York: Cambridge University Press, 1991.

Bromiley, G. W. *Zwingli and Bullinger*. Philadelphia: The Westminster Press, 1953.

Clanchy, Michael, ed. *The Letters of Abelard and Héloïse*. London: Penguin Classics, 2004.

Cox, J. E. *The Works of Thomas Cranmer*. London: Parker Society, 1846.

Furcha, E. J. (v. 1) and H. Wayne Pipkin (v. 2). *Huldrych Zwingli: Writings, The Defense of the Reformed Faith.* Allison Park: Pickwick Publications, 1984.

Janz, Denis, ed. *A Reformation Reader: Primary Texts with Introductions.* Minneapolis, MN: Fortress Press, 2008.

Jackson, Samuel M. *The Selected Works of H. Zwingli.* Philadelphia: University of Philadelphia Press, 1972.

Liechty, Daniel. *Early Anabaptist Spirituality: Selected Writings.* New York: Paulist Press, 1994.

Lull, Timothy F., ed. *Martin Luther's Basic Theological Writings.* Minneapolis: Fortress Press, 2005.

Manschreck, Clyde L., ed. *Melanchthon on Christian Doctrine: Loci Communes.* New York: Oxford University Press, 1965.

McNeill, John T., ed. *Calvin: Institutes of the Christian Religion,* 2 v., Translated by Ford Lewis Battles. Philadelphia: The Westminster Press, 1960.

Pipkin, H. Wayne and John H. Yoder, eds. *Balthasar Hubmeier: Theologian of Anabaptism.* Scottdale, PA.: Herald Press, 1989.

Schultz, R. C., ed. *Luther's Works.* Philadelphia: Fortress Press, 1967.

Scott, Tom and Bob Scribner, eds. *The German Peasants' War: A History in Documents.* New Jersey: Humanities Press International, Inc, 1991.

Thompson, Bard. *Liturgies of the Western Church.* Philadelphia: Fortress Press, 1961.

Wicks, J., trans. *Cajetan Responds: A Reader in Reformation Controversy,* Washington D.C.: Catholic University of America Press, 1978.

*Secondary Texts*

Alfeyev, Archbishop Hilarion. *Christ the Conqueror of Hell: The Descent into Hades from an Orthodox Perspective.* Crestwood: St. Vladimir's Seminary Press, 2009.

Balmer, Randall. *The Making of Evangelicalism: From Revivalism to Politics and Beyond.* Waco: Baylor University Press, 2010.

Bebbington, David W. *Evangelicalism in Modern Britain: A History from the 1730s to the 1980s.* London: Unwin Hyman, 1989.

Belloc, Hillaire. *Cranmer: Archbishop of Canterbury 1533-1556.* Philadelphia: J. B. Lippincott Company, 1931.

Brecht, Martin. *Martin Luther: His Road to Reformation, 1483-1521.* Translated by James L. Schaaf. Minneapolis: Fortress Press, 1985.

_____. *Martin Luther: Shaping and Defining the Reformation, 1521-1532.* Translated by James L. Schaaf. Minneapolis: Fortress Press, 1990.

_____. *Martin Luther: The Preservation of the Church, 1532-1546.* Translated by James L. Schaaf, Minneapolis: Fortress Press, 1993.

Bromiley, Geoffrey. *Thomas Cranmer: Theologian.* New York: Oxford University Press, 1956.

Brown, Christopher Boyd. *Singing the Gospel: Lutheran Hymns and the Success of the Reformation*. Cambridge: Harvard University Press, 2005.

Burgess, Joseph, *The Role of the Augsburg Confession: Catholic and Lutheran Views*. Philadelphia: Fortress Press, 1980.

Courvoisier, Jaques. *Zwingli: A Reformed Theologian*. Richmond, John Knox Press, 1963.

Davey, Colin. *Pioneer for Unity: Metrophanes Kritopoulos (1589-1639) and Relations Between the Orthodox, Roman Catholic and Reformed Churches*. London: British Council of Churches, 1987.

Dayton, Donald and Robert Johnston. *The Variety of American Evangelicalism*. Knoxville: University of Tennessee Press, 1991.

Duffy, Eamon. *The Stripping of the Altars: Traditional Religion in England c. 1400-c. 1580*. New Haven: Yale University Press, 1992.

_____, *Saints and Sinners: A History of the Popes*. New Haven: Yale University Press, 2006.

Estep, William R. *The Anabaptist Story: An Introduction to Sixteenth Century Anabaptism*. Grand Rapids: William B. Eerdmans Publishing Co., 1996.

Evans, G. R. *John Wyclif: Myth and Reality*. New York: IVP, 2006.

Farner, Oskar. *Zwingli the Reformer: His Life and Work*. Translated by D. G. Sear. Hamden: Archon Books, 1968.

Fischer, Austin. *Young, Restless, No Longer Reformed: Black Holes, Love and a Journey In and Out of Calvinism.* Eugene: Cascade Books, 2014.

Forell, George W. and James McCue. *Confessing One Faith: A Joint Commentary on the Augsburg Confession by Lutheran and Catholic Theologians.* Minneapolis: Fortress Press, 1982.

Fossier, Robert, Stuart Arlie and Roby Marsack, eds. *The Cambridge Illustrated History of the Middle Ages. 950-1250 AD.*, v. 2. Cambridge: Cambridge University Press, 1997.

Frame, John. *Evangelical Reunion: Denominations and the Body of Christ.* Grand Rapids: Baker Book House, 1991.

Furcha, E. J. and H. Wayne Pipkin, eds. *Prophet, Pastor, Protestant: The Work of Huldrych Zwingli After Five Hundred Years.* Allison Park: Pickwick Publications, 1984.

Gäbler, Ulrich. *Huldrych Zwingli: His Life and Work,* Translated by Ruth C. L. Gritsch. Philadelphia: Fortress Press, 1986.

Geffert, Bryn. *Eastern Orthodox and Anglicans: Diplomacy, Theology and the Politics of Interwar Ecumenism.* Notre Dame: University of Notre Dame Press, 2010.

Gritsch, Eric W. *Reformer Without A Church: The Life and Teaching of Thomas Muentzer 1488? – 1525.* Philadelphia: Fortress Press, 1967.

Hadjiantoniou, George A. *Protestant Patriarch: The Life of Cyril Lucaris (1572-1638) Patriarch of Constantinople.* Richmond: John Knox Press, 1961.

Hatch, Nathan O. *The Democratization of American Christianity.* New Haven and London: Yale University Press, 1989.

Heers, Peter Alban, *The Missionary Origins of Modern Ecumenism: Milestones Leading up to 1920.* Greece: Uncut Mountain Press, 2007.

_____. *The Ecclesiological Renovation of Vatican II: An Orthodox Examination of Rome's Ecumenical Theology Regarding Baptism and the Church.* Greek edition by Apostoliki Diakonia, 2014. (English edition forthcoming)

Hodge, A. A. *The Confession of Faith.* Carlisle: The Banner of Truth Trust, 1869.

Jackson, Samuel M. *Huldreich Zwingli: A Rerformer of German Switzerland, 1484-1531.* New York: AMS Press, 1972.

Jensen, Robert W. *America's Theologian: A Recommendation of Jonathan Edwards.* Oxford: Oxford University Press, 1992.

Jones, Martin, *The Counter Reformation: Religion and Society in Early Modern Europe.* New York: Cambridge University Press, 1995.

Kelly, J. N. D. *The Oxford Dictionary of Popes.* London: Oxford University Press, 1986.

Kolb, Robert. *Martin Luther as Prophet, Teacher and Hero: Images of the Reformer, 1520-1620*. Grand Rapids: Baker, 1999.

Kolbaba, Tia M. *Inventing Latin Heretics: Byzantines and the Filioque in the Ninth Century*. Kalamazoo: Medieval Institute Publications, 2008.

Langford, Rev. H. W. "*The Non-Jurors and the Eastern Orthodox,*" (1965): Accessed June 20, 2014. http://www.anglicanhistory.org/nonjurors/langford1.html.

Lathbury, Thomas. *History of the Non-Jurors*. London: W. Pickering, 1845.

Lee, Philip J. *Against the Protestant Gnostics*. Oxford: Oxford University Press, 1993.

Lindberg, Carter. *The European Reformations*. Oxford: Blackwell Publishers, 1996.

Loades, David. *Thomas Cranmer and the English Reformation*. Bangor, Gwynedd: Headstart History, 1991.

MacCulloch, Diarmaid. *Thomas Cranmer: A Life*. New Haven: Yale University Press, 1996.

_____. *The Boy King: Edward VI and the Protestant Reformation*. Berkeley: University of California Press, 2001.

_____. *The Reformation*. New York: Penguin, 2004.

_____. *Christianity: The First Three Thousand Years*. New York: Viking, 2010.

McGrath, Alister. *Evangelicalism and the Future of Christianity*. Downers Grove: InterVaristy Press, 1995.

Mastrantonis, George. *Augsburg and Constantinople: The Correspondence between the Tübingen Theologians and Patriarch Jeremias II of Constantinople on the Augsburg Confession*. Brookline: Holy Cross Orthodox Press, 1982.

Maynard, Theodore. *The Life of Thomas Cranmer*. Chicago: Henry Regnery Co, 1956.

Meyendorff, John. *Rome, Constantinople, Moscow: Historical and Theological Studies*. Crestwood: St. Vladimir's Seminary Press, 1986.

Oberman, Heiko. *Luther: Between God and the Devil*. New York: Yale University Press, 1990.

O'Malley, John. *The First Jesuits*. Cambridge: Harvard University Press, 1993.

Pelikan, Jaroslav. *Reformation of Church and Dogma (1300-1700)*. Chicago: University of Chicago Press, 1984.

Potter, George Richard. *Zwingli*. London: Cambridge University Press, 1976.

Phillips, Melanie. *Londonistan*. New York: Encounter Books, 2006.

Rodopoulos, Met. Panteleimon. *An Overview of Orthodox Canon Law*. Translated by W. J. Lillie. Rollingsford: Orthodox Research Institute, 2007.

Rose, Archimandrite Seraphim. *Little Russian Philokalia*. v. 1. St. Seraphim, Platina: St. Herman Press, 2008.

Ryrie, Alec. *The Origins of the Scottish Reformation*. New York: Palgrave, 2006.

Schaff, Philip, "Prolegomena to the Works of St. John Chrysostom," in *Nicene and Post-Nicene Fathers* v. 9. Peabody: Hendrickson Publishers Inc., 1889.

Scouteris, Constantine. *Ecclesial Being: Contributions to Theological Dialogue*. ed. by Christopher Veniamin. South Canann: Mount Thabor Publishing, 2006.

Selderhuis, Herman J. *John Calvin: A Pilgrim's Life*. Downer's Grove: Intervarsity Press, 2009.

Siecienski, A. Edward. *The Filioque: History of a Doctrinal Controversy*. Oxford: Oxford University Press, 2010.

Spinka, Matthew. *John Hus: A Biography*. Princeton: Princeton University Press, 1968.

Stephens, W. P. *The Theology of Huldrych Zwingli*. Oxford: Clarendon Press, 1986.

Sweeney, Douglas A. *The American Evangelical Story: A History of the Movement*. Grand Rapids: Baker Academic, 2005.

Swete, H. B. *On the History of the Doctrine of the Procession of the Holy Spirit from the Apostolic Age to the Death of Charlemagne*. Eugene: Wipf and Stock Publishers, 1876.

Trenham, Josiah B. *Marriage and Monasticism according to St. John Chrysostom*, Platina: St. Herman Press, 2013.

_____. "The Antiochian Withdrawal from the NCC" in *Faith and Freedom* 24, no. 4. Institute on Religion and Democracy, 2005.

Vedder, Henry C. *Balthasar Hubmeier: The Leader of the Anabaptists*. New York: AMS Press, 1971.

Ware, Timothy (Bishop Kallistos of Diokleia). *The Orthodox Church*. London: Penguin Books, 1997.

Warfield, B. B. *Calvin and Augustine,* ed. Samuel C. Craig, Philadelphiad: Presbyterian and Reformed Publishing, 1956.

Wendel, François. *Calvin: Origins and Development of His Religious Thought*. Translated by Philip Mairet. Durham: The Labyrinth Press, 1987.

Yannaras, Christos. *Orthodoxy and the West*. Translated by Peter Chamberas and Norman Russell. Brookline: Holy Cross Orthodox Press, 2006.

Yoder, John H. *The Legacy of Michael Sattler*. Scottdale: Herald Press, 1973.

Zacharou, Archimandrite Zacharias. *The Hidden Man of the Heart.* Essex: Stavropegic Monastery of St. John the Baptist, 2007.

# Index

## A

Abelard, Peter 5
Abraham 113–115
Africa 193–194
Albert of Mainz, Archbishop 15
Alcuin of York 280
Alexander IV, Pope 12
Alexander VI, Pope 201
Alexandria (Patriarchate) 6, 156
Amish 108–109
Ammann, Jakob 108
Amsterdam 102
Anabaptism
 confessions of faith 53,
  103–104, 105–107
 ecclesiology 105–107
 experientialism 103
 factionalism 102, 106–107, 107
 pacifism 101, 102, 105, 106, 108
 politics 91–92, 94, 98–99, 104,
  105
 sacraments 100–101, 105,
  106–107
Andreae, Jacob 63
Anglicanism. *See also* Episcopal
  Church
 Anglo-Catholicism 173, 178,
  184–185
 confessions of faith 56, 173,
  175–176, 178, 179–181,
  183–185

 dissidents 151, 186–187
 influences 148, 175, 178,
  181–183
 liturgy 175, 178
 modern 189–192, 193–194,
  220–221, 227
 politics 167–168, 173, 182
 sacraments 180, 183
 as Western Orthodox 186–187,
  187–189, 365–369,
  371–380
Antioch (Patriarchate) 6
apocalypse. *See* eschatology
Apocrypha. *See* Scriptures
Aquinas, Thomas 280
architecture 140
Arian heresy 133, 256
Arminianism 153–156, 227–229
Arminius, Jacob 153–156
Arsenios the Cappadocian, Saint
 190
Athanasius, Saint 76, 131, 280,
 296
Augsburg 21, 55, 204, 205
Augustine of Canterbury, Saint
 165
Augustine of Hippo, Saint 12, 14,
 42–44, 50, 60–61, 76, 78,
 131, 137, 279–280, 287
Augustinians 11–12, 13, 198
Austria. *See* Holy Roman Empire

391

# P

# T

Τέλος
καὶ τῷ Θεῷ Δόξα.

NEWROME
PRESS